Scaffold
of
Shame

Antony W. Rogers

DEDICATION

For Grandpa.

CONTENTS

IMAGES

ACKNOWLEDGMENTS

A debt of gratitude is owed to the Staff of the Queensland State Archives without whose expertise in uncovering the information held within their records it would not have been possible for this story to be told.

Also Bob Brown for his encouragement and inspiration.

INTRODUCTION

Those that remember my grandfather will recall his love of reading. Detective and western novels featured heavily on his reading list. As well as subscriptions like Readers Digest and National Geographic. I was fortunate that at the age of seven or eight he had enough confidence in me to let me have a copy of the National Geographic. I read the magazine from front to back, curiously the only thing I remember of it now was an advertisement for a colour television. I asked my mother why we didn't have a colour television. Her response being 'don't be silly there is no such thing'. I went back to the magazine and reread the ad, looking for the disclaimer, that there was indeed no such thing. I learnt a few life lessons that day. Just because it's written down doesn't make it true. Adults don't know everything. Poor people lie. That was my awakening to the fact that we were poor. Instead of truthfully saying we could not afford a colour television, it was easier for my mother to lie and tell me there was no such thing. Poor people lie to themselves. They don't admit they need help. They harbour shame for being poor. Once I was awakened to the fact we were poor it seemed everything in life occurred purely to reveal the shame.

I hated going back to school after holidays. It seemed to be the teacher's way to unveil the truth. Write an essay on what you did during the school holidays. Words that would fill me with dread. I remember one poor bastard asked what they should write about. The teacher offered outings, movies, trips to the beach. I thought I was the only one that spent their breaks trying to fashion sticks into toys. I started to fall behind in my schoolwork. Then another life lesson. A school sports carnival. My mother was talking to my teacher and they called me over. My mother told me that they thought I needed an incentive to improve my marks. If I did well, I could have a bike. My first thought was, 'yeah like we can afford that'. But knowing that I had to keep up the pretence I jumped up and down and yelled 'Oh Wow!'. I went from twenty-fourth to fourth in my class at the next exam. The other students gasped when my name was called. I didn't get a bike. The lesson? Never, ever, admit that you are poor. Education is the springboard out of poverty.

When my Grandfather got too old for blacksmithing and baking he took up a ward-man's job at the hospital. Eventually he was asked to provide a birth certificate for superannuation purposes. There wasn't one. He found out on his sixtieth birthday that he was adopted. When he asked about his birth parents he was told they were aboriginal.

I thought that would be the point that made me special, unique, not just poor. How naive. I proudly announced an aboriginal heritage at high school. My olive complexion and dark, wavy, shoulder-length hair was consistent. Then the jibes started. I hadn't learnt the racism lesson from my football days as a kid. At the start of one season we were assigned a young aboriginal man, Brian Williams, as coach. The second night of training parents arrived in their cars to remove their sons. The team manager walked out. So Brian's father took over the role. I asked my mother why the other boys couldn't play? My mother said because the coach and manager were Aboriginal. I didn't comprehend the answer. They were good people. Softly spoken and kind. Another of life's lessons. Racism is taught.

Then I started work. The corporate world was not all that friendly. The interviews horrendous. What school did you go to? State School. Oh. What does your father do?

He's a boner at the meat works. Oh. You could hear it in their voices. Oh, that's a shame. I was lucky, eventually I got a cadetship. I got to work in the office attached to a factory during the day and study at night. God bless Gough Whitlam and free tertiary study. Otherwise I would have spent my life pulling the guts out of chickens or digging holes. Not that there is any shame to those occupations. It's just I'm too lazy for hard physical work.

The office was set out classroom style seating five of us. I had my back to everyone else but that didn't stop the conversations. They were a great bunch and we had very meaningful conversations. Then I made some comment about eating bread and dripping for lunch, every day going to school. Or perhaps I mentioned being told to never accept food and drink from relatives when we visited them. My parents feared that we might reveal we were hungry and poor. Then one of my co-workers said, 'you either have a very vivid imagination, or it happened, which is sad'. Another of life's lessons. Never reveal that you were once poor, people treat you differently. I didn't want sympathy. I just wanted to tell my story.

Uni kept me out of the sun and my skin paled. My wavy locks transformed with a corporate cut. The old man would tease me mercilessly about my attempts to stop the corporate cut from becoming an afro. So I wore a hairnet to bed, big deal. I laugh about it now. It was an attempt to deflect the shame others wanted for me. Poor and black. Fuck that. I didn't want any special treatment. If I was to achieve anything in my life I wanted people to say 'you did well'. I never wanted to hear the suffix, 'for a black fella'. I wanted to know that in everything I did I was equal to everyone else. My grandfather taught me that.

But never talking about those times outside of the family created a desire to learn about the past. To delve into the family history. To understand how the family got to that point. Or find the hero in the past to attach some pride. I started foraging about with genealogy. Researching, cross referencing, multi-source validation became my hobby. One thing about genealogy is that you discover many brick walls, rabbit holes and side tracks. It is a process of looking for patterns.

My Grandfather had his birth certificate changed by deed poll. It gave his birth mother's name but not a father. One of my Grandfather's dying wishes was for his birth mother to be found. With just the name Eileen Gladys Christ to go by, I picked up the search from my Aunt.

During my research I discovered the story of her passing, in 1926, murdered in the company of a policeman, in the process of sexual intercourse. Some would have left it there, not wanting to know anything further. Others cautioned me against judging her too harshly, 'who are we to condemn' they said. They had accepted what was reported as true. Just because it's written down doesn't make it true. By not judging her, there would be no need to delve further.

Eileen Gladys Walsh had been condemned to stand on the scaffold of shame for eternity, along with Acting Police Sergeant Marquis Cumming. The crime committed in Brisbane became known as Australia's Greatest Double Murder Mystery. The person or persons responsible for the murders have never been identified.

As I began to delve further, I unearthed a series of coincidences. I kept reminding myself that these were only coincidences, there was no pattern. This became increasingly difficult and I was consumed by conspiracy theories. Is it a tendency we all have, to erroneously recognize a pattern where none exists? We do tend to be uneasy with chaos and chance. But the tendency to see patterns everywhere means that we are susceptible to seeing them when none exists. But what if there was a pattern? That is when I realized that the truth, as they say, 'is stranger than any fiction'.

Why was I so quick to dismiss these patterns? Was I overcompensating in recognition of my bias that there are no coincidences? At some point with enough coincidences present do we all establish a pattern? Should trying to make sense of an event such as murder ever make sense to a rational mind? Or did I just not want to believe?

The recognition of patterns has been applied to the most heinous of human action, murder. Detectives have used the established pattern of motive, means and opportunity, to uncover numerous guilty parties. Yet, there remains unsolved those murders where no perceivable pattern can be found. Even when no motive can be determined investigators will normally pursue the other factors, means and opportunity, to uncover the perpetrator of a random act of evil.

Was it this human condition to question coincidence and our suspicion of conspiracy theories that prevented the police from solving the murder of Acting Police Sergeant Cumming and Eileen Walsh in 1926? Or were those involved part of a conspiracy too horrendous to be considered plausible?

This book is my journey of discovery for answers.

1 BELT, HANDCUFFS, AND KEYS

Research revealed the city of Brisbane, Queensland, during the 1920's as a far more subdued metropolis than the more populous Australian capital cities. It wasn't known as having any organised crime presence, in fact, some considered it conspicuous that there was a complete absence of organised crime reported. It wasn't without petty crime, a gang of safe blowers was operating and there had been a few discrepancies with the Golden Casket (an art union with a healthy first prize of £5,000, the equivalent of 30 years of a worker's wage). But this didn't appear organised by any means. This façade of normality was tested though. A series of events, seemingly unrelated, unnerved the reserved Brisbane folk. And it all started with a chance discovery in the lead up to Christmas 1926.

At 6:45 am on Christmas Eve a locomotive approached Park Road Station. The railway line linked the Suburb of Sunnybank with South Brisbane Station, the terminal stop in the city. Park Road Station was one of the few last stops before the terminal. The line passed between the Diamantina Hospital, that sat atop a hill on the right of the inbound train, and the Boggo Road Gaol to the left atop a higher hill. The ground from the prison sloped down to the railway station and a reserve occupied an area of about 200 yards by 100 yards. The reserve was used as a sports ground and goal posts had been erected for a football pitch, as the ground closest to the train line was as near level as required for such activity.[i]

The reserve was well-known as a rendezvous for canoodling couples. As a trysting place it was, in fact, a most uninviting centre, surrounded as it is by unpretentious factory sheds, frowned upon by the high walls of the famous Gaol, and skirted by a rubbish strewn track called Railway Reserve. The railway line passes along the edge of the paddock. A scrub covered embankment leads down to the rails at one end of the reserve, while the other end is cut off short by a paling fence, on the other side of which the residential area begins.

The engine driver and fire-man saw what they thought was a couple seemingly preoccupied in their passion. They called out. There was no response. The engine driver gave a blast of the steam whistle. Still no response.

The fireman jumped from the moving train and made his way towards the pair laid out on the reserve. They both laid on their backs about a yard apart, 10 yards from a set of the goal posts, with their heads pointed to the Gaol, their feet towards the rail-line.

As the fireman drew closer, he could see that their clothing was disarranged. The gentleman on the left appeared to be in a blue policeman's uniform, tunic, trousers and black regulation boots. His legs were fully extended and the feet separated by about ten inches. The arms extended down alongside his body, the forearms and hands slightly inclined outwards. The tunic was unbuttoned and both edges opened out a few inches. The braces were unbuttoned from the front of the trousers, being drawn up to the chest. The shirt and flannel were also drawn up to just above the waistline. The fly of the trousers was completely unbuttoned and were drawn down to about midway between the buttock and knees. His white plump stomach formed a mound that cast a shadow over his private portions.

The woman lay parallel to the policeman. Her legs were fully extended with the feet spread out about two feet apart. Both arms were extended downwards along her side with the forearms towards her body. She wore a brown cotton material frock with a white petticoat. She had black shoes on her feet. Her black stockings were about her knees with the front of her dress scrunched up to just below her waist. Her left leg had been removed from her silk bloomers and these had been thrown across the right leg. A small white handkerchief lay on the ground between her legs, above her knees. She wore a light coloured straw hat on her head. Nine inches from her left hand lay a police blue uniform cap, top facing up.

As the fireman drew closer he could see that their open grey eyes stared unblinking into the morning sun. He saw that the clothing about the neck and shoulders of the policeman were saturated in blood with a pool of blood on the ground about his head. The woman had congealed blood about her face concentrated on the right hand side about level with the lower part of the nose, almost directly under the right eye, with blood across her arm. He turned and ran back to the train, waving his arms wildly for the train to progress to the station.[12]

The train was particularly well occupied on this Friday

---

[1] Figure 1 – Murder Scene photograph.

[2] Figure 3 – Map of Brisbane in 1926 with Murder Scene indicated.

morning, as people were making their way into town to take advantage of the last few hours of shopping before Christmas. Passengers crowded to the open carriage windows on the left of the train, drawn towards the macabre sight. Mothers covered the eyes of their children.

As the engine arrived at the platform the fireman again jump out and run to the station master. The Station Master called the Woolloongabba Police Station stating that the body of a policeman and a woman had been discovered lying on the railway line between Park Road and Dutton Park Railway stations. At 7:45 am Woolloongabba rang South Brisbane Police Station and told Acting Sargent William Bonis. Bonis had been in charge of the third relief the previous day (his hours were from 10:00 pm to 6:00 am) and he quickly organised four constables to accompany him to Park Road Station.

At the rail station the group encountered a number of constables from Woolloongabba Police Station on the platform. One of the men pointed down the rail tracks in the direction that the Station Master had given him.

Bonis had made contact during the night to inform them that Acting Sargent Cumming[3] had not put in an appearance when the second relief was due to hand over. At ten past ten on the previous evening the Sargent in charge of the South Brisbane Police Station at the time, gave instructions to search for and determine the whereabouts of Cumming. Even a Sub-inspector from Roma Street had joined in the search when news had reached him. But they had found no trace.

While they had been out searching for Cumming, South Brisbane received a call at about 3:45 am. It was Frederick

---

[3] Figure 6 – Photograph of Acting Sergeant Marquis Cumming.

Christie of Stephens Street to the effect that his sister, Eileen Gladys Walsh[4], had been missing from around 8:00 pm the previous evening.

Bonis knew both of them. Eileen Walsh was separated from her husband and was living with her mother and siblings at Stephens Street. Bonis had heard rumours that Cumming had been inclined to demand 'favours' from women in exchange for relief payments. But as far as he knew Eileen Walsh was not in receipt of relief payments, or a pension.

They walked in silence for a distance of some 25 chains along the rail tracks. The sun was now quite warm in the early summer mornings, the air still, laden with the smoke of recent bushfires. On beholding the grotesque sight Bonis bowed his head, it was them.

*

The train arrived at South Brisbane Station at the scheduled time and the alarm went out from there as well. By 8:45 am a car-load of police from Roma Street also arrived at the reserve, led by Sub-Inspector Lipp. The sub-inspector called for pickets to be posted along the fences and at the entrances to the reserve. Railway Parade, which runs alongside the reserve was also guarded.

As the constables got into position the Government Medical Officer, Dr. Joseph Espie Dods arrived.

At first Dods suspected it may have been a murder suicide with the weapon obstructed from view under one of the bodies. Before he examined the bodies he asked for the police to start looking for tracks.

---

[4] Figure 7 – Photograph of Eileen Gladys Walsh nee Christie.

The police began to look for tracks, between where the bodies lay and Dr. Dods. The ground however was hard and stony and gave them nothing. Bonis sent for the black tracker, George Munro. Lipp instructed Bonis to commence a door knock to find out if anyone heard or saw anything.

Dods knelt down between the bodies to examine them. 'On first examination it appears that they have both been shot in the back of the neck, the bullet appears to have entered at the base of the skull, penetrating the brain, death would have been instantaneous', Dods was attributed as saying.

Or as 'The Truth' reported him as saying, "It appears obvious, this pair have been surprised in an illicit attitude, and whoever committed this murder must have crept up behind them and despatched them to the land of everlasting shadows".[ii]

Dods reported there was no signs of a struggle, just a little dirt on the toe of his right boot, the same as the ground around them. There was nothing on the heels of either of the woman's shoes, nothing to suggest they had been pressed into the ground. Dods presumed he was shot first. He'd know more when he had a look at them back at the morgue and organised for the undertakers' wagon to come and collect them.

Dods then remarked that the policeman's belt, handcuffs, and keys appeared to be missing. Sub-Inspector Meldon, Officer in Charge of Criminal Investigation Branch, and Detective Henderson, arrived shortly after.

Bonis commenced the task of searching the bodies. He padded down the policeman's body removing a white handkerchief from his left trouser pocket, police memorandum book from his bottom tunic pocket, a pair of spectacles, in their case, from the inside tunic pocket.

From his top tunic pocket, he recovered a fountain pen, handcuff key numbered 15, and a typewriter rubber.

In his other trouser pocket they found a purse containing a five-pound bank note, one shilling, a six pence, and threepence. On his left wrist Cumming wore a wristlet watch that bore the correct time. Meldon ruled out robbery as a motive.

The handcuff key was not the key that they were looking for as Cumming was known to have had a ring of keys, which he used for his locker, attached to his belt.

Bonis examined Eileen and noted her hand was bare, with no wedding ring. He had spoken to the family earlier that morning and had been told she was separated from her husband. Police had already been dispatched to try to locate her husband.

Bonis had spoken to Eileen's family at about 4 o'clock that morning, as the station had received a call reporting Eileen as missing. Bonis went himself to get a description and other particulars, what she was wearing, where she was going when she left home. He states that the family was frantic, her mother and siblings had been up all night roaming the streets looking for her.

Bonis recalls that her mother, Mary Christie, stated that she last saw her between seven forty-five and eight o'clock last night. She told her mother that she was going out to post a letter at the pillar box, and that she wouldn't be away five minutes. She had asked her niece, thirteen-year-old Ruby Jones, to go with her, but the niece said she was too tired. They thought she may have been with her husband, she had met up with him once before and remained with him till about nine thirty on that occasion. If that was the case they expected her at home no later than quarter to ten. When ten o'clock came and she still hadn't returned, her sisters went out looking for her.

*

Shortly they were joined by the black tracker and he commenced his parade of the reserve followed closely by a troop of police constables. At times the Aboriginal would be on all fours around spots were tracks were likely to have been left. Then he would rise, walk a few steps in one direction with a hunched back, his hands behind his back, only to return to his starting position seemingly baffled. The tracking sleuth seemed to meet obstacles at every turn. Tracking in the bush would have been a comparatively easy task compared with the tracking he was called upon to do here. The footprints that he did come across told him nothing. The paddock was crossed and re-crossed innumerable times by railway employees and residents of the district.[iii]

Around 11:00 am as they searched around the bodies, about ten feet from Mrs. Walsh's head at an angle to the right, they found a spent automatic cartridge shell. Bonis estimated that this lay at an angle of about 45° from a line drawn through the body and head. Then in the same direction about four feet further away another cartridge shell, similar to the first. Bonis took possession of them.

Henderson was dispatched to Eileen's home and told to check her room for her ring before telling them what had happened. He was also asked to search for a weapon.

Meldon then received word that a tramway man had a recollection of hearing three shots the previous night and concluded that they might have a murder suicide. Meldon called on the men to widen the search, checking the adjoining mud dump, the gullies, the bushes surrounding the reserve, all conceivable hiding places for a third body.

*

Henderson, in the company of four detectives, arrived at the home of Mrs. Eileen Walsh and her family. He had joined the force in 1910, three months before his twenty third birthday. He was a tall lean man with hazel eyes and brown hair. His fresh complexion revealed him as a Scotsman who had served a year and eight months with the Dumfries-shire Constabulary before immigrating to Australia.

He asked if they could inspect her room and the rest of the house, at first telling them that Eileen had met with a serious accident, but found nothing that could be of assistance in their investigations. Henderson spoke to Eileen's mother, Mrs. Christie and the other members of the household disclosing to them the tragedy that Eileen was dead, but would not say where it had occurred. Eileen was the youngest of Mary Christie's four children.

Henderson informed them that he had heard that Eileen was separated from her husband and asked for further information.

Mary Christie informed Henderson that Eileen was indeed separated from her husband, James Samuel Walsh, and had left him on three different occasions, the last time about two and a half years ago, and had been living with her ever since. When asked why she had left him Mary responded that on the first occasion, that she knew for a fact that Eileen had had quarrels with him, but she only left him for a few days. Walsh had been in destitute circumstances, he hadn't been working, they were existing on Government Relief, he had some sort of row with his mother and when Eileen interfered, Mary stated that she got it! The second occasion wasn't long after the first, but again, only for a few days.

Mary Christie revealed that her relationship with Walsh was strained. From the outset she had forbade Eileen to marry him, she was never friendly with him and never on good terms. She didn't quarrel with him, and would help the family out by taking fruit and vegetables round, for her daughter's sake. When he visited her place he was always well received, when he was sober. Mary related that at times Walsh would come to her home drunk and she would refuse to let him in.

When asked if Eileen had left him the last time on account of the drunkenness, Mary responded no. Mary stated that Eileen told her it was for the ill treatment she received from him, and his not being able to support her.

Mary states that Eileen left him on a Tuesday, the Friday before she had been discharged from the Mater Hospital and they had told her when she left that she was to stay in bed for a fortnight. Walsh pulled her out of the bed and gave her a thrashing, he said his mother had kept her long enough, and she was only on an old aged pension. Eileen got dressed and tried to go over town to get some rations for them, but she collapsed in Vulture Street. Mary had a phone call to say go down immediately, that she was wanted and Walsh brought Eileen to as far as the gate and left her there.

Mary had no idea as to the whereabouts of Walsh at that time.

*

The two stiff corpses, stretched out as they were on blood soaked grassy beds laid out in the heat of the sun unprotected, now became an even more ghastly spectacle. The detectives discussed the lack of footprints that suggested that the perpetrator must have crept stealthily along the railway track. Adjacent to the railway line and near the fatal scene was a heap of stones about four feet high that could have provided a handy hiding place for any would be attacker. It was possible that the killer had crept from behind this screen and worked his way behind the couple.[iv]

The questioning by police had alerted local residents of the activity and with curiosity driving them, they huddled at the fence to behold a sight unfit to be seen. In consequence of this, Lipp called for a tarpaulin.

*

Not long afterward the undertaker's wagon arrived and was driven down the paddock to where the bodies lay. Each was lifted in turn onto the tray and driven away to the morgue.

2 THE MORGUE

At midday Acting Sargent Bonis attended the city morgue for the post mortem examination to be conducted by Dr. Dods. The morgue was a timber framed building clad with galvanised iron situated at the end of Alice Street that backed onto the Brisbane River. The location had been chosen so that the floors could be cleansed of blood which was washed into the river. The building was divided into three sections. The first section consisted of an office and vestibule. The central section contained a table with a metal cover to which was attached a funnel that ran up to the roof, this is where the post mortems were carried out. This table was also used to store decomposing bodies as the funnel allowed the odours to escape the building. This section had to be passed through by members of the public when they would be escorted by police to the end room for the identification of deceased persons. Refrigeration was a prohibitive cost at the time with the preferred method for handling deceased persons being to move the bodies through as quickly as possible. The climate in Queensland was not conducive to the storage of bodies for any length of time. Sticky flypaper dangled from the rafters.

Bonis met Dr. Dods in the middle room and noted that the wounds on the bodies were as he had found them at the scene. He watched as the Doctor examined Cumming then rolled the body onto its back.

"This appears to be a bullet wound," said Dods, "with powder marks, two inches to the left of the spine on a level with the top of the shoulder. The skin is grazed upwards, and the bullet entered three inches up in the middle line."

He made a small incision.

"It's fractured the cervical vertebra, injuring the spinal cord, and here it is, sitting between the anterior portion of the vertebra and the base of the skull."

Dods handed the bullet to Bonis, who rolled the nickel plated automatic bullet in his palm before taking possession of it as evidence. Dods continued the examination. Bonis decided to check the clothing that the doctor had removed from the bodies. He picked up the tunic that Cumming had been wearing and noted a hole about five inches from the neck band. He counted six perforations altogether. The perforations were all in line and parallel with the neck band of the tunic. He surmised that the tunic must have been scrunched up when the bullet passed through it. He checked the shirt the deceased had been wearing and found two perforations that corresponded with two on the tunic.

-O-

When I first read the report by the Government Medical Officer I was a little sceptical. Power marks on the skin through six layers of a tunic did not seem plausible. I researched the GMO's record and found that he was a highly respected medical practitioner. Nothing untoward. Yet according to modern forensic pathologists, when there is clothing between the firearm and the skin, you will not find soot and powder on the skin, and searing is lessened or can be prevented.[v]

*

Just shy of an hour later, Dods turned to Bonis and said,

"I've determined that all other organs were sound. I would conclude from my examination that the cause of death was a gunshot wound to the neck."

Dods then turned his attention to Mrs. Walsh. Bonis noted that her body had two wounds, one on the right hand side of the face about level with the nose and a second wound at the back of the neck, at the base of the skull.

"There is a bullet wound with powder marks on the face," said Dods, "on the right of the nose, bullet has fractured the upper jaw," he turned the skull in his hand, "and the odontoid process of the second vertebra, as well as the posterior portion of the first cervical vertebra, coming out in the centre of the neck, just below the base of the skull."

The hat worn by Mrs. Walsh, at the time she was found, had been worn with the back pulled down onto the back of the neck, as was the fashion. It was saturated with blood. There was a hole in the rim of the hat, at the back, that corresponded with the wound at the back of her neck.

Bonis observed that the hole in the hat appeared to have been made from the inside and not the outside of the hat.

"All other organs are healthy," said Dods, "the cause of death is a gunshot wound to the face."

"What are you doing now?" asked Bonis.

"Just collecting a sample from the vagina," said Dods, "for microscopic examination."

Bonis turned his head and spoke to the Medical Officer

as he prepared the sample.

"Have you developed a theory Doc?"

"Death would have been instantaneous in both cases. I think that the deceased Cumming was lying on his face when he was shot, and that the person who fired the shot would have been standing at his feet, and the deceased Walsh was probably shot when sitting up," said Dods as he adjusted the focus of the microscope.

"Spermatozoa here," said Dods, "and they're recent."

-o-

From the records I cannot find a follow up question. My question would have been, 'what did he mean by recent?' I can only assume that he meant that the sperm was still live when he examined it. We now know that a woman's cervical fluid provides the sperm with the nutrients they need to survive during their journey to the ovum. The typical lifespan of sperm in a woman's body while fertile cervical fluid is present is three days, but in the right conditions sperm can even live up to five days. In the absence of cervical fluid, sperm have a brief lifespan of a mere few hours. The only inference that can be drawn then is that Eileen was close to ovulating and had sexual relations sometime during the five days leading up to her death. However the inference drawn by those at the time was that Cumming and Eileen had been murdered during sexual intercourse.

*

"Assuming that the person that shot Cumming was at his feet then Mrs. Walsh must have been sitting up, if that same person was still in the same position. There must have been two shots fired. From everything I've seen, the position of the bodies at the scene, the post mortem, I believe that he was shot after having connection with her."

"Really?" quizzed Bonis.

"Yes," replied Dods, "I think that the position of Cumming, and Walsh, is quite consistent with his being shot on top of her, and rolling to the position at which he was found. The same size bullet caused the injuries to both. I definitely think Walsh was sitting up when shot."

"The bullet could be anywhere then!" said Bonis.

"Not necessarily," said Dods, "I would think that it would not have travelled very far after passing through her head."

"But definitely sitting up?"

"Well no, not definite," responded Dods, "there is a possibility that the woman was shot while lying down on the broad of her back, but in my opinion it is more likely that she was sitting up. She may have sat up immediately Cumming was shot. But if she was shot while on her back the bullet would be in the ground immediately below where her head was found resting."

Bonis made a note to search the reserve again, the bullet may have been buried beneath the blood soaked patch that was below Eileen's head.

"If Cumming had been shot where I saw him, and the person who fired the shot was standing at his feet, then the cartridges would probably have been ejected to the right front of the automatic. That's where you found them, right?"

Bonis nodded.

"What are your thoughts on either wound being self-inflicted Doc?" he asked.

"Murder Suicide you mean?" responded Dods.

Bonis nodded.

"Well, I don't think the shooting of Cumming was self-inflicted, no I can be stronger than that, his wound was not self-inflicted, but it is possible that a wound such as Mrs. Walsh's could have been. And given my earlier assumption regarding Cumming's being on top of her, I should say that he was shot first."

The morgue keeper stepped into the room.

"There's a Mrs. Cumming here with her son to identify her husband."

"Not right now," said Dods, "please ask them to come back later this afternoon, there's a good man."

*

By four thirty that afternoon Dods had completed his examination and prepared the bodies for identification, having them moved to the room for such purpose. As he was adjusting the white linen sheets draped over each body, the morgue keeper entered the room, followed by Detective Constable Campbell, Constable Cook, Mrs. Cumming and her son Stanley.

According to records, Detective Constable Kenneth Campbell asserts that the following conversation took place.[vi]

"It is terrible," said Mrs. Cumming, "I have often warned him that he would meet with a sudden end, but he took no notice of me."

"Are you ready for this?" asked Dods.

Mrs. Cumming and Stanley nodded.

Dods pulled back the sheet from the deceased policeman's head.

"Oh Daddy, Oh Daddy," wailed Mrs. Cumming, "I knew it would come to this. I have warned you that you would meet a terrible end."

She bent over the body of her husband and kissed his forehead a number of times.

"Daddy, God forgive you," she said in a calmer tone.

She straightened her back and said pointing, "There, is that the woman?"

Campbell nodded and drew back the sheet from Eileen's head. Mrs. Cumming looked at her and then at Stanley who was standing on the opposite side of the morgue table.

"That is not the woman he was with at the pictures, she is too stout!"

"The other woman was thinner," agreed Stanley.

Mrs. Cumming lent in at the body of Eileen Walsh and examined her features.

"It is a bit like her," she said to Stanley, "No, she is too stout!"

"Where was he shot?" asked Mrs. Cumming turning towards her husband's body.

"In the back of the neck," responded Campbell pointing to the wound at the back of the head of Cumming's deceased body.

Mrs. Cumming did not look at the wound, instead she snapped at Campbell,

"It is the woman's fault! I hate all women!"

She returned to her husband's side and again kissed his forehead.

"Daddy, God forgive you."

"I have to ask formally Mrs. Cumming," said Campbell, "is this the body of your husband, Marquis Cumming?"

Mrs. Cumming sobbed and nodded while Stanley placed an arm around his mother's shoulders and said, "Yes."

"Could you tell me please Stanley," asked Campbell, "have you any firearms at your home."

"Yes," said Stanley, "My father had a revolver and I have an automatic."

"If you wouldn't mind, before we go back to C.I. Branch for a few questions," said Campbell, "could we stop at your place."

Campbell nodded to Constable Cook and he left the morgue to turn over the motor-car.

*

Shortly thereafter Henderson arrived at the morgue, and he escorted Mr. James Samuel Walsh, Eileen's husband, into the identification room. Walsh had been found at the Labour Bureau around midday. He was a stocky man of five feet three inches in height.

Henderson walked over to the corpse of the woman and pulled the sheet back from her head.

"Do you know whose body this is?" asked Henderson.

"Yes," said Walsh, "that is my wife." He began to sob.

"Poor Eileen, I swear to God that you didn't meet your death at my hands!"

Henderson gave him a moment before softly asking, "Have you got any idea as to who would have caused her death?"

"No," said Walsh, "I don't know of anyone living who would have done such a thing."

Henderson moved on to the body of Cumming and pulled the sheet from his head.

"Do you know whose body this is?"

"Yes," replied Walsh, "that is the sergeant from South Brisbane."

"Did you know him?"

"Only from seeing him on duty from time to time."

"Did you know he was on friendly terms with your wife?"

"What do you mean?"

"That he had a habit of going out with her?"

"No," replied Walsh shaking his head with a furrowed brow, "this is the first that I have heard of it."

3 CRIMINAL INVESTIGATION BRANCH

Records state that Campbell escorted Mrs. Cumming and her son Stanley to the C.I. Branch offices in George Street. They were led to separate rooms for questioning. Campbell handed a revolver and automatic pistol to Constable Cook and asked him to have it locked up in the property room. He took the tin trunk to his office and placed it on the desk. He had decided to start his questioning with the dead policeman's wife. Mrs. Cumming sat behind a wooden table, her purse in her lap, with her hands resting on the straps. She wore a black felt hat pulled down over her ears and neck covering the shorter hairstyle she had adopted some 12 months prior. She wore black horn-rimmed spectacles. The room was stark, save for the table and chair that she occupied and a chair opposite. The room had no natural light.

Mrs. Cumming was said to visibly upset, sniffing and reaching for the handkerchief tucked into the sleeve of her blouse. She expressed concern for her son Stanley who was in a similar room further down the corridor.

Campbell took down Mrs. Cumming's particulars. She

was Theresa Jane Cumming nee Howden. She married the Acting Sergeant in Brisbane on the 11th May 1904. He had turned 47 years of age on the 28th May. His father was David Cumming, a retired farmer, and his mother was Mary, maiden name Hammill and he was born at Felton on the Darling Downs. They resided at Wilton Street, Woolloongabba with their five children having lost two children, a boy and a girl.

Their eldest son was Marquis David James Stanley Cumming, known as Stanley, twenty-one years of age in March. Their eldest daughter was Theresa Jane Margaret Mary Cumming, known as Tessie, sixteen years old. Followed by Mary Angela, eleven in January. Reginald Francis, ten in October. With the youngest Cecil Joseph turning five in September.

Detective Campbell asserts that the following conversation took place.

"Can you tell me about yesterday," said Campbell, "did you have lunch with your husband?"

"Yes, we lunched at between one and one thirty and my husband left home at about one forty, dressed in his Police Blue Uniform to take up his duty at two pm."

"Was he wearing his belt?"

"Well he usually wore a belt, but I didn't see him getting dressed, so I cannot say if he had one on."

"What about his handcuffs?"

"I did not see him with them, but he usually had them."

"Did he have his keys?"

"He always carried his keys with him," said Mrs. Cumming rolling her eyes.

"How many keys did he carry?"

"I don't know, about six, more or less."

"Did he have these keys on him when he left the

house?"

"I don't know, I didn't see them."

"How was your husband's demeanour?"

"He was in the best of health and spirits, when he left."

"What did you do after he had left?"

"I went into town, to McDonnell & Easts in George Street,[5] to do some shopping, that would have been between three and four o'clock."

"What time did you get home?"

"A little after six."

"Was your husband home?"

"No."

"When did you next see your husband?"

"Well we had arranged to meet that afternoon, so I walked from McDonnell & Easts, over the bridge, you know, the tram stop opposite Delaney's Hotel, at Victoria Place."

Campbell nodded.

"I noticed my husband on duty, on the right hand side, as you go from the city, at the Delaney's Hotel side."

"Did you approach him?"

"No, he appeared busy, and a section car came along so I got that."

"So you didn't speak to him?"

"No, I did not speak to him, and the section car was a Juliette Street car, before you ask."

"What time did the Juliette Street car have got you home?" he asked.

"It would have been about twenty past six that evening when I got home."

Campbell nodded without looking up from his note

---

[5] Refer Figure 5 - Refidex Directory 1926 Map 25

pad.

"What did you do then?"

"I got the tea ready just in time for my husband's arrival at six thirty."

"How did he greet you?"

"He asked me what I had been doing, and I told him I stood there and waited for him at Delaney's Hotel as we had arranged, but after waiting I decided to go home. He replied that he was very busy that afternoon, so much so that he was running late, and that he did not have much time for tea as he would have had otherwise."

"Was anyone else at home?"

"Yes, all the members of the family were then home and all sat down at the tea table but myself, I gave them their tea and went to my bedroom, as I wanted to open the parcel I had brought home with me from McDonnell & Easts."

"What was in the parcel?"

"Some drapery, and Christmas gifts for my husband and son."

"Did anyone see you open the parcel?"

"My daughter, Mary Angela, followed me into the room and she saw me open the parcel, and she saw what it contained."

"Continue please," said Campbell.

"I removed braces, shaving soap, and shaving cream from the parcel and wrapped them in paper, oh, and three handkerchiefs, then I removed three more handkerchiefs and shaving cream, I think, for my son, and I also wrapped that up. I handed the two parcels to Mary and said to her, 'give this one to your father, and this one to Stanley' and I think I told her to say 'from mother and the family with love' to father. She left the room and I followed closely behind hearing her say what I had told her. Then I took my place at the table with the family."

"What happened then?"

"Well, shortly after that my husband had finished his tea and he remarked that he did not have much time and he would have to be going. Mary had been crying, as he finished his tea, as she found out I had not brought her home anything and she expected something from me. My husband was now standing at the door saying goodbye to everyone in general then he said to Mary and Tessie, 'you girls meet me down the street tomorrow' meaning Christmas Eve, 'I will buy something for the girls, and mother can buy for the boys', then he said again that he would have to be going and with that he said, 'Hooray I'm off'. That was all he said. He left us all sitting at the table."

"Where was he going," asked Campbell.

"He went off to resume duty."

"Do you know if he had any money on him?"

"Oh yes, before he left he handed me £13 and he said there was some more he had to give me but he would wait till he got some change."

"Was it payday?"

"I can't say whether he said it was payday or not."

"How much did your husband earn?"

"I don't know what salary he was receiving!" said Mrs. Cumming with indignation.

"Was your husband receiving a pension."

"My husband is not in receipt of a pension!" said Mrs. Cumming excitedly.

-o-

On first reading this I thought this to be an unusual question. Why would Mrs. Cumming be asked this? Why would a serving policeman be in receipt of a pension?

*

"So you know nothing of your husband's financial schedule?"

"He gave me to understand that it was payday, and if it was payday then it would have been his fortnightly pay."

"How did your husband leave you?"

"When he left he was in the best of health and spirits, and he was on the best of terms with me and the family."

"Did you see your husband again?"

"That was the last time I saw my husband alive."

"Was he in possession of his belt when he left?"

"I cannot say whether my husband had his belt, his handcuffs, or his keys!"

"What did you do after your husband left?"

"We finished tea and the washing up was done."

"Did you remain home after your husband left?"

"No I went to see my mother, in the Valley."

*

Campbell reports he returned to his office and saw Cumming's tin trunk sitting on his desk. He worked the key in the lock. The key had been removed from the duchess of the bedroom used by Acting Sargent Cumming. It did not work, so he forced it open. He slowly removed its contents, examining each carefully, clothing, private papers, bank slips. Nothing contained in the trunk seemed suspicious. He called Constable Cook into his office and directed him to see if Mrs. Cumming and Stanley would like refreshments or a meal.

Campbell made his way to South Brisbane Police Station and opened Acting Sergeant Cumming's locker. He states he took a cardboard box and hurriedly scooped the contents of the locker in to it. On his return to C.I. Branch Campbell placed the cardboard box on Henderson's desk.

He then returned to the interview rooms. He entered the room furthest along the corridor from where he had left Mrs. Cumming. There sat Stanley Cumming alone in a room similar to the one his mother occupied.

"Sorry to keep you," said Campbell, "just have a few questions for you."

"That's all right," said Stanley, "it has been good to have the opportunity to sit and reflect on what has been quite a shock."

"I'm sure it has been," said Campbell, "could I start with your full name please."

"Marquis David James Stanley Cumming."

"Married?"

"No Sir, I'm a single man."

"Residence?"

"I live with my mother at Wilton Street, Woolloongabba."

"Occupation?"

"I'm a salesman employed by Finney Isles & Co. of Queen Street."

"How did you know the deceased whose body we saw at the morgue this afternoon?"

"The deceased, Marquis Cumming, was my father."

"Tell me, what time did you arrive home last night?"

"Well, I returned home at about six fifteen."

"Who was at home?"

"My father was then home, and mother, and the other members of the family."

"What were they doing?"

"They were about to have tea, I had general conversations with father and other members of the family."

"Did anything happen while you were having tea?"

"My sister brought in a parcel for my father, containing handkerchiefs, shaving cream, and braces, if that is what you mean," said Stanley.

"Did she say anything?"

"I can't recollect if Mary said anything to father when she handed the parcel to him."

"Please continue," requested Campbell.

"Well, there's not much more to tell, father finished his tea and the last words I heard him say as he went out the door was, 'You, Boy, the presents for the two boys, I will look after the girls', then he said 'Hooray' and left by the back door.

"What sort of mood was your father in when he left?"

"Oh, he was in the best of spirits and on good terms with the whole family, including me," said Stanley smiling.

*

According to records Detective Henderson was in a similar room, further along the corridor, sitting opposite Eileen's husband who gave his particulars as James Samuel Walsh, boot clicker, residing at Cairns Street, Red Hill when the following conversation ensued.

"You have identified the body in the morgue as Eileen Gladys Walsh, how do you know her?"

"She was my wife."

"When and where were you married?"

"That was the 26th of November 1920 at the Congregational Church in Vulture Street, South Brisbane."

"That mustn't have been long after you got back?"

"Got back, from the war you mean?"

"Yes, you're a returned serviceman, ain't you?"

"Yes."

"Tell me about that."

"I was young and stupid, so I enlisted, got captured at Reincourt and held as a prisoner of war for over eighteen months, end of story!" said Walsh agitatedly, "that's all I have to say on the matter, anyway."

It appears as though Henderson was trying to gauge Walsh's knowledge of firearms, and his state of mind, but thinking better of it, did not pursue that line of questioning.

Walsh reported that Eileen's father was John Christ and her mother Mary Mulholland. She had been born in New Farm 29 years earlier on the 2nd February. They had two children, James Frederick, who would be six in a few days, on the 28th, and, Ronald Samuel, who was three on the 4th July. He reported they had one child that died before they were married.

-o-

When I read this information I immediately though that my grandfather's father must have been Walsh, who had been told that the child had died. I subsequently found a death certificate listing Eileen as the mother. Her daughter Gladys Delacour Christie was born in November 1919 and passed away in early March the following year. No father was listed. Eileen and her family had also Anglicized their Germanic surname of Christ to Christie, no doubt as a result of the First World War.

Walsh lied to the police about the parentage of Eileen's daughter but later in a newspaper interview he agreed that it was not possible for him to be the father. It is assumed that he had done so to protect Eileen's honour.

My grandfather was born in 1912, when Eileen was 17 years old. Eileen named him Leslie Christie. This information was not recorded on her death certificate but provided by the Queensland Department of Adoption Services.

*

Henderson continued his questioning of Walsh.

"Was your wife in receipt of a pension?"

"No, not that I am aware of," said Walsh frowning.

"You said you last saw your wife alive on the 22nd, two days ago?"

"Yes, she then being in a tram going along Stanley Street towards Vulture Street."

"What time was that again?"

"Six pm."

"Was she with anyone?"

"She had a child in her lap."

"Where were you?"

"I was on the footpath, she was riding in a passing tram, that was the last time I saw her alive, I've told you this!"

"Just want to make sure I got it down correctly Mr. Walsh. You told me earlier that you last spoke to your wife in October, do you remember when exactly?"

"Well, no, oh, hang on, we did discuss the Golden Casket, you know, the raucous in parliament and the fraud allegations, when was that?

"That was early in October," responded Henderson.

"Right, so it would have been a week after that, on a Friday," said Walsh.

"When did you first learn of your wife's death?"

"When you guys arrived at the Labour Bureau and brought me here, you told me then."

"How did you come to be at the Labour Bureau?"

"I came up from Manly this morning, got into Brisbane

at about eleven at the Melbourne Street Station."

"You caught the train from Manly?"

"Yes, the twelve minutes past ten train."

"And you have been living apart from your wife?"

"Yes, since about July of 1924, that being the first separation, and we have been living apart ever since."

"The first separation you say, you have never been separated before that?"

"No, we had separated before that, twice, but that was only for a few days."

"When was that?"

"Sometime in 1923, she left me."

"Why, did you have a quarrel?"

"Well, yes, I resented her visiting her mother's people so frequently, on account of them having a grudge against me."

"Did you keep in contact with your wife while separated?"

"Sometimes I would meet her by accident, other times she wrote me, to make an appointment with me, and I used to see her, but we never lived together since we separated."

"Why did she write you?"

"She was trying for us to get back together, and when she had any news of importance, she would tell me."

"What did she last write about?"

"She seemed anxious for us to get back together, I always gave her to understand that she could come back any time she wished, and she said she would, but that she would have to give the eldest child to her mother to adopt."

"Why would she say that?"

"I always contended that if we came together we would have to have the children."

"When did you last arrange to meet her?"

"That was in early October, as I said, and on that occasion I, I co-habited with her."

"Did you know she had been on friendly terms with others?"

"No, I never knew she was on friendly terms with anyone else since we have been married."

"Did you know of the relationship between your wife and Acting Sergeant Cumming?"

"I had no idea there was any relationship between them!"

"Where were you yesterday?"

"I was staying at the home of William Morris, my brother-in-law, I have been for some time."

"What were you doing last night?"

"Harry Morris and I went to the 'Waterloo Bay Hotel' in Wynnum, about five thirty and remained there till about eight o'clock."

"What did you do after that?"

"Harry Morris and I, and another chap, whose name I can't remember, the three of us, we left the Hotel, we came down the street towards the beach and the other chap said he was going to the pictures, and I said to Harry Morris, 'Come down to the fair', as there was a fair down near the beach, and we got to the fair and stayed there till about nine thirty last night."

"The man that was with you, can you tell me anything about him?"

"He was a lorry driver."

"Had you met him before?"

"No."

"What did you do after he left you?"

"We went down to the Liberty Fair, that is Morris and I, and remained there indulging in the various games being played until about nine thirty."

"What did you do then?"

"We then went to the Kiosk, and Harry Morris and I then drank a bottle of beer under a shed, and then we went up to town at Wynnum South and went into a cake shop, but it was closed, so we had to knock, and there we had tea and scones, that being just about ten o'clock."

"Who served you?"

"A girl."

"Can you describe her?"

"She was wearing a dress, a red dress."

"What did you do then?"

"We proceeded towards our home at Manly, and on the way Harry bought some cake and bananas, and then we went on our way home arriving there about eleven pm."

"What did you do when you got home?"

"We had a bottle of stout, that is Harry Morris and I, oh, and my mother, my mother was residing with us, and I retired to bed about eleven thirty."

"Did you get up during the night?"

"No, I remained there, and didn't get up until seven thirty this morning, I had breakfast, then caught the twelve past ten train."

"Did you speak to anyone at the Hotel?"

"I spoke to a man named Menzies, and another man there, Souter, the barman, I spoke to him there."

"And how many times have you assaulted your wife?"

"I never assaulted my wife on any occasion!" said Walsh indignantly.

"Never?" questioned Henderson.

"I was on very good terms with my wife, always."

"But she left you?"

"It was all through her mother, as I objected to my wife going to her mother's place, I never, ever, had rows with my wife, well, not until the morning she left."

"Do you know who may have wanted to murder your wife?"

"I have no idea who shot my wife, or Cumming."

*

According to reports, Henderson returned to his office where he met Campbell and Constable Cook. On his desk sat the small cardboard box collected from the South Brisbane locker of Acting Sergeant Cumming. Cook peered into the box, and his back must have straightened in shock.

He removed a woman's undergarment made from delicate silk lace. Campbell scrummaged in the box to extract a quantity of letters and Christmas Cards. He flicked quickly through the letters looking at the signatures. The letters were all from women. Henderson stood behind him reading the cards as Campbell flicked through them.

Henderson, on recognized one of the names asked to be left alone then instructed Cook to organise a check of the pawnbrokers to see if anyone had purchased an automatic pistol lately.

4 DOMESTIC TROUBLES

Campbell reportedly returned to the interview rooms, this time entering the room of Mrs. Cumming. She appeared to be a little agitated.

"Is Stanley still alright?" she asked as she straightened her back.

"Yes your son is fine," said Campbell, "do you mind if I ask where your husband has been stationed."

Mrs. Cumming nodded as she slumped back into her chair.

"Several places before South Brisbane, Mareeba, Capella, Emerald, North Rockhampton, Marmor Westward, and Mt. Morgan, he came to South Brisbane from Mt. Morgan."

"Would you say you lived happily?"

"Yes," said Mrs. Cumming somewhat reluctantly.

This is it, Campbell must have thought to himself.

"Are these yours?" he may have asked, dangling a woman's undergarment from his index finger.

"Oh! my stars!" Mrs. Cumming may have exclaimed turning her head, "I should think not, why would you show me such a thing!"

"Would you be surprised if I said these were found in your husband's locker at the Station?"

Mrs. Cumming said nothing, her eyes darting around the room trying to avoid the sight of the undergarment.

Campbell returned them to his coat pocket.

"When did the domestic trouble start?" he asked.

"The first sign of domestic trouble started at Mt. Morgan."

"How long were you there for?" said Campbell in a conversational way, so as not to upset Mrs. Cumming any further.

"We were over three years at Mt. Morgan."

"Really, and when did the trouble start?"

"About five years ago. For about six or eight months there my husband was in charge of the police station, at Mt. Morgan, during the absence of Senior Sergeant McKenzie. He, McKenzie, went off on long service leave before retiring. My husband was instructed to live in the Senior Sergeant's quarters, but he decided not to, as it was only a short distance away from our residence. But he was instructed to occupy the quarters with me and the family. In the end he decided to sleep on the premises and I remained in the house, with the family. The Mt. Morgan house was spacious with two stories. Then I heard that my husband had been visiting a particular woman's house, and so I asked him, at first he denied it. Then I questioned him further about visiting this woman and he said he had to go to her place to make inquiries. At this period my husband used to go out a lot, but I did not know where he was going, I used to take exception to that."

"That's only natural," said Campbell.

"He didn't agree with me, and continued going out. I always took exception to his going out, not telling me where he was going, and not taking me out with him."

"And you took exception," said Campbell.

"It was his going out at night alone that I took exception to, when he was off duty, then I found out that that woman had sent vegetables to our house, so I went to see her I told her about the exception I took, at first she denied that my husband had been there, then she said when one did her a good turn she liked to do them one back. After that, I was doing the laundry, and I found a little note in my husband's trouser pocket written to him, reminding him not to forget an appointment that was made at 8 o'clock that night. I did not make my husband any the wiser that I had seen it."

"What impression did that leave you with?"

"It was definitely a females handwriting so, well, that created an impression in my mind that my husband was, not treating me as he should, it created the impression in my mind that my husband was, spending his evenings with other women!"

Mrs. Cumming sobbed again, reaching for the handkerchief folded into her blouse sleeve.

"I never believed him when he said he was going out with a party of friends or men, I was always asking him to stay home with us, and not go out every night."

"Did anyone ever see this?"

"Oh yes, we had a married cousin of my husband's stay with us, Mrs. Jessie Cumming, and one evening Jessie Cumming said, 'What about some music?' and I said 'Yes, yes, let's have some music!' but my husband was all dressed up ready to go out. He was in the first room and I said 'Dadda, are you going out?' and he replied 'Yes'. I begged him to stay home and join in the evening, but he said 'I'm going out' and with that he went to go down the stairs, to go to the dining room, and I ran to the bannister. Over the bannister there was a heavy strip of canvas. I called out to him, 'Dadda, why don't you come back and have some music?' I put my hand on the canvas accidentally causing it to fall on his head, he got very annoyed, he accused me of doing it intentionally, I hadn't, but he rushed back up the stairs, and took hold of me by the shoulders, and he pushed me against the wall. Then Jessie sang out, 'Oh Mark, Don't hit Totty', meaning me, then he let me go and went out."

Campbell underlined the name Mrs. Jessie Cumming in his notepad.

"What can you tell me about this person," he said, slipping a piece of paper in front of Mrs. Cumming.

She adjusted the glasses on her face, to sharpen the focus of the name she had been shown. She turned pale.

"That's not the woman I spoke of," she said, "that's different to the one I told you about, that I suspected my husband of visiting, but I will not speak her name either!"

Campbell had been instructed 'that under NO circumstances were the names, attributed to the letters he found, to be uttered'. Nor the locations, such that doing so may tend to identification of persons in the letters. So wide, it is reported, were the illicit amours of the dead police sergeant, that the names of dozens of women appeared. Some were young girls, but most of them married women, none of whose names were to be revealed, in order that no happy household would be sundered, the good names of respectable families impugned, and tragedy follow tragedy tenfold'.[vii]

"Tell me more about this one."

"Well, shortly after we arrived in Brisbane, the family and I didn't come down straight away from Mt. Morgan with my husband, it was probably three months afterward, I had to sell the house, so I remember him coming home from work and he took some letters from his pocket."

"When was this?"

"We came down here in October of 1923, so it was probably the July after that."

"Continue, please."

"He put the letters on the table in front of me, and he went outside and he left the letters on the table. Amongst those letters I noted that there was a letter in a woman's handwriting."

"Where was your husband?"

"He went out the back."

"And the letters were on the table."

"Yes, I could see all the letters on the table."

"Did you read them?"

"No, I did not read them, at that time, my husband subsequently put those letters away in a box, which he kept locked. I opened the box and I got the particular letter with the ladies' handwriting, and I saw that the letter was signed with certain initials, and I learned from that letter, that my husband, was, was the father of another woman's child."

Campbell gave Mrs. Cumming a moment to gain her composure before asking,

"Where was the letter from?"

"Mt. Morgan."

"What did you do with the letter?"

"I kept it."

"How did you open the box?"

"I used the key from his duchess."

"Continue, please."

"Later on that day my husband missed the letter and he asked me if I saw any letters about, he asked me if I saw a letter knocking about, he did not indicate what letter it was, and after a while I said to him 'I think I know the letter you are looking for', and I related to him that I noticed the letter in the morning, and that I opened his box, and I said to my husband 'I have found out all your secrets now, if I had waited for 20 years, I could not have learnt more!' then he demanded the letter from me."

"Did you give it to him?"

"No, I refused, I accused him of what I had read in the letter, him being the father of this woman's child, but my husband denied it, but I retained the letter."

"What did you do with the letter?"

"I believe I showed Stanley that letter when he came home, and Stanley made some inquiries about the initials,"

"Initials?" interrupted Campbell.

"Yes, the letter bore no signature just signed with initials."

"What did Stanley do?"

"He made some inquiries about the initials and he located a name, and he wrote a letter to that address."

"How did finding out this news make you feel?"

"I was upset and annoyed by this matter and I told my husband that I would make arrangements for a judicial separation, and I consulted a solicitor."

"What did the solicitor say?"

"That I needed more than that letter, so some months later Stanley went to Mt. Morgan, in the course of his occupation, and on his return he told me that he had seen this particular woman, and he told me that he got a signed statement from her, admitting that my husband was the father of her child, and he gave me the statement."

"What did you do with it?"

"I destroyed it."

"Did you tell your husband?"

"Oh yes, and he got quite annoyed about the information Stanley had obtained."

"How annoyed was he?"

"Well he came home the next night and appeared to have taken some drink, and he came into the room where

Stanley and I were and said, 'I could shoot the two of you if I liked', and he placed his hand towards his hip pocket, where he usually carried his revolver, and I said, 'Oh Dadda, there is no necessity for that!' but it had upset me. The following night he had a quarrel with Stanley and in consequence, Stanley left home, and went to reside at Stephens Road."

"Your son is back with you now though isn't he?"

"Yes, he eventually came home, after some weeks."

"So there was no domestic trouble after that?"

"No, after the incident my husband and I made it up, I consulted a friend of mine and they advised me that for the sake of the children I should forgive him."

"Were there other occasions here in Brisbane when you were suspicious of your husband?"

"I remember a time when we were living in Gladstone Road, I heard that my husband was going out to meet a woman and I decided to follow, and I followed him to a house off Annerley Road."

"Can you tell me the name of the street?"

"No, no, I don't know what street it was, but I went into the house and I saw my husband sitting on the edge of a bed talking to a man and woman and I said, 'Is this were you are', or words to that effect, and he replied 'What brought you here?' and I said to him, 'If you can find time to come here you can surely find time to come out with me!' Then I left, leaving my husband there."

Campbell slipped another piece of paper in front of Mrs. Cumming.

"Was this the woman?"

Mrs. Cumming bowed her head and looked into her purse before she said embarrassedly, "No."

"Can you tell me about this woman?"

"It was about two months ago and my husband had

come off night duty and had gone to sleep, but about twelve thirty he got up in a hurry and dressed in his civilian clothes and I said to him, 'Daddy are you going to have some lunch?' to which he responded, 'No, I am going out and I don't feel inclined'. He finished dressing and he went out, he didn't tell me where he was going, but I suspected he was going to the pictures as he had been speaking about going to see a picture called 'Greenhide', but when he previously spoke of going to see 'Greenhide' he did not approve of me going with him."

"Why?"

"He didn't say."

"Continue, please," said Campbell.

"It was about quarter past one when he left home, sometime later in the afternoon, I got dressed and went over town."

"What time was that?"

"About three thirty, I had to go on business. I was also suspicious as to where my husband was going, and who he was with! So I went down to 'His Majesty's Theatre', where this picture was being shown, and when there for a while I saw my husband come out of the dress circle entrance. He appeared to be alone when I saw him and he came out and he looked up and down the street."

"Did he see you?"

"No I don't think so, not at that time, he turned round towards a woman who was following him out, and she joined him."

"Did you know the woman, at that time?"

"No, she was a perfect stranger to me."

"Continue please."

"They both walked down into Edward Street, round the corner, and then into a Café, in Edward Street, going towards the Gardens."

"What did you do?"

"I followed them, after I saw them go into the Café I went up to Finney Isles where my son was employed, and I saw Stanley, and I told him of what I had seen, and I asked him to come with me to find out who the woman was."

"Did he agree?"

"Yes, and when we got to the Café my son Stanley stood outside the door while I went in, and I saw my husband sitting at a table with this woman, and I walked up to the woman and said, 'Good evening, do you know who your gentleman friend is?' and that woman replied 'Oh No', and then I said, 'That! is my husband!' and when I said that the woman stood up and left the table, and she walked out into Edward Street, and I followed, leaving my husband in the café. When I got out of the café I said to the woman, 'This is my son', pointing at Stanley, and the woman said, 'I am very sorry, I never met your husband before, I only just met him at the pictures, and he asked me to have afternoon tea.' I then said to her, 'You would do more than I would, taking tea from a stranger!' and the woman then said, 'Please don't make any fuss about it, for the sake of my crippled child'."

"What did you say then?"

"I believe I said to her, 'Do you come from Mt. Morgan?' and she replied 'No', and I think Stanley asked her name and address, and she said Mrs. Page, and that she lived at Dutton Park, and then I said to her 'Did you ever see my husband before!' and she said 'On the Dutton Park tram, going out of town' I was annoyed and stepped away and Stanley continued a conversation with her. Then I turned back and said to her, 'I am as pleased as if I found a fiver to have caught him with a woman, he is always telling me that he is out with men pals!"

"How did she react?"

"She was very upset, so I took her into a Café in Queen Street and gave her a drink and some refreshments, she was so upset, I believed what she had told me. Then we saw her catch an Ipswich Road tram, and Stanley said something to me and I became suspicious, that she may have been telling a lie as to her name and address, seeing that she got onto an Ipswich Road tram after telling us that she lived at Dutton Park."

"What did you both do, you and Stanley?"

"Stanley decided to follow her and I went home."

"Where was your husband?"

"I left him at the Café."

"What happened then?

"I was at home preparing tea when Stanley arrived home, he said that he had followed her to a street in Dutton Park, but had lost sight of her."

"What did you say to your husband?"

"I did not see him when he came home that night, I spoke to him the next day and said, 'You have always told me that you have been going out with gentlemen friends, and I can see now that you have always been telling me untruths!' He then wanted me to believe that he had only just met this woman by accident! But I did not believe him."

"What did he say?"

"Nothing, it ended at that."

Mrs. Cumming was now almost inconsolable as she sobbed heavily.

"I should think we should be getting you home now," said Campbell.

"What about Stanley?" said Mrs. Cumming sniffling as she spoke.

"Don't you worry about Stanley," replied Campbell, "we'll take care of him, he should not be too far behind you."

*

Detective Campbell left Mrs. Cumming and returned to Stanley who was still waiting in another interview rook. As he sat down he looked directly into Stanley's eyes and asked,

"Who is Mrs. Page?"

"Mrs. Page?" asked Stanley uncomfortably.

"Yes, your mother has just told me of an incident with Mrs. Page, could you tell me about her," said Campbell in a matter of fact way, "your mother came to your place of employment."

"Yes, she did," said Stanley reticently, "about two months ago, she asked me to go with her as she had found my father in a Café with another woman."

"What did you do?"

"I went with her."

"Did you enter the Café?"

"No, I remained outside while my mother went into the Café."

"What then?"

"I saw a woman come out ahead of my mother."

"And your father?"

"I saw him come out of the Café afterwards."

"What did the woman do?"

"She spoke to me, she said, 'Are you the son?' and I replied 'Yes' and added 'It's pretty hard on a man to have to leave his work and witness a thing like this', and she replied 'I am very sorry but this is the first time I have met him'. I asked her for her name and address and she told me that her name was Page and that she lived at Dutton Park. I didn't believe her, so I said, 'I want to know where you are living and if you don't tell me I will call a policeman!' and the woman said, 'I have not been here long, I have just come from Sydney' and I said 'I don't believe that, where are you living now!' and she said again 'Dutton Park'."

"Did your mother talk to her?"

"Yes my mother did converse with that woman."

"What did they do then?"

"My mother and she then walked up Queen Street, and after that the woman went to catch a tram, one that goes up Stanley Street, but not the tram to Dutton Park, and on seeing that, I, I decided to follow her."

"Why?"

"I believed then that she was telling me lies all the time."

"So you followed her?"

"Yes, I caught a Yellow Cab and followed the tram to North Quay, then I caught the tram that the woman Page was on."

"And then?"

"Then she got off the tram at the intersection of Stanley Road and Annerley Road, and I alighted from the tram as well. She went into a shop and then when she came out she proceeded up Annerley Road, and I followed her, and after about fifty yards I overtook her and I said to the woman that she was telling me lies, and that I had decided to follow her, as far as I can remember, she said, 'I don't live very far up the road' and she requested me not to come any further. I told her that 'I decide to go as far as I like'. After a short distance up Annerley Road she took a turn to the right, and we went along a path to an overbridge on the railway line, we crossed that, and went about another 200 yards, when she said, 'I only live at the corner house of this street' and that she wished I did not come any further. By this time I thought she was telling the truth so I left her. I walked across the street to the opposite corner, and decided to watch where she went and she was passing the house that she had indicated to me that she lived in, and I came out from where I was standing, being unobserved by her up to that time, that I was watching her. She half turned round and looked back, and she saw me watching her, then she came back a few paces and then stopped. Then she suddenly rushed up to the corner. I lost sight of her and I have no idea where she lives."

"Have you ever seen this woman after that day?" asked Campbell.

"About a month ago," replied Stanley, "It was a Saturday night, I can't remember the exact date, but a Saturday, I went out with the intention of keeping an appointment with a young lady from Merivale Street, at Carisbrooke boarding house, to go to a dance next door at St. Mary's School and it turned out the young lady was sick in bed, so I stayed with her till about nine o'clock then I came down Melbourne Street. As I was passing the old skating rink I noticed my father standing on the opposite side of the street, talking to the woman I had previously seen him with at the Café, and to make sure that it was she, and to let my father know that I knew he was out with her again, I walked across the street, and passed within a few paces of them. Just as I was passing, my father noticed me and with that he said, 'Are you following me!' and he rushed at me, and I ran away from him, and cut across the street and I got away."

"What did you do then?"

"I went home and I told mother about it."

5 CHRISTMAS EVE

Accounts suggest that Henderson received word from South Brisbane Police Station, that a local resident from a cottage across the street, had reported a strange occurrence from the night before. Only when he read of the murders in the paper had he decided that the police should be informed. The previous night he had been sitting on his verandah, 'musing on things in general, idling away a few moments in the cool of the evening breeze' when a friend passing by the front gate hailed him and invited him down the street for a drink, urging him to hurry up as it was fast approaching closing time, eight o'clock.

The resident of the cottage hurried up, and hastily strode down the path to join his friend on the footpath. Together they had walked off to the 'Plough Inn' in Stanley Street, not far from the gate of his cottage. The hotel bar had been thronged when they arrived and they barely had time for a couple of 'shouts' and a brief yarn before eight o'clock struck and the bar was cleared.

They had chatted for a few seconds at the gate to the cottage and then parted. As the resident was about to step into the cottage he heard the hum of a conversation on the other side of his garden fence. Two men were speaking. But he recognised the voice of his friend whom he had just left.

'Go on! Has it?' he heard his friend exclaim, 'Well that isn't my home. You had best ask the chap who has just gone inside'.

The resident on hearing that he was mentioned in the conversation, turned and returned to the gate. The figure of a man appeared at the opening of the pickets where the gate stood.

"I say," the stranger had said, "My hat has blown over your fence. Can I go and get it?"

The resident readily gave his permission and walked across the lawn with the stranger who commenced searching for his headgear. The resident had mused 'How the deuce could his hat get over there. There's not enough wind to stir up the dust." He didn't bother sharing his observation with the stranger and smilingly remarked 'That fixes you up' when the stranger retrieved his hat from a rose bush.

The resident hadn't paid much attention to the appearance of the stranger up to that moment, though he had casually noticed that he seemed to be a very nervous fellow, apparently agitated over the temporary loss of his hat. The stranger moved towards the gate and the resident stepped cautiously around his flower beds to hold the gate open for the stranger.

But the stranger hesitated outside the gate, he looked across at the dull grey outline of the South Brisbane Police Station then made a gesture towards it and said, 'Someone over there will get knocked tonight'.

The resident observed as the stranger dipped his hand nervously into a pocket for a handkerchief with his lips trembling violently. The resident questioned the stranger on his manifestation of excitement, 'A woman in the case, eh?' 'Yes' agreed the stranger, 'bloody oath!' and with that the stranger turned and moved off down the street.

Later in the evening the resident relayed the incident to several acquaintances and while it was agreed that the man's behaviour was peculiar, to say the least, the vague threats were reckoned to be the irrelevant babblings of some 'half shot' reveller who was getting an early start on the festive season's refreshments.

The resident learned from his acquaintances that a bleary idler had been hustled along the street by a constable just prior to the incident, for holding too conspicuous a conversation with some of the free and easy Magdalen's of the highway, who are somewhat prevalent in that part of the locality.

The next day when the resident studied the daily newspaper reporting the occurrences of the night before, he had wondered if there was a connection. He had contemplated how the stranger had gestured 'over there' and knew Acting Sergeant Cumming as one of those 'over there' at South Brisbane Police Station, and now Cumming was dead, murdered. 'What did it all mean?' he thought to himself. Could the stranger have been hiding behind the fence itself, and in his hurry to scramble outside when he heard himself and his companion on the footpath, lost his hat in the rose bush? But then it was hardly reasonable to presume that a man would advertise his feelings and betray his intentions by such a paltry ruse if he was contemplating murder. On the other hand, his behaviour could have been that of a man caught in the throes of jealousy, a man 'mastered by his temper and irrational in his hate'.

For a moment the resident thought he might have dreamed of the stranger and went to inspect his garden path, and there, in the soft soil of a garden plot he found the plain impression of a man's boot. The imprint clearly disclosed that the sole which had trod the mark was that of a square-toed shoe. The home dweller's own shoe was of a pointed shape and therefore he was not responsible for the impression. He then came to the quick determination that the police should know of what had happened.[viii]

A woman had also presented to South Brisbane Police Station. Volunteering the information that she had observed two men acting strangely on the previous evening. She related how she had been on the lookout for her husband, expected home soon after dinner. she had strolled down towards the tram stop corner with her two children several times, in the hope of meeting him.

To her discomposure she noticed two men, one a tall fellow, who carried a parcel under his arm, and the other a shorter man, skulking in the shadows of the railway bridge.

Both were in earnest conversation, and she said they spoke in hushed whispers.[ix]

Henderson arranged for the resident and the woman to be brought to C.I. Branch as he arranged a line up. The resident closely examined the men in the line-up, he studied their features with lengthy care and finally he went up and placed his hand upon a man's arm.

Henderson requested the resident to be led away for a moment and the men in the line-up were reshuffled, being moved from the original places in the line.

The resident was brought back and again he scrutinised the men and again he placed his hand on the arm of the man whom he had first selected, as the stranger he had seen the previous night.

The woman also inspected the line-up but failed to identify anyone as either of the two men she had seen the previous evening.

Henderson called the identification test a complete

failure, as the man selected was a dummy placed in the line.

As Henderson asked for Walsh to be escorted back to the interview rooms, the resident expressed the thought that he had made a mistake, and that Walsh appeared to be something like the man who had lost his hat.

*

By all accounts Henderson had sent word to Wynnum Police Station to detain the men that Walsh had said he had been with the previous evening and to bring them to C.I. Branch for questioning, or rather, to assist with their inquiries. He spoke to Constable Cook and was told which interview room held Henry Morris.

"For the record please," said Henderson, "could I have your name, occupation, and address."

"I'm Henry Morris, a labourer, residing with my brother and sister-in-law at Manly."

"Do you know James Samuel Walsh?"

"Yes."

"How?"

"He is a brother-in-law of mine; my brother being married to his sister."

"Were you in his company yesterday?"

"Yes, I was, from about three thirty."

"And what did you do together?"

"We left home and made our way out to the gas works, he then residing at my brother's house, as I had to go to the gas works to get my pay. After I got my pay we left and walked up towards Wynnum, to the 'Waterloo Bay' Hotel and were there till eight o'clock. Why all the questions?"

"We just want to establish some facts, that is all you need to know at this time," said Henderson, "What time did you get to the 'Waterloo Bay' Hotel?"

"We got there about seven o'clock."

"What did you do between leaving the gas works and entering the hotel?"

"We stayed in the street, looking at the shops."

"What did you do at the 'Waterloo Bay' Hotel?"

"We had a drink together and stayed in the bar till eight o'clock."

"Just one drink?"

"No, we had several drinks there."

"And when did you leave the Hotel?"

"We left at about eight o'clock and then we went down to the fair at the beach."

"Did you speak to anyone at the Hotel?"

"I saw a barman named Frank."

"What did you do after attending the fair?"

"After that we went on our way home."

"Did you stop anywhere?"

"We had some refreshments at Wasse's Café and got home at about, eleven, eleven thirty."

"What did you do when you got home?"

"We went straight to bed."

"The two of you went to bed?"

"I sleep in separate rooms from Walsh," said Morris annoyed with the question.

"Yes, of course," said Henderson, "when did you next see Walsh?"

"This morning, near seven o'clock, as soon as he got up."

"Where was this?"

"He was outside the house."

"Did he sleep there the night?"

"As far as I know, yes, he slept in a room inside the house and I slept on the back verandah."

"How much beer did you bring home with you last

night?"

"None that I recall."

"So Walsh didn't bring home a bottle of stout?"

"No, he bought a bottle of stout, down at the fair, but he drank that down there."

"Who was at home?"

"There was only two of us there at the time."

"So you don't recall drinking stout at home?"

"The only thing I can remember was having a drink at the shelter shed last night."

"Do you think Walsh could have been in Brisbane at eleven o'clock last night?"

"No, and he wasn't there beforehand!"

"How long is the walk to the gas works from your residence?"

"It takes a good hour."

"What did you do before heading off to the gas works?"

"We were home before noon, then went out fishing before we set off for the gas works."

"Did you meet anyone at the gas works?"

"No."

"How far is Manly from town?"

"From Brisbane?" Henderson nodded and Morris replied, "thirteen miles".

"Thanks Morris," said Henderson, "nothing else to ask at this time, but if you stay put we'll organise a car to take you home."

-o-

There are a few discrepancies with Morris' alibi of Walsh. They state that they went to the gas works to collect Morris' pay, yet they met no-one. If they had collected a payment then it surely would have been given to them by someone. If there was no one at the gas works at that time then surely they would have checked before setting out on a two hour round trip to go there.

Walsh also stated that he shared a bottle of stout with his mother and Morris at home after the fair. Yet Morris refutes this occurred.

*

Henderson opened the door of the adjoining interview room.

"Mr. Souter?"

"Yes," said Frank Souter.

"Come with me please."

Henderson walked a little further down the corridor with Frank Souter behind him, and thrust the door open.

"Do you know this man?"

"Yes," replied Souter.

Henderson closed the door again.

"Right, let's go back to the interview room," he said pointing back along the corridor the way they had come.

"Take a seat please Mr. Souter."

"For the record, could I have your name and occupation please."

"I am Francis Joseph Souter, a barman, employed at the 'Waterloo Bay Hotel' in Wynnum South."

"And you say you know that man in the other room?"

"Yes."

"Can you tell me who he is?"

"No, I only know him by sight."

"How's that?"

"I used to serve at a Hotel in the Gabba, my present employer used to keep a Hotel there, and I would see him there."

"How long have you known him?"

"About five years, by sight."

"When did you last see him?"

"In the bar of the Waterloo Bay Hotel, at about seven forty last night."

"Was he with anyone?"

"A chap named Morris I believe."

"How long was he there?"

"Morris?"

"No Walsh."

"Walsh, is that the name of the chap I know by sight?"

"Yes."

"Walsh was in the hotel till closing time, which is about 8 o'clock."

"What were you doing?"

"I served them a drink."

"Did you see him after eight o'clock?"

"No, no, I did not see him after eight o'clock."

"How long where they there, Walsh and Morris?"

"About twenty minutes."

"Are you sure, they weren't there longer than twenty minutes?"

"They could have been there longer, but I only saw them for about twenty minutes."

"Did you interact with them?"

"I shouted for them."

"You bought them a drink?"

"Yes, I was speaking to Walsh, and knowing him from sight, from the 'Gabba', I shouted him and his companion."

"Alright then," said Henderson, "if you go and see Constable Cook he will arrange transport to take you home, thank you for your assistance."

-O-

The police had good reason to suspect Walsh. In July 1925 Eileen charged that Walsh had unlawfully left her and the children without adequate means of support. Simultaneously with this charge Walsh was further charged with desertion of his family as Eileen had been compelled to leave his residence under reasonable apprehension of danger to her person.

Eileen stated on oath that she had not been living with Walsh since July 22, 1924. Since leaving her husband she had the care of the two children. They had at that time no means of support and neither did she. Prior to leaving Walsh she was living in a three roomed cottage in Clarence Street South Brisbane with the only furniture being a bed, a double stretcher, and two chairs. There had been three chairs but one got broken and was put under the house.

During her time with her husband she states that she would not have had any clothes if her mother had not given her some. She admitted to having little tiffs with her husband like everyone else. But during the last twelve months she lived with him she described the relationship as very unhappy. He would not work. At the beginning of that time Walsh had been working but of the 33/- a week he was making Eileen was lucky to get 5/- a week.

Eileen stated that on many an occasion Walsh would punch her in the face using language that would not be heard in the lowest part of Brisbane. One another occasion she was struck with a broom after Walsh had a bit of dust on his face from the floor while having breakfast. Eileen states that she had to stop many a punch and nearly every day he would call her a ____ _____. The words were not recorded but according to the police deposition it was the vilest of language.

Eileen stated that he used the same language towards their eldest boy while he was kind to the youngest. One night he came home drunk and gave the boy an unmerciful hiding. Pay nights were the worst drinking nights. At times when drunk he would spit in Eileen's face and would threw the food from his mouth into her face and the faces of the children. He used to get more like a beast than a man when drunk.

She stated that she left him in July 1924. The previous Friday she had just come out of hospital where she had been for 12 days. Although he was at home when she arrived he did not come into the room to see how she was. The following Tuesday she was not feeling well and said that she would stay in bed for a while. Walsh went and had breakfast then returned to the room and said 'Aren't you getting up today you lazy ___.' He also said 'Do you want a blanky servant to look after you'. He then grabbed her by the throat with one hand and with the other he caught hold of her hair and pulled her out of bed. He then told her to get out of the house as his mother's old age pension had been keeping her long enough. Walsh called Eileen a prostitute. She hurriedly washed the youngest child's clothes and left the house with sixpence in her purse. She told Walsh she would be coming back for her clothes. 'That is just what I want' she reports he said, 'When I am finished with you nobody else will want you'.

Eileen applied for support through the courts to which Walsh agreed to on the condition that she brought the children to see him every Saturday. Eileen complied but after two months she arrived at the home to find Walsh speechlessly drunk from spirits. When Eileen asked for the money Walsh had said, 'you will not get any money until you come and live with me'.

Eileen states that she had said she would go back to

Walsh if he gave up drinking and provided a home. Since she left her husband she had been in receipt of Government relief and was informed that Walsh had tried to have it stopped. Walsh had made an offer to provide a home but Eileen stated that she considered the offer like those he had made previously. 'They all end in smoke'. Eileen closed her statement by saying, 'I repeat, on the last occasion I took the children to see him he was drunk'.

In the course of cross examination Walsh also gave evidence in the case which was in fact a denial in toto of the allegations made by Eileen. He stated that at no time had he drunk to excess but later admitted that he had been fined for drunkenness and further that a conviction had been recorded against him in the Brisbane Police Court for calling his mother-in-law a black _____!^{ix}

I had a lot of emotions after reading this. The violence was all too frequent amongst returned servicemen of The Great War. They had trouble ridding themselves of the demons of war. So, in part, I felt sorry for Walsh, but then again, I also hoped that he wasn't Grandpa's dad. I felt sorry for the situation Eileen was in but also marvelled at her strength. Taking Walsh to court and making her statement must have been very difficult. But the thing that stood out to me the most? The very last line. He called his mother-in-law a black whatever.

It appears as though Eileen's family was poor and black.

I have checked Mary Mullholland's birth certificate and it states that her father was James Mulholland born in Belfast Ireland, and her mother Ann Smith of County Westmeath in Ireland. Ann signed the certificate with her mark. It appears as though she could neither read nor write. Did she know what she was signing? Their wedding certificate, which indicates they were married in Alfred Village of the Colony of Queensland in 1865, records their place of birth as the same as Mary's birth certificate. Another mystery.

*

The following is one of the letters reportedly found in Cumming's locker from the mother of his illegitimate child.

11 A.M. Friday
Morning &
The Conceit Bitch

To Sergeant Cumming,
Your letter received and more than concerned contents - but greatly insulted, How dare you write to me like that – you never addressed me in the first place as you shoved off and the second it was easy seen, out of sight out of mind, but remember you have cut me to the very core, but I should have known better. I had no need to do what I did. But whatever power you have over me is invisible. I know I love you and always did. We would never perhaps of come together only through rations, fun etc, but I just couldn't help it.

Will you please forgive and forget me as I am sure I feel this lot and cannot endure it much longer. I can't expect anything else as the way you addressed me is most insulting & an escaped mole would only escape such liberal terms. However I wish you all sorts of good luck and health as I love every inch of you & I know this much I have made my own cross & am prepared to shoulder it alone, unexplained things do happen! I seen no show, but went down last Friday on a very sad mission. Mrs Arthur Mee, Bob's Sister had the misfortune to lose her little child 2 ½ years old with gastritis. Passed away at ¼ past one last Saturday morning. So I seen nothing of the show.

"They are high up in the world" He is manager of Headricks Rockhampton I promised her to go down tomorrow midday but will phone her not too well. I couldn't go now after receiving that nasty one from you. Thank heavens your little son is healthy & a little picture of love but I will care for him & always look after him, He is just beginning to talk & not only today did he call me D. but two days ago & that hurts most now. I have a hard role to play but will play the card for the man. I always admired & respected & love too much just to be cast aside for others. They say love is blind, but not here. I am just beginning to wake up & remember could write pages.

I have a lot to say but I don't know why I can't write anymore. So there is just one thing left to forgive & forget me. But not your <u>Baby</u> as he speaks for himself. Now I hope I am not intruding on too much space, if so, you can count that as a slip with the pen & I hope you will more than enjoy yourself with your new friends as life is short. I know I have made a real slip & it is only a judgement on me, I am fully prepared to bear it all. The path is stony & rough but I will go through everything for you only.

I can't write any more perhaps I will have another try when this fever works off. So I remain

Your affectionate Friend,

F.A.D. Broken Hearted

Love from Baby

C xxx

S.W.M.T.

P.S. That Beautiful memory "A cradle of Peace lovely tears, left behind, <u>B</u> is too good for this rotten earth. He is too intelligent & forward & such a Kid." I n<u>eve</u>r h<u>a</u>d o<u>ne</u> li<u>ke</u> <u>him</u> no trouble at all. I co<u>ul</u>d n<u>o</u>t th<u>in</u>k of c<u>o</u>ming

down your way now as I am only classed with the low set
in your estimation. But will try from now on to hold my
spirit up a bit. It is not quite crushed all of me yet. I
intended after the exhibition was over to come but will
cancel it. I forgot to mention there was nothing on the
Casket Ticket another little debt of mine But will not
forgetting it all the same. But will forward you what I owe
you in full all what I got from you. You will meant it all for
pastimes now. N.B. No they never made any comment on
that at P.G. Re Hegarty I intended to make my B.Cake but
it is made & too rigid more than dough. You don't know
what that letter meant to me, but there is only one way out
and that is the easiest, the Grave is the Sweetest.

*

Meldon decided he needed to gather together all
correspondence between the pair, quickly, but discretely.
He instructed Detective Martin Elford to travel to
Rockhampton. There, he was to report to Detective
Sergeant McCarthy and they were to travel together to
Mount Morgan.[xi]

The thirty-six year old Martin Elford had been promoted
to Detective earlier in the year after spending twelve
months as a plain-clothes constable at Roma Street Station.
He had been recruited from Sandgate Station where he was
serving as a constable. Prior to being deployed to Sandgate
he had spent time at the Mount Morgan Station under
Sergeant O'Grady and Acting Sergeant Cumming.

-o-

The first aspect of this letter to strike me was the tone in which it was written. It seems to have been written after the arrival of another from Cumming. It would appear that Cumming was not too flattering of her as she resents being referred to as being 'classed in the low set'. I have concluded that Cumming must have written to end his relationship with this woman. This is somewhat supported by the ending of the letter which is either a suicide reference or a threat to Cumming's life. The other thing I found curious was, that in such a letter, Cumming would include a Casket Ticket. Why? And is there any significance in the note after the casket reference, 'they never made any comment on that at P.G.? Why are there letters and words underlined? Was there a code?

The letter was said to be from a woman in Mount Morgan and does have sufficient information to identify the writer. Mention is made of the death of the son of Bob's sister, Mrs. Arthur Mee. A search of the death certificates around that time reveals that Neville Arthur Mee passed away in 1924. The son of Arthur Mee and Elizabeth Carol Doak. Elizabeth Doak had a brother Robert. Robert was married to Francis Annie. The letter is signed off with the initials F.A.D. I therefore believe the author of the letter to be Francis Annie Doak.

At this juncture I apologize to the family of Francis Annie Doak for any issues this may create. I understand that the child she had with Cumming may have never been aware of this fact. Growing up believing Robert Doak to be his father.

With the Casket Ticket reference in the letter I researched this a little further. More out of curiosity than believing it to be a factor in the murders. The history of the Golden Casket commences with its establishment in March of 1917. The Queensland Patriotic Fund requested permission to hold an inaugural art union to raise money for the Australian Soldiers' Repatriation Fund. Termed the 'Golden Casket', the first prize was £5000, the equivalent to 30 years of a skilled tradesman's wage. Although such gambling was unlawful at the time, the Queensland Government approved the request. Due to this illegality, the first Prize was paid as bullion, a solid gold casket, and bought back from the committee immediately in cash. The gold coming from the Mt. Morgan mine.

Due to the success of the art union the Labor held Government assumed control three years later. Administration of the Golden Casket Art Union being transferred to the Home Secretary's Office in a controversial move dismissed by opponents as official gambling. Initially profits were raised for housing of nurses, bush nurses, a cancer campaign and the Tuberculosis Soldier's Housing Scheme. By 1922 most of the monies raised went to improving the health of mothers and babies under the Maternity Act 1922. By 1924 sales of Golden Casket tickets exceeded £500,000 per annum with less than half being returned as winnings.

It was lucrative, and the Government did everything to ensure the confidence of the people in the probity of the now weekly draws. In August 1922, the then Manager of the Golden Casket Committee, Mr. Lucas, left suddenly for Sydney without the knowledge of the Home Secretary's Office. The State Opposition made much of the fact in parliament, especially after an Auditor General's report, issued afterward, discovered an amount of £265 had been stolen. Investigations were made by Detectives attached to C.I. Branch but no arrest was made. Neither was there any form of prosecution.

However, it was a series of incidences in 1924 that raised the most concerns. Fraudulent practices had been uncovered within the Casket Office, when members of the staff had been found to have altered the official results slips to tickets that they held in their possession. This had been supressed with the Government ascribing irregularities to printer's errors. There were also allegations of undue interference in connection with the office administration, the filling of vacancies and other administrative matters. That the situation had become so unbearable that a determined stand was required to be taken at the Casket Headquarters. The opposition further alleged that a report had been furnished to the Minister requesting a review of the whole situation. Furnished with this information the Opposition moved a resolution in Parliament for a searching inquiry to be conducted. But the motion was talked out by the Government enraging the Opposition who made loud protests and called for the Government Member to sit down.[xii] As the newspapers of the day reported, anything adversely affecting the Casket would be a calamity, the public hospitals that greatly benefitted from the Casket money they received would suffer grievously, should anything happen to shorten this welcome and necessary source of support.[xiii]

The Opposition continued to accuse the Government of 'hushing up' any notion that there were fraudulent activities and practices within the Golden Casket Office. In 1926 the Auditor General's Department uncovered further irregularities when conducting a check of the discs used in the drawing of the Gold Casket. And again a call for an inquiry into the management committee, who they said displayed gross negligence and carelessness in such continued accusations.

The Home Secretary, Mr. Stopford, or Stoppy as his mates at the Miners Union called him, Member for Mt. Morgan, held that there was constant inquiry into the affairs of the Golden Casket Office as it was subject to continuous audit by the Auditor General and therefore the opposition were merely grandstanding, and in fact, jeopardised the assistance rendered to the country hospitals, the sick and afflicted, by their political propaganda. He asserted further that there was no need for any query, for the Golden Casket had the confidence of the people of the state.[xiv]

It should be remembered that on 23 March 1922, legislation to abolish the Upper House (Legislative Council) was passed and Queensland became the only unicameral state parliament in Australia. The Legislative Council had opposed many of the reform measures of the Ryan Labor Government which was elected in 1915. This resulted in the government formulating a policy to abolish the Council. This proposal was continually rejected by Upper House Members and was defeated in a referendum. However, the Acting Governor, William Lennon, then appointed 14 Labor Members to the Council giving the Government a majority in the Upper House. The Council sat for the last time on 27 October 1921, where it voted in favour of passing the Constitution Act Amendment Bill, the purpose of which was to abolish Queensland's Upper House. At the time the Opposition protested that the abolition of the chamber would result in the Assembly being 'able to do what it thinks fit' and becoming unaccountable.

6 CHRISTMAS DAY

Christmas Day in the Christie home must have been a subdued affair. Both of Eileen's sons were too young to understand why their mother had not attended the morning church service with them. They would have been confused by the lack of cheer that they had been promised by their Grandmother, Uncle, and Aunts. The build up to Christmas Day would have promised so much, but as young as they were, they must have sensed that all was not well in the household.

In the early afternoon Mary Christie states that she stood on the verandah of her home in Stephens Road. I imagine that she had her forearms placed on the balustrade to take her weight. Her head was bowed as she stared into the flower bed at the front of the house. A small tear plummeted from her face and flicked the petal of a geranium causing it to quiver in unison with her lip. She dabbed at her eyes with her handkerchief before straightening her back and wiping her hands down the front of her apron to steady herself for Christmas Dinner preparations. As she straightened she became aware that she was being observed.

She states that at the front gate stood a middle aged woman with black horn rimmed glasses, a hat pulled down to cover her ears and the back of her neck. Beside her stood a young girl.

"May I help you?" said Mary.

"Are you Mrs. Christie?"

"Yes," said Mary following the words with a deep breath.

"I am Mrs. Cumming," said the middle aged woman before her, "I came to you to offer my sympathy," before adding, "I don't know if you will accept it?"

"Yes," responded Mary, "I do accept the sympathy and I am awfully sorry for you."

"Did you know my daughter?"

"No," said Mrs. Cumming, who added after a pause, "Where is the body?"

"I buried my daughter yesterday afternoon," replied Mary.

"You got rid of her quick didn't you?"

Mary chose not to respond.

"Has my husband ever been here drinking, or playing cards here?"

"Never!" Mary exclaimed agitated by the questioning.

"If not here it must be a place further down the street," said Mrs. Cumming casting a glance down the road.

"How long have you been living in this house?"

"Over sixteen years."

"Oh no, you were living further down the street a few years ago."

"No, I have never been out of this house for over sixteen years," said Mary, becoming more annoyed with the questions.

"If it's not you, it must be someone else," said Mrs. Cumming, "I have always warned my husband that this would be his end, and he only laughed and said, 'it will be a good man that will get me'. Evidently the good man has got him, but got him from the back!"

"He was always so fond of beautiful women and girls, but let him go and look at them lying at the morgue twenty-four hours afterwards, with the paint and powder off!"

"My daughter had no occasion to use paint or powder!" said Mary with indignation.

"It was a strange coincidence," said Mrs. Cumming again casting an eye down the street, "that was the only night that he went out without his revolver, and he left it at home, on the table. Are you aware that his belt and handcuffs and keys were missing?"

"No," said Mary, "I did not know that they were missing."

Mary was thoughtful then asked,

"Have you got any idea who murdered my daughter Mrs. Cumming, and your husband?"

"No," said Mrs. Cumming, "Don't you think the husband did it?"

"No!"

"Or did he pay for someone else to do it?"

"He had no money to pay someone else to do such a terrible crime!"

"My idea in coming up to your place today is to see what kind of people you are."

Mary did not respond, leaving it for Mrs. Cumming to judge for herself.

"My husband was so particular in life, about this, and that, and everything, look at the headlines he has left in the papers now."

"Have you seen them?" quizzed Mary.

"Yes, they're shocking!"

"I remember Mrs. Walsh," said the sixteen-year-old

Tessie Cumming, "she goes to the same church as I do every Sunday, with her little boy."

"I don't give that," said Mrs. Cumming clicking her fingers, "for him or his relations."

Mrs. Cumming pushed her glasses up the bridge of her nose before setting off down the road. She said something that Mary did not quiet hear, but it sounded like Mrs. Cumming had said she needed to see a big woman down the street. Mary ventured back into the house and proceeded to the kitchen. She had two little boys to take care of now and that was her only priority.

*

Henderson and Campbell took the revolvers they had found at the Cumming residence to Mr. Joseph Bauman, a gunsmith, that carried out business on the Corners of Albert and Elizabeth Streets. Bauman thoroughly inspected the pistols that had been collected from the Cumming's residence. He looked through the barrel noticing that the grooves and rifling of the barrel had a polished surface, which he took to indicate that the pistol had been fired recently. He asked the Detectives if he could keep the weapons overnight, as he wanted to carry out an experiment. He asked them for the spend cartridges found at the scene of the crime so that he might compare the cartridges resulting from a test firing from Stanley's weapon. The Detectives agreed and also handed him the cartridges that Stanley stored with his revolver.

The detectives followed up a lead given to them by Constable Cook. A pawnbroker visited by Cook had reported the sale of an automatic pistol the day of the murders. They arrived at the pawnbroking business of Samuel Hawgood in George Street and inquired as to who there had spoken to Constable Cook. Walter Frederick Hawgood identified himself as the pawnbroker's assistant that had provided Cook with the information.

"Constable Cook tells us you sold a revolver recently," said Campbell, "is this correct?"

"Yes," replied Hawgood.

"When was this?"

"Two days before Christmas," replied Hawgood, "between four thirty and quarter past five."

"Please tell us what transpired between you both," said Henderson.

"Well, he came in and said to me 'Have you got any revolvers?' and I replied that I had, and I said, 'Do you want one?' and he said 'Yes' so I went to the draw and got one for him, and he had a look at it."

"How many revolvers did he have a look at?" asked Campbell.

"I only had the one," replied Hawgood.

"What transpired after he had a look?"

"I told him it was 32/6, and he took it, and he paid for it."

"Did he inspect the condition of the weapon, the barrel perhaps," quizzed Campbell, "did you show him how to load it?"

"No," said Hawgood, "he just took it, I did not show him any of the points of it."

"How did he pay for it?"

"He gave me two £1 notes, and I gave him the change 7/6."

"What type of weapon was it?"

"An F.N. 25 20, one of those small ones that you could put in the palm of your hand and very nearly hide it!"

"Have you seen this man since?"

"No."

"How would you describe him?" asked Henderson.

"He was of bushy appearance, badly in need of a shave, about six-foot-tall with shallow hollow cheeks, sharp features, probably about 40 years of age, an Australian."

"What makes you say he was Australian?"

"He had that Australian twang when he spoke."

"What was he wearing?"

"Oh, a dark coloured suit or serge, but it was of a dirty appearance."

"Was he wearing a hat?" quizzed Campbell.

"I didn't take much notice of his hat except that it was a felt hat."

"How long did you interact with this man?" asked Henderson.

"Well he was only here for about five minutes, if that!"

"How was his demeanour," asked Campbell, "did he appear nervous at all?"

"No, he was quite normal. Just in a desperate hurry, he was no sooner in than he wanted to get out."

"What makes you say that?"

"He did not examine the pistol, I showed it to him, told him the price, and he took it!"

"How did you come to have the pistol in the store?" queried Henderson.

"I'd have to trace that back, could take some time," replied Hawgood, "I'll ring it through to C.I. Branch when I find it if you like."

"That would be appreciated Mr. Hawgood, thanks for your time.

As the detectives walked back to C.I. Branch they agreed that a description of the bushie should be circulated widely, the Police Gazette being preferred.

*

Henderson and Campbell set out to locate the woman, who had been mentioned by Mrs. Cumming and Stanley, as going to the Picture Show with Acting Sergeant Cumming, that was also followed by Stanley to Dutton Park. The woman known to them as Mrs. Page. According to their accounts the detectives accomplished this rather quickly and led her to C.I. Branch for interrogation.

She is reported as having told them that she had been at work up until eight thirty and arrived home, where she was boarding at Spring Hill, at about nine o'clock. After that she had played cards with the other people in the house. She also told them that on three occasions she had visited an allotment, about one hundred yards from the scene of the tragedy, and had sexual intercourse with Acting Sergeant Cumming on each occasion. The last occasion being two nights before the murder. She described her mode of meeting Cumming was that he would arrange to meet her at the Dutton Park tram terminus at a certain time and on each occasion this was twenty minutes past eight. She would arrive there at the arranged time and Cumming would be there waiting for her. The precise meeting place was Pound Street near the South Brisbane Pound Yards and the Dutton Park Tram Terminus. They would then proceed along Pound Street onto the Railway Terrace making their way to the vacant allotment to the east of the Brisbane Gaol. She was also reputed to have informed them that on each occasion Cumming had intercourse with her he would remove his belt with his handcuffs on it and keys and would place them aside. When about to return home he would walk with her until about one hundred yards from the tram line when he would tell her to go ahead and catch the tram. She would not see him again that night. He never travelled on the same tram with her and she presumed he would catch the next tram. It was further alleged that she had told the detectives that she had been at the Picture Show with Cumming, and that she had been followed by Stanley. She is then reported to have recalled how Stanley had said, 'My father is no damn good, he has been causing a lot of trouble at home, the man ought to bloody well do time for it!'

7 BOXING DAY

Detectives Campbell and Henderson state that they arrived in Wilton Street, the residence of Mrs. Cumming just before half past eleven. There they found Stanley, Mrs. Cumming, and a brother of the deceased policeman, David Cumming. David Cumming had arrived in Brisbane on Christmas Eve coming from somewhere near Kingaroy.

Mrs. Cumming appeared to be in an excitable state and before Campbell and Henderson could say anything she turned to David Cumming and ordered him from the house.

"It has got nothing to do with you, it is private business that we are talking, just wait outside!"

After David Cumming left the house, Henderson stated his line of questioning regarding Mrs. Cumming's movements on the night of the murders, after her husband had left the house.

"I visited my mother," said Mrs. Cumming, "I am satisfied that somebody from the underworld has done this. All policeman have enemies. My husband was all that a husband could be in his own home. He never stopped out at night and he always gave me all his money. I am quite satisfied that he has been trapped into this. He would never have gone to a place like that with a woman in his uniform! He has often told me that he had to visit that place round about the Lock Hospital on account of complaints being received about fellows hanging about there. What I want to know is how the police didn't find the bodies before daylight, they couldn't have looked very far! You won't find the murderer on this side, you will find them on the woman's side!"

"I understand there was a very thorough search for your husband that night," said Henderson, "and I understand that there were no record of complaints being made to the South Brisbane Police that night that would cause your husband to go there. It is my understanding that that place falls within the jurisdiction of the Woolloongabba Police."

"Stanley," said Henderson moving his focus away from Mrs. Cumming, "I would like you to come over to the office with us, I'd like to get a statement from you as to what you can tell us about your movements and anything we want to know about the murder."

"Alright," responded Stanley, "I will get ready and come with you."

As they waited for Stanley, Henderson and Campbell went outside and did a sweep of the property looking for the belt, handcuffs, and keys. They searched the water tank, the water closet including the pan, and looked for freshly dug earth for suggestions that something had been recently buried. They found nothing.

*

At C.I. Branch, Stanley was again escorted to an interview room and was joined this time by both Campbell and Henderson.

"Please Stanley," said Henderson, "after your father left home, what did you do?"

"I left home sometime between seven and eight o'clock."

"Why?"

"I had an appointment to keep, with a lady friend."

"Who is this lady friend?"

"Miss Josephine Clutterbuck."

"Where does Miss Clutterbuck live?"

"At 'Carisbrooke' boarding house, kept by Mrs. Melican, at Merivale Street South Brisbane."

"What time had you arranged to meet?"

"Between seven forty-five and eight o'clock."

"How did you get there?"

"I caught a tram at the five ways, at Woolloongabba, and travelled in that tram as far as the 'Palace Hotel', where I got off and went in to the hotel."

"Alone?"

"Yes, I went in alone and had a drink, a shandy, and proceeded from there up Melbourne Street to the boarding house in Merivale Street."

"What time did you get there?"

"It would have been between seven forty-five and eight o'clock."

"Continue, please," said Henderson.

"I waited outside and Miss Clutterbuck joined me there and we both walked down Melbourne Street, towards the Victoria Bridge, and when we passed the 'Palace Hotel' I noticed that my father was standing almost on the edge of the footpath, just around the corner in Stanley Street."

"Did you speak to your father?"

"No, he was about 15 yards away from us, with his back towards the Bridge, side on to us. As we passed I said to Miss Clutterbuck, 'That is my father standing there.' And she asked 'which one?' and I said, 'the one with his back towards the bridge', then we walked over Victoria Bridge and crossed over to Costa's Cigar Store, and I bought a cigar."

"Who served you?"

"A young lady."

"Did you know her?"

"No?"

"Would she remember you?"

"Probably, she was trying to cut a piece of string off a roll and mentioned something about the scissors being blunt, so I volunteered to show her how to break the string with her fingers, and I did, and she passed a remark mentioning being in the trade for years and had never learnt the correct way to break a piece of string with her fingers."

"What did you do then?"

"We proceeded to the Empire Theatre and I purchased two tickets for the dress circle."

"Did you speak to the cashier?"

"There was a remark passed, when the young lady passed me the tickets, I asked which part of the theatre they were to be used for, and when being informed that they were for downstairs, I asked for tickets to the dress circle."

"Then what occurred?"

"I received the tickets, and when we arrived upstairs at the dress circle, the usher escorted us to two seats towards the far end of the left hand wing of the dress circle."

"Where were the seats?"

"They were in the fore most row, as near as I can recall about eight to ten seats from the extreme end."

"What time was this?"

"We got to the theatre shortly after eight so that would

have been about five past, there were still advertisement slides on the screen when we sat down, so the programme hadn't started."

"Did you leave there at any time?"

"No, I stayed until the end of the programme, till about ten thirty."

"Did anyone see you at that time?"

"Well there was an old gentleman sitting next to me that was deeply interested in Mary Laurence from the singing point of view, I did consider him to be a bit of a nuisance."

"Then what did you do?"

"After we came out we went to a Café, about two doors down from the Empire, in Albert Street towards Elizabeth Street, and we had a drink each. Then we left."

"Where did you go then?"

"We proceeded up Elizabeth Street to North Quay, across Victoria Bridge, along Melbourne Street to Hope Street, and then into Peel Street, going up there to the corner of Merivale Street to St. Mary's School."

"What did you do then?"

"We went under the verandah and sat down on some seats till about ten past eleven."

"Then?" asked Henderson.

"We left the school," continued Stanley, "and went to the gate of Melican's boarding house, and remained there till about eleven thirty, and I left Miss Clutterbuck there and I went down Melbourne Street to Stanley Street to catch a tram."

"Did you? Catch a tram?"

"No, there were no trams then so I walked down Stanley Street to the Reel Cab Depot, I asked about a cab and was told that there was no chance of getting one, so I walked along Stanley Street and while doing so a Yellow Cab passed me. I hailed the driver but when I reached him he said he had a fare, but if I liked I could stand on the running board for a short distance then I would be able to have the cab."

"Did you?"

"Yes, and in the cab was a man dressed in Naval uniform, as worn by a ship's officer, and he alighted from the cab at Burt's Wharf, I think, at Musgrave Wharves, but I am not entirely certain which, and then I got in the cab and we went up Stanley Street, and when we got to the intersection with Vulture Street I noticed a tram car passing, so I ordered the driver to overtake the car which he did at the intersection of Stanley and Annerley Roads, and I got on the tram and proceeded to the five ways at Woolloongabba, and proceeded to my home."

"What was the time then?"

"A little after midnight, maybe quarter past."

"Once you got home, what did you do?"

"I came in by the back door and I found mother home, she appeared to be very upset and rushed to greet me. She informed me that my father had been reported missing, and also mentioned that Sub-Inspector Bergin and other members of the force had been to my home inquiring for my father. She mentioned something about a conversation regarding a likelihood of my father being at my grandfather's place at Red Hill. I understood from that conversation that Sub-Inspector Bergin was going to make inquiries at Red Hill and let us know the results later in the night, or early in the morning as it was then."

"Proceed, please," instructed Henderson.

"I retired to my room and fell asleep, then shortly afterwards was awakened by a footstep on the front verandah of the house. I got up and noticed that mother was getting up also, and that there was a constable at the front door. He informed us that the investigations at Red

Hill had been unsuccessful."

"What were you thinking at that time?"

"I began to fear for my father's safety, and my mother became very ill. She asked me to try and get some brandy, so I proceeded to the 'Five Ways Hotel' in company with the constable, and I succeeded in getting the brandy and returned home alone. On returning home I poured out a nip of brandy for my mother, and one for myself. We drank same and we both decided to go to bed."

"When did you next see your mother?"

"Just as I got out of bed, between six and seven o'clock, my mother came in and informed me that she had been to the South Brisbane Police Station and that no further tidings had been received regarding my father's whereabouts."

There was a knock at the door, as it opened all three of them looked up. Before them stood Sub-Inspector Meldon with David Cumming. It was approaching eight o'clock in the evening.

"Are you alright Stanley?" asked David Cumming.

"Yes, I'm alright Uncle," said Stanley.

"I'll be waiting for you."

"Don't worry about me, you need not wait, I'll go home when I am finished."

"Mr. Cumming has come with someone I think we should talk to," said Meldon, addressing Campbell and Henderson, "Miss Josephine Clutterbuck."

"We would love to have a chat," said Henderson.

"I should think the time is getting on," said Meldon, "Miss Clutterbuck would you mind returning tomorrow please. Chaps if you could finish up with young Stanley there, and while you're doing that, I'll take these two for a spot of tea."

*

At ten thirty that evening, Stanley Cumming was allowed to go home after agreeing to return the next day, after his father's funeral, to complete his statement. His Uncle had waited for him, and so had Miss Clutterbuck. They walked home together.

8 ESTABLISH THE TIMELINE

Miss Clutterbuck returned the next morning and was escorted to an interview room by Henderson and Campbell. Henderson established that she was a single girl, that came down from Warwick to work as a domestic at 'Carisbrooke' boarding house. She had arrived during August that year and had met Stanley at a dance at St. Mary's School in South Brisbane, sometime during September. She said they had become friendly after that and Stanley would take her out to plays of a night time or picture shows.

"Did you meet Stanley two nights ago?" asked Campbell.

"Yes?"

"When?" asked Henderson.

"At about quarter to eight, opposite 'Carisbrooke' in Merivale Street."

"Why?"

"That was the appointed time."

"Could you be precise with the time?"

"I didn't look at my watch."

"What did you do?"

"After meeting, we both walked down Merivale Street

into Melbourne Street, on the same side as the 'Palace Hotel'. When we got to the 'Palace Hotel' my attention was attracted by Stanley to three policemen in uniform and a civilian, and referring to one of them he said, 'That is my Dad'."

"Had you seen Acting-Sergeant Cumming before."

"No, I had never seen him before."

"What were these policemen doing?"

"They were standing on the footpath near the gutter, in Stanley Street."

"Had you seen Stanley's father before this?"

"No, as I said, I have never seen before the man he pointed out as being his father."

"What of the others, did you know any of them?"

"No."

"Then what did you do?"

"We continued walking, and walked over the Victoria Bridge."

"Which side?"

"The right-hand side, and we went into the vestibule of 'Poulson and White', the photographers in Queen Street at North Quay, and I did my hair, then Stanley said he was going to buy a cigar."

"Did he say where?"

"No."

"Continue please," said Henderson, "what did you do after Stanley left you?"

"I went out onto the footpath where I saw a man named Bob Adamson with whom I had a conversation until Stanley came back."

"How do you know Bob?"

"He is a brother of the son-in-law of Mrs. Melican at the boarding house."

"What did he do?"

"Well, Stanley came along, so he raised his hat and said good night and Stanley and I walked away."

"Where did you walk?"

"We proceeded down Queen Street as far as the Strand Building and went from there to the Empire Theatre, Stanley got the tickets and we went upstairs to the dress circle on the left hand side, facing the stage, in the front row of seats."

"What time would that have been?"

"It would have been about eight o'clock when we arrived, the picture slides were showing when we arrived but the programme had not started."

"Were you shown to your seats?"

"Yes, the usher showed us to our seats."

"What can you tell me about the usher?"

"He was fairly young, medium build, not too tall, I couldn't tell you what colour hair he had."

"Was he wearing a uniform?"

"He did not have any particular kind of dress that I recall, I really didn't take that much notice."

"Did you leave at any point?"

"We remained there during the evening until the show terminated at about half past ten."

"Did Stanley leave you at any occasion during this period?"

"No, Stanley did not leave the theatre on any occasion, neither did I."

"Did anything happen while you were there?"

"When the lights went out a lot of boys from the back came into the front seat, but the usher put them back."

"Do you remember anything of the performance?"

"I remember a girl singing on the stage that night, I think her name was Mary Laurence, well that was the name on the programme, my attention was specially drawn to

Mary Laurence by a man sitting next to Stanley, he said that he knew the girl and she was a great singer."

"What did you do then?"

"After coming out of the theatre we went into a shop next door and we had a drink each there and Stanley produced the two butts of the tickets. He was going to throw them away so I asked him for them, I said, 'Don't throw them away, give them to me, and so I put them into the lap of my handbag."

"Did anything happen in the Café?"

"A person behind the counter gave a plate of fish over the counter to a girl, if that's what you mean."

"What did you do then?"

"We left the shop and proceeded down Elizabeth Street to William Street and crossed over the bridge, then after crossing the bridge we went over to the 'Palace Hotel' corner then continued along Melbourne Street to Hope Street."

"Then?"

"Then we went up Hope Street into Peel Street and from there to St. Mary's School."

"What did you do there?"

"We went inside the school and sat down on a form under the verandah."

"What time did you arrive there?"

"I have no idea," said Josephine Clutterbuck.

"Do you think it could have been eleven o'clock?"

"Well, it was about half past ten when we left the theatre, we were in the shop for about ten minutes or quarter of an hour, it probably took us fifteen minutes to walk from the shop to St. Mary's School, so, yes eleven sounds right."

"How long were you there for?"

"About half an hour, then we walked down next door to

the boarding house where I am employed and we stood there for about ten minutes. I told Stanley that I intended to go home the next day, to Warwick, and that I would ring him up the following Wednesday from there."

"Then what did you do?"

"We departed at that point."

"What time was this?"

"When I got inside my room I had a look at the clock in my room and it was quarter to twelve then, and I know that clock to be accurate."

"But you didn't go to Warwick."

"No, as it turns out, the lady of the house had some additional boarders and she asked me to remain on, when I saw her the following morning."

"When did you hear of the tragedy?"

"I remained on there yesterday so it would have been between three and four o'clock when I heard, one of the boarders was sitting at the table and had a paper in his hand. He read it out aloud and I had a look at the paper myself and read it over."

"What was the boarder's name," interrupted Henderson.

"Archie McKissock."

"Continue, please."

"After I read the paper I realised that one of the deceased was the father of Stanley."

"Thank you Miss Clutterbuck, you have been very helpful, I think we should like to see the ticket butts, do you still have them?"

"Yes, there at Melican's, but we will have to go to Hayden's first."

"Why?"

"I will have to collect my bag, it's not far from Melican's, on the corner of Hope and Peel Street, I left Melican's on the night of Christmas Eve, the boarders were a rowdy lot and some of them had drink in them. A girl friend of mine also works at Melican's and we decided to go to Hayden's as Mrs. Hayden is her Auntie."

"What is your girlfriends name?" asked Henderson.

"Eileen Deeks, she and I left Melican's together and went to Hayden's."

"I think we should take you there now," said Campbell.

Henderson and Campbell escorted Miss Clutterbuck to the residence at the corner of Hope and Peel street, where Miss Clutterbuck retrieved her bag. They then proceeded to Melican's where Detective Henderson entered the boarding house to interview Eileen Deeks. Campbell and Clutterbuck remained on the footpath. Miss Clutterbuck foraged in her handbag. She then produced two ticket butts from her handbag, No.'s A. 58 and 59, with the date 23rd December printed on them, and handed them to Detective Campbell.

*

Campbell and Henderson returned to the shop of gunsmith Joseph Bauman, where they were joined by Detective Meldon. They wanted the gunsmith to conduct a test firing from the weapons they had provided him with. He placed six cartridges into Stanley's revolver and fired the rounds into a water barrel designed for such tests. When completed he retrieved the shells.

"Have you got anything for us Bauman?" asked Henderson.

"I'm just comparing these shells, that I fired out of this revolver, with the shells from the scene."

"And?" quizzed Campbell.

"And, they no way correspond with each other."

"What do you mean?" asked Henderson.

"Well they compare in make and calibre, in that regard they are similar, but look here," he pointed at the rim of one of the shells found at the scene, "the firing pin has struck a different position to these," offering the test fired shells to the detectives.

Bauman then extracted the bullets from the water barrel and took them to his microscope. He placed a bullet under the lens and focused on the markings and serrations, making notes in a pad that sat beside the instrument. He then replaced the bullet with the one that had been extracted from Cumming's skull and made notations.

"What have you got for us Bauman?" asked Meldon.

"Well this bullet that was retrieved from the body, it clearly shows that it passed through the barrel of a pistol that was clean, whereas these bullets, from the test firing, they show signs of passing through a barrel that was rusty."

"What's your conclusion then?" quizzed Henderson.

"This bullet," he held up the item extracted from the body, "was never fired out of this gun," he said pointing to Stanley's revolver.

"What about that one?" asked Campbell, pointing to the weapon of the deceased policeman.

"That's a 38," said Bauman, "you could not fire this out of it!" He still had the recovered bullet in his palm.

"How long would it take for the barrel of that revolver to rust up?" asked Henderson.

"That depends on the weather," said Bauman, "in dry weather it might take six months, in wet weather possibly only a week after being discharged, but I inspected this revolver when you bought it in and the lands of the barrel were very rusty, looks like it has been neglected for some months, and the recent weather would not have altered the condition of the barrel to this extent."

"The shells from the scene," asked Campbell, "are they

from the same weapon?"

"Yes, the position of the firing pin markings on both are the same, indicating to me that the same weapon fired both."

"Looks like your Cumming's is in the clear then," stated Campbell.

"Let's not be too hasty men," said Meldon, "I've had word from Mt. Morgan and Elford is sending through some information which might change your mind. I would be seeking collaboration of his story if I was you!"

*

Detective Henderson states he entered Costa's Cigar Store in Queen Street and asked to speak to the woman that had been serving in the store last Thursday night. The woman behind the counter said that she had been in the store that evening.

"Could I have your full name please," asked Henderson.

"Miss Maud Mary Crowley, what's this all about?"

"Just wanting to verify the movements of a young man that says he came into your store on Thursday evening, says he showed you how to break string. Do you recall this incident?"

"I do," said Miss Crowley, "I was serving in the shop when a young man came in to purchase a cigar."

"What time was this?"

"About seven forty-five, when he came in I was serving another customer, and I was wrapping it up with paper and tying it with string. I had tied the knot and went to cut the string with scissors, and the scissors came away in halves, so I went to find a penknife to cut the string and I remarked to the young man that 'I have been a shop assistant for seventeen years and I can't break string yet', and the young man said, "show me a piece of string Miss, I am a shop assistant and I will show you how to break it,' and with that he tied the string round his finger and he showed me how to break it."

Henderson read through his memorandum pad, flipping through the pages before asking if she had said that the scissors were blunt.

"I may have said they were blunt, but I don't recollect saying that."

"What did he do then, this young man?"

"He bought two cigars and he left straight away."

"And you are sure this was seven forty-five?"

"Yes."

"Was the young man wearing a hat?"

"No."

"How did he seem to you?"

"He seemed quite normal, very polite."

"Have you seen him before that night?"

"Yes, he comes in and out, being a customer, I would say I've seen him about a dozen times."

"Do you know his name?"

"No."

"Would you recognise him again if you saw him."

"Yes, I'm certain I would."

"Did you notice him acting strangely on that night?"

"No, he was the same as always, I did not notice anything unusual in his demeanour."

"What was he wearing?"

"He had a suit on, of dark colour, one of those sack coats of black material, that men have evening suits made out of."

"What about his shirt, what type of collar did he have?"

"No, I could not describe his shirt, nor his collar or tie, I didn't even notice if he had a vest on."

"What did he wear on his feet?"

"I'm sorry, I couldn't tell you if he wore boots or shoes."

"So there was nothing out of the ordinary on that night?"

"Well, now that you mention it, that was the first time I had seen him without a hat."[xv]

*

The detectives state they decided to interview Fannie Howden, mother of Mrs. Cumming, to verify Mrs. Cumming's visit to her home on the night of the shootings. Mrs. Howden verified her daughter had visited her that evening at sometime between seven and eight that night and stayed with her for about two hours.

"Could you be more precise with the time?" queried Henderson, "could it have been after half past seven?"

"No, now that I think about it, it wasn't as late as half past seven, it was probably only a few minutes after seven."

"How could you know that?"

"Well on that day I was residing with Mrs. Gregory, at her place in Constance Street, and my daughter arrived just after I had my tea, and Mrs. Gregory's clock struck seven just before she arrived."

"Why had she come to see you?"

"She talked over the Christmas festivities, and the presents she had bought that day, and that she was sending up the children to me the next day to take me up to the Valley."

"What time did your daughter leave Mrs. Howden?"

"A little after nine."

"When did you next see your daughter?"

"The next day, Christmas Eve, she came and told me about the tragedy. I was waiting for my grandchildren to come and take me out as she promised the night before. She came up the steps, and when I saw her dressed in that attire, I knew something was wrong."

"What attire?"

"She was dressed all in black."

"What then?"

"She was carrying a newspaper and she said to me, 'Don't be shocked at what I am going to tell you, Marquis has been shot' and I said 'God bless and save us, who shot him?' and she said 'I don't know but here is the paper' and she left me the 'Telegraph'."

"That was the first you had heard of it?"

"Yes, I knew nothing about it until she told me."

"What did she do then?"

"She left me."

"Was anyone with her?"

"Her son was, and he put his hand on my shoulder and said 'Don't be frightened Granny'."[xvi]

*

I have assumed that Campbell and Henderson returned to C.I. Branch to compare notes, and to review the statements taken from the public in the vicinity of the murder scene. They should have wanted to establish an accurate timeline. Constable Cook probably collected the details for them and they would have used one of the interview rooms to go over the material.

"Who do we start with?" asked Henderson.

"Let's start from the top of the pile," responded Campbell.

He took the first statement from the pile and began to read to Henderson.

"This one is from a William Witt of Annerley Road,

sixteen years of age, lives with his parents, mother has a shop at that address, says he's known Cumming for about two years, and states that on the night he, 'saw Cumming at about eight thirty who passed the shop in Annerley Road at that time."

Henderson placed a book on the table.

"What's a Refidex," quizzed Campbell, looking at the cover.

"Refidex Directory Maps," said Henderson, "the company claims it to be the first of its kind for any city in the world, a directory of seventy-eight maps," Henderson fanned the pages as he added, "it shows all the streets, roads, railways, parks, schools and other features of Greater Brisbane."

He flicked through the book until he reached the Dutton Park map and marked the location where the bodies had been found.[6]

"Where's about in Annerley Road is the shop?"

"Um," responded Campbell, "he says here about midway between Clarence Corner and Boggo Road."

"He was at the front of the shop when Cumming passed, walking faster than usual, alone, he appeared to be normal in every way, he was in his blue Police uniform and had his cap on. That was the last time he saw him. States that he calculated it was eight thirty as it was some time after closing time at the hotel."

"Also states he knows Mrs. Walsh as a customer of his mother's, but did not see her that evening. He goes on to state that at nine thirty he heard two reports, like shots from the direction of Merton Road."

Campbell checked the map.

---

[6] Figure 3 - Refidex Directory 1926 Map 35

"Merton Road runs somewhat parallel to Annerley Road and East of Park Road Station," he said.

"He states that when he heard the shots he said to his brother Charlie, 'Someone's shot themselves' and his brother laughed but did not say anything."[xvii]

"Not much to go on there," said Campbell, "next."

"Next up is James Jamieson," said Henderson, "waterside worker from 171 Annerley Road.[7] He has known Cumming personally for the past two years. He finished work at New Farm Wharf about eight forty-five and took the thirteen minutes to nine tram to Dutton Park. He got off the tram at the Corner of Annerley and Gladstone Roads."

Campbell marked the position on the map.

"He states he proceeded to his home in Annerley Road when on the way he saw two figures, standing in the dark, dressed in men's attire, about 15 yards from his home, and they were looking towards Gladstone Road, the way he had come. He went inside his front gate and he noticed they appeared to be anxious, looking round towards the roadway for a few seconds, then turning round sharply to look the other way. They didn't see Jamieson inside his gate but he could see them as they were under the electric street light, he didn't know who they were. One was taller than the other, and appeared to be five foot nine inches in height, well built, he wouldn't say stout, dressed in a dark grey suit with a felt hat, the shorter of the two was dressed in dark clothes and also a dark suit."

"That's fairly precise," said Campbell.

"Yes," said Henderson, "he goes on to state that he considered their actions suspicious and so he continued to

---

[7] Figure 2 - Aerial view of Boggo Road Gaol, Brisbane, 1929

observe them. States here he wasn't sure of the time but the tram should have been at his stop at nine twenty-six and his house is only five doors down so it would have been shortly after that."

"Five doors down," said Campbell marking up the roadmap.

"He says these two then moved towards the roadway about seven or eight yards and continued looking up Annerley Road in the direction of the tram stop up on Gladstone Road. They then walked back down the road closer to where he was standing. After a few moments he saw two people walking down the middle of the road from Gladstone Road, and when they got under the electric light he recognized Cumming in the company of a woman. Cumming was in his uniform, with his cap off, his tunic was unbuttoned. Jamieson was on Cumming's left as he walked along and the woman was on the other side, on Cumming's right. The woman was short, stout, and appeared to be thick set. He didn't see her face as Cumming cast a shadow across her. Cumming and the woman continued to walk down Annerley Road toward Woolloongabba, but then turned right and went up the Gaol Lane that leads into Burke Street."

Campbell consulted the map.

"At the time Cumming was passing," continued Henderson, "Jamieson states that the two he had seen earlier shifted their position and walked over closer to where he was standing, on the footpath, about two yards from him. They were close together and did not speak. In his opinion, based on what he could see, they appeared to be watching Cumming and the woman. As Cumming got about thirty yards down the road, after having passed him, the two men then shifted onto the roadway, towards a shop on the left hand side of the road, the same side as

Jamieson, walking fast, going in the same direction as Cumming and the woman. As Cumming and the woman turned to go down the Gaol Lane these two men started walking faster still going up the lane in the direction that they had gone, then they disappeared from his view."

"That lane would take you directly to the reserve," said Campbell, "where the bodies were discovered."

"Jamieson then states," said Henderson, "that he checked the clock inside and it was nine forty, and that corresponded with his watch. He then went to bed, after having a wash and a cup of tea, estimating the time as nine forty-five or ten to. Then his wife and he heard the report of firearms a few seconds after he went to bed. He says the two shots came from the direction of where he now knows that the shootings took place. He states he can tell the difference between the report of a gun, and a revolver, and the report of a backfiring motor-car. He passed a remark to his wife at the time that he had heard two shots and she thought it was a motor-car but he told her 'No it was not'.

He then remarked that he thought the shots came from the Gaol and that someone might be escaping. He states that the two reports were in quick succession, he no sooner had the words out of his mouth on hearing the first shot that he heard the next."[xviii]

"That's quite interesting as well," said Campbell.

"Last one for now," said Henderson, picking up the final statement from the table.

"This is reportedly from Leonard Johns, in the employ of the Queensland Government Railways as a signal man and he was on duty at the signal box at Park Road from seven forty-five till eleven-fifty and states that between nine fifteen and ten on that date while in the signal box he heard two sharp reports, like revolver shots, and then a duller report afterwards. The first two shots were in quick succession, about three seconds between the two, and about a dozen seconds between those two shots and the third shot. There was a wind blowing from the South East that night. He estimates that the signal box is about three hundred and fifty yards from where he understands that the bodies were found."[xix]

"Well, that's been a great way to spend a Sunday afternoon," said Campbell, "I think I'll call it quits and mull over that information till tomorrow."

"Well, at least we have some sort of a timeline," said Henderson, "the time of death must have been between the hours of nine and ten."

Henderson and Campbell were interrupted by a knock at the door. Constable Cook entered the room.

"Excuse me Detectives," said Cook, "I was asked to pass on a message from the lads at Sandgate Station. They want you to know that Cumming was seen at Scarborough on Sunday a few months before Christmas in the company of a woman and her two small boys. They state that the description of the woman in regards her height and figure was markedly like that of Mrs. Walsh. She was wearing a floral voile dress."[xx]

*

The detectives state that at eight o'clock that evening they decided to visit the Cumming household to find out why Stanley had not made his appointment. When they got there they were greeted by David Cumming, Stanley was lying on a bed on the verandah sleeping. Mrs. Cumming was absent. They left word with David Cumming for Stanley to come in the next morning.

9 LEGAL ADVICE

After the funeral for Acting-Sergeant Cumming, his son, Stanley, had felt unwell after returning home and elected not to return to C.I. Branch as he had been instructed. Detectives Campbell and Henderson returned to the Cumming's home the following day to request that both Mrs. Cumming and Stanley accompany them to C.I. Branch to complete their statements. They were met with a very agitated Mrs. Cumming when they arrived at midday. The detectives stated that the following conversation took place.

"Mrs. Cumming would you accompany us to C.I. Branch please, to complete your statement," requested Henderson.

"I won't go near your office, or make a statement!" said Mrs. Cumming, "I have told you all I know. You won't find the murderer here! He got his desserts, and I will say no more!"

"Stanley," said Henderson, "are you coming over to finish your statement?"

"I do not want Stanley to go to your office," said Mrs. Cumming, "you had him for over ten hours on Sunday."

"What's brought this on?" quizzed Henderson.

"I have had legal advice on the matter, and will say no more!" said Mrs. Cumming, "It appears you are trying to make us out guilty!"

"I won't say any more," said Stanley, "I have just got my senses now, and I am sorry I have told you so much. Why don't you go and get somebody else for the job! Whilst you are questioning me, he or she who has did the murder are going free."

David Cumming then joined the group.

"We have been advised by our solicitor to keep away," he said, "and we have decided to take his advice."

"Who is your solicitor?" asked Henderson.

"Gerald McGrath," said Mrs. Cumming, "you can go to the office of W.J. McGrath Solicitors and ask him there! By the way you men keep coming here it looks as if you are trying to make us out guilty. Now if you don't mind could you leave us please!"

"We are not trying to make you out guilty but your attitude now wouldn't impress anyone that you are not guilty," said Campbell.

Mrs. Cumming stormed out of the room.

"Stanley," said Henderson, "you don't have to come with us now but please give some thought to clearing yourself, come to C.I. Branch at two o'clock this afternoon."

Stanley gave tacit acknowledgement of compliance to Campbell and Henderson. The detectives descended the stairs of the home to return to their car.

"What do you make of that?" quizzed Henderson.

"We need to find more evidence, try and disprove their alibi's," said Campbell, "their certainly not doing themselves any favours!"

"Let's head over to the office of W.J. McGrath, they're

in Adelaide Street."

*

Henderson and Campbell subsequently reported to the office of W.J. McGrath to be told that Gerald McGrath was out of the office. The detectives left a request for him to contact them immediately he returned.

According to Henderson and Campbell they decided to run out the Walsh alibi and headed to Wynnum.

*

Campbell and Henderson arrived at the 'Waterloo Bay Hotel' mid-morning and began to make inquiries. Soon they were talking to Mr. Elgin Menzies.

"Mr. Menzies" said Henderson, "could I have you confirm what you have just told us. Last Thursday you left home at about seven thirty-five and arrived at the 'Waterloo Bay Hotel' at about seven fifty, you went into the hotel and had a drink with a man named Harry Morris, a man you have known for about three years, along with a chap named Walsh."

"Had you met Walsh before?" asked Campbell.

"No, that was the first time, when Morris introduced him to me."

"You then state," continued Henderson, "that you walked out of the hotel at about eight o'clock and you walked a couple of hundred yards to Irvine's Store, conversing with Morris and Walsh as you went."

"That's correct," said Menzies.

"Were you drunk?" asked Campbell.

"No, I only had the one drink."

"What about Morris and Welsh, they had been

drinking?"

"Yes they had had a drink but I would call them sober."

"What did you do, after reaching Irvine's Store?" asked Henderson.

"I left them at the corner at about eight o'clock."

"Why?"

"Morris told me he was going down to the Liberty Fair, down on the beach."

"Did you see them again that evening?"

"No, that was the last I saw of them."

"Thank you Mr. Menzies," said Campbell, "could I ask though, would you know Welsh if you saw him again, to identify him as the man you had a drink with on that night."

"Yes, I think so."

"Alright, we'll be in touch to arrange for you to do that at the Wynnum Police Station."

*

Soon their inquiries led them to Charles Clyde, a carter, employed by James Hamlet of Wynnum. He had been at the Liberty Fair the previous Thursday night and knew Henry Morris by sight having seen him at the Gas Works. He had arrived at the Liberty Fair about 8 o'clock that evening in the company of Dennis McKee. Mr. Clyde stated that he had seen Morris at the fair between eight forty-five and nine forty-five and he was in the company of a man he had not seen before. He had taken him to be a man from Sydney. He was playing a game of 'Roller' and they remained there for about an hour. Campbell also asked Clyde if he would be able to identify him if he saw him again and arranged for him to attend Wynnum Police

Station.

*

They were also able to locate Frederick George Chapman, a tiler, resident of Melville Terrace at Manly. He had personally known Henry Morris for about two years. He described to the detectives how he had been at the fair on the Esplanade at Wynnum South, arriving there about eight fifteen the prior Thursday and had a game of 'Rollum'. He had seen Henry Morris there, in company of another man that he had never seen before. It had been about ten o'clock when he left and Morris and the other man were still there at that time. Chapman was also asked if he would be able to identify the man he saw with Morris that night if he saw him again and it was arranged for him to also present at Wynnum Police Station.

*

Henderson and Campbell arrived at Stephens Road, at the home of Mrs. Mary Christie. The detectives state that they asked Mary Christie if she knew of anyone that would want to do her daughter harm.

"I do not know of anyone that threatened my daughter's life in any way. The only one that she was unfriendly with was her husband."

"Why do you say that?" asked Campbell.

"He had threatened her once."

"When was this?"

"About three or four weeks after she left him the last time, that would be about two and a half years ago."

"How did he threaten her."

"He said he had something in his pocket, that he would settle her if she came outside the gate."

"You heard him say this?"

"Yes."

"What did he have in his pocket?"

"He did not say, he just wanted her to come out and see him, but she was in bed at the time and could not come out, he said he would force his way in so I rang the South Brisbane Police, and they came and arrested him."

"Was that the only time?" asked Campbell.

"No," said Mary, "about twelve months ago, my other daughter, Mrs. Jones, she told me that she and Eileen were in Edward Street when they came across Walsh and he pulled a razor from his pocket, and he threatened her with it, 'this is what I got for you' he said."

"Tell me," said Henderson, "did your daughter, Eileen, wear her wedding ring?"

"Yes," said Mary, "I could not swear that she had it on her finger that evening, but I am sure she had it on that day, I saw it on her hand when she came home after being out that afternoon."

"Did it fit tightly on her finger?" asked Campbell.

"No," said Mary, "the ring was loose, but not that loose that it would slip off, actually I think a little bit of force was required to get it off."[xxi]

"Thank you Mrs. Christie, would you mind if we speak to your daughter, Mrs. Jones."

"I'll just fetch her, would you like some tea?"

I imagine that both men nodded and sat silently in the reception room of the home. They knew Madeline Jones was two years older than her sister Eileen. That she was now divorced from her husband, Harold Jones, and had two children. A third child, Marie, had passed away when quite young. She now resided at her mother's home with her two surviving children, Ruby and Dorothy.

"Good afternoon Mrs. Jones," said Henderson rising to

his feet along with Campbell, "would you mind answering a few questions?"

"Not at all," said Madeline gesturing for the men to return to their seats.

"Your mother was just telling us about an episode with Walsh, when he threatened your sister, can you tell us about that," said Henderson.

"That was last Christmas, well Christmas 1925, I was with my sister going down Edward Street, to the Returned Soldiers and Sailors League, to collect a parcel, when my sister met her husband and he asked if she was coming back to him, she said 'No' and he said 'If you don't you'll be getting this' and he pulled a razor out of his pocket, I said to him 'Put that away now!'" and then he said, 'I only done it to frighten her'"

"Was the razor in a case?" asked Campbell.

"No."

"Did he open the razor?" asked Henderson.

"No," said Madeline again.

"You knew Acting-Sergeant Cumming, didn't you?" quizzed Henderson.

"Yes."

"Did your sister?"

"She would be with me when I spoke to him."

"How's that?"

"On several occasions," said Madeline, "we would be waiting for a tram together, when he would come and speak to me, and my sister too, but mostly to me, as he knew I had a child in hospital and he would inquire as to how she was."

"Was your sister on friendly terms with Cumming?"

"No, she never told me she was."

"When your sister and Cumming spoke did they arrange to meet?"

"No, I never knew my sister to meet Cumming by appointment or otherwise, except as I said, when she was with me."

"Did Cumming ever tell you he was on friendly terms with your sister?"

"No, as I said, he would ask after my sick child."

"Do you know if they would write to each other?"

"No, I do not know if he wrote to her, or she to him."

"What can you tell us about her wedding ring?" asked Campbell.

"She always wore her wedding ring, on her left hand."

"Have you ever known her to go out without her ring?" asked Henderson.

"Only once, she pledged it, for the purpose of getting a summons for her husband, but the first payment she got, she redeemed it."

"Thank you Mrs. Jones, you've been most helpful," said Henderson closing his memorandum pad, "anything else you need Campbell?"

"Your sister's ring," said Campbell, "could you describe it please."

"It was a plain gold narrow band."[xxii]

I imagine Mrs. Christie entered the room with a tea service on a tray and placed it on a small table in front of the detectives.

"You wouldn't happen to have a photograph of your daughter Mrs. Christie?" asked Campbell.

Mrs. Christie went to the room occupied by her daughter, Ruby May, and removed a small black and white postcard from the top of the chest of drawers. On returning she presented it to Detective Campbell. He tilted it so that Henderson could see the image of a woman, with fine yet dark wavy shoulder length hair, that had been parted on the left, falling across her forehead to be twisted into a loose bun above her right ear. There, it was held in place by a round black hairclip. Her oval shaped face framed almond shaped eyes that were crowned by thick dark eyebrows. There was just a hint of a smile on her thin lips. She wore a white blouse with a lace collar fastened by a small brooch.[8]

"When was this taken?" asked Henderson.

"Oh, I'm not sure, about eight or nine years ago, something like that," said Mary.

Campbell turned the postcard over in his hand and noticed the inscription.

"Did your daughter write this?" he asked Mrs. Christie.

"Yes," she responded.

"February 29th To Ruby from Eileen," Campbell read aloud.

"So it must be ten years ago, 1916," said Henderson.

The others stared at him blankly.

"February 29th," explained Henderson, "you only get a 29th of February on a leap year, and a leap year has to be divisible by four."

"Would you mind if we kept this?" asked Campbell.

Mary Christie appeared reluctant.

"It will help us tremendously in finding your daughter's murderer," said Henderson before Mary nodded in the affirmative with reticence.

"Do you know if your daughter may have been in Scarborough one Sunday a few months back?"

"Definitely not," said Mary Christie, "she seldom went anywhere, every spare penny she could scrap together she spent on her boys."

"Did she own a floral voile dress?" asked Henderson.

---

[8] Refer Figure 6

"No," responded Mary, "She only owns the two dresses, and they're both of the same colour and fabric, but it's curious, you're asking about a floral voile dress."

"Why is that curious?" quizzed Campbell.

"Well," said Mary, pausing to rub her chin with her index finger, "a few months back Frederick, my son, was on a tram-car in South Brisbane when he says saw a woman in a dress, like you described, with two small boys, about the same ages as Ronnie and Jimmie. At first, he thought it was Eileen, but as the tram-car drew closer he could tell it wasn't her."

"He was certain that it wasn't your daughter?" asked Henderson.

"Yes, very certain," replied Mary, "he teased her about it at the dinner table that night. We knew it wasn't Eileen for the boys were with me that whole day. Do you think it possible that Eileen was mistaken for this woman in the floral voile dress?"

"Is your son Frederick home?" asked Campbell to avoid Mary's question.

"No, but he should be home shortly," said Mary, "you could wait for him, he really shouldn't be too far off."

"Could you have a look at something for me Mrs. Christie," said Campbell extracting an envelope from his pocket and handing it to Mary.

"Do you think that is your daughter's handwriting?"

"It resembles her handwriting, but I would not swear that it is hers, the 'South Brisbane' is more like hers, but the 'Sergeant Cumming' is not."

"Thank you Mrs. Christie," said Campbell returning the envelope to his pocket, "if you don't mind we shall wait by the gate."

"You're more than welcome to stay."

"That's all right, just need a bit of fresh air," said

Henderson.

"Well, suit yourselves," said Mary, "I did offer."

Henderson and Campbell were keen to share their thoughts and didn't want to do that in front of Eileen's family. They made their way out of the house and stood at the front gate.

"Any ideas?" quizzed Campbell.

"Jealous husband motive looked good, but Walsh's movements that night seem to be panning out for him. The three we interviewed today say they can identify him, so if they do then I'd say he's looking safe, even though from what we have heard here we can't be blamed for suspecting him and we would have to prove that Walsh was the jealous husband. But so far there seems to be no connection between Cumming and Walsh, well not as so explicitly described in the letters from others in his locker. I'm beginning to consider the possibility that jealousy is not gender biased."

"Where did the envelope come from?"

"It contained a Christmas Card, under the printed verse and the word 'From' was the name Eileen, as simple as that, arrived the day after the tragedy, I'll check the card when we get back."xxiii

Campbell was looking up the street and saw a man approaching them. He turned to Henderson, and Henderson nodded.

"Frederick Christie?" asked Campbell.

"Yes," said Fredrick, Eileen's brother.

"We have a few questions before you step into the house," said Henderson, "did you know Acting-Sergeant Cumming."

"No," replied Fredrick.

"Could you tell us please what you were doing on the night of last Thursday."

"I was at home, but left about ten to seven and went to a mate's place."

"What is your friends name?" asked Campbell.

"Mr. Slaughter of Highgate Hill."

"What time did you arrive there?"

"It would have been about seven by then."

"Was your sister, Eileen at home when you left?"

"Yes, she and mother, and my other two sisters were at home when I left."

"Did your sister tell you of her intentions that night?"

"No, but I don't think she intended to go out."

"Why do you say that?" quizzed Henderson.

"She had her ordinary house dress on, she would never go out in that."

"Why did you go to your mate's place that night?"

"I go there every Thursday night, to listen to the wireless."

"What time did you leave there?"

"I would have left there about nine thirty, and then I came home and went to bed."

"When did you first have concerns for your sister?"

"I was sleeping on the front verandah and my mother came out and told me that Eileen was missing, then my other sisters, both of them, they went out looking, but they returned with no tidings of her, so then my mother and I went out looking till about two the next morning, we got no trace of her."

"What then?"

"I remember Acting-Sergeant Bonis came to the house at about four that morning, to take down particulars."

"Is that when you found out about your sister?

"No, I had to leave home at eight thirty to head into town."

"Did anyone see you in town," quizzed Henderson.

"No, I don't recall, anyway I was home by midday, and that was when I was informed that my sister had been found shot in company with Acting-Sergeant Cumming."

"Did you know your sister was on friendly terms with the policeman."

"No, I did not, to my knowledge she did not have any male admirers, she was a woman that generally stayed home at night."

"Did she keep company with other men?"

"She did not keep company with any men whatsoever as far as I know!" said Fredrick annoyed by the line of questioning, "now, if you'll excuse me, I'd like to freshen up!"[xxiv]

"Before you go," said Henderson, "what can you tell me about the altercation you had with Walsh last February?"

"Altercation," responded Frederick, "he blanking well hit me from behind!"

"We know," said Campbell, "that is what you told the court, can you tell us why?"

"I have no idea."

"Walsh said at the time that you struck him in the face and knocked him down three times."

"He started it and I blanking well finished it, now, if you will excuse me!"[xxv]

*

Campbell and Henderson returned to C.I. Branch for the meeting arranged with Stanley for two o'clock. Stanley Cumming did not keep the appointment.

*

By three o'clock Campbell and Henderson decided to visit the home of Mr. Slaughter, the retired coachbuilder who lived in James Street at Highgate Hill. What he told the detectives seemed to support Frederick Christie. Yes, he knew Frederick Claude Christie, for about two years, he came to his home regularly about once a week to loan books, or listen to the wireless. He took great interest in the wireless last Thursday night from when he arrived at about seven until he left around nine forty. Yes, he appeared quite normal and in his usual frame of mind.

*

I imagine the two detectives decided to return to C.I. Branch as it was late afternoon. They would have greeted at the counter by Constable Cook who told them that Sub-Inspector Meldon wanted to see them immediately upon their return. It had been a long day and Henderson and Campbell slowly made their way to the muster room which adjoined Meldon's office. They knocked at the door and Meldon called for them to join him.

"Ah, men," said Meldon, "glad to see you're back, I assume your day has proved fruitless."

Campbell and Henderson looked at each other in acknowledgement that although they had gathered some good information it really had not bought them any closer to the culprit.

"You haven't seen these papers, have you?" said Meldon.

He passed them the statement that had been collected. Campbell and Henderson shared the document between them.

"I'll be well fucked!" exclaimed Campbell, "that's enough to make an arrest!"

"Not so hasty," said Meldon, "Let's keep this to ourselves for the moment. I'd like you both to concentrate on gathering more physical evidence while we wait for further information from Mt. Morgan, and we are getting a number of leads from the public, this tragedy hasn't been off the front page!"

*

At half past seven Henderson and Campbell were alerted to the presence of Stanley Cumming at the counter. He greeted them with 'I have come here to clear myself but I am not going to answer any questions', but the detectives escorted him to the interview rooms regardless. Meldon joined them. Each detective in turn put questions to Stanley and he refused to answer any of them. It was pointed out that 'he was taking a very foolish attitude if he had nothing to hide and if he was innocent', but still he remained mute. After several hours Stanley asked if he could go home. This was allowed and Meldon called for Constable Cook to escort Stanley from the building. I imagine Meldon was frustrated by Stanley's reluctance to answer questions.

"Can't we just arrest them both?" Campbell may have asked.

"You haven't told them about the information?" asked Meldon.

"No, up to this stage there has been no suggestion blaming either of them with having committed the murder," said Campbell.

"And nothing said or done to cause them to become refractory," added Henderson.

"All we've got so far is circumstantial," responded Meldon, "go out and get me some physical fucking evidence! I want to nail this pair!"

*

The next day, Henderson and Campbell returned with Bonis to the scene of the crime to re-examine the ground where the bodies had been found. They sieved through the soil below the blood stain where Eileen's head was found resting, but found nothing. They continued turning over the soil and sieving it. They worked on a line out from this spot on one that corresponded to a line taken from the blood stain and where her feet had been. They worked on Dr. Dode's hypothesis that she may have sat upright before she was shot, by a perpetrator standing at her feet. Surmising that the bullet would have passed out through the back of her neck and into the ground behind her. Save for a rusty nail and a three penny piece, they found nothing, the second bullet alluded them.

*

The detectives then decided to interview a member of the public that had come forward. Frank Waygood was a motorman employed by the Tramway Department of the Brisbane City Council and Henderson and Campbell made their way to his home in Tottenham Street which was about five hundred yards from the scene of the crime.

"You're here for my report," said Waygood greeting the men that stood on his verandah. Campbell frowned. "Well ya don't look like none bible bashers," said Waygood.

"Francis Beauchamp Waygood I presume," said Henderson.

"Yes."

"We've heard you may have information that may be of assistance to us," said Campbell, "in relation to the shooting last week. Did you know Acting-Sergeant Cumming?"

"Yes," said Waygood, "I knew him, but not the woman."

"Did you see him that night?"

"No."

"So what information do you have?" asked Campbell rather coolly.

"Well, I'm a motorman, and that night I handed over my last car at eight forty-eight, that was an Ipswich Road tram, and I handed it over at the Five Ways, at Woolloongabba. I would catch a car eight minutes afterwards, at Woolloongabba for Tottenham Street. That night I did not go back to the depot to sign off. It was eight minutes' travel from the Five Ways to Tottenham Street. When I got off the tram I walked home, that took me about two minutes, so that would make it eighteen minutes after I left the Five Ways, making it about six minutes past nine. I took about three or four minutes before I actually took off my cap, when I heard three shots."

"Three shots?" quizzed Henderson.

"Yes, the first two were in quick succession, then there was a pause, I should say for inside a minute, when I heard the third shot."

"What time was this?"

"Based on my calculations I would say ten minutes past nine but definitely not later than nine fifteen."

"You know where the shootings took place?" said Campbell.

"Yes," replied Waygood, "those shots that I heard definitely came from the scene of the tragedy, three snappy shots similar to what would be made by an automatic pistol."

"And how might you know the sound of an automatic pistol?" quizzed Campbell.

"Why I say an automatic pistol was because during the war I was issued with five different makes of revolvers, and made good use of them! Four of them were automatics and I had been taught to distinguish the sound between automatics and other arms."

"How long did you serve for," asked Henderson.

"I have had five years of war experience," replied Waygood.

"Did anyone else in the home hear these shots?" asked Henderson.

"My wife was home at the time and I remarked to her that there must have been another South Side tragedy or someone escaping from Boggo Road, out of curiosity I walked back out to the verandah and listened for any further shots that might be fired. Hearing nothing further I took no further notice."

"Why did you say, 'another South Side tragedy?'" quizzed Campbell.

"You know, that chap after the card game, and Spider Raper."

-o-

Detective Campbell knew Spider Raper all too well. It had only been the June of the previous year when he had put his revolver to Spider's head as he sat in a motor-car outside the Macartney Bros. produce store at the Five Ways. Campbell had been called there around midnight on reports of a burglary in progress. Campbell, in company with Detective Moore, had arrived just in time to glimpse a motor-car setting off. Campbell pushed his revolver into the 'chauff's' face and cried 'HALT'. There was no denying who the chauffeur of the motor-car was, Spider bore on the side of his face a livid looking scar reaching from the ear-tip, right across the cheek, and ending on the chin, the handiwork of a jealous rival armed with a razor. As he held the gun at Spider the back seat passenger fell headlong into the street and fled. He was later identified as Henry Alfred Kendall, a young crook recently bought to the attention of authorities. Beside the chauffeur was a gentleman well known to police, 'Come out of that, Tommy,' Campbell had said. It was Tommy Hood, alias William George Ellis, alias William George Parsons, alias William Jones, alias Rawson, alias Mansden.

In his pockets, Hood had a plug of gelignite and other paraphernalia included in the 'kit' of every burglar. Raper vehemently disclaimed any knowledge of an attempt to get away with the safe which was lying awaiting removal in the laneway beside the store.

Police alleged that Hood was true to the traditions and code of the underworld as he stoutly exonerated Raper, whose innocence he zealously proclaimed. This allowed Raper escape from being arrested. When Kendall was captured a few weeks later he unceasingly expressed the opinion that he and Hood had been 'shelved' for the 'Gabba tank' robbery by their accomplices, Raper and Atterbury.[xxvi]

Just five days before the bodies of Cumming and Walsh were discovered, William Kirby, otherwise known as Spider Raper, was found shot dead. His body lay in front of a house in Blakeney Street in Highgate Hill. Set upon by an unknown attacker on the night of the 18th of December 1926. Hood was doing time for the 'Gabba tank' job and would have been within earshot of the murders.[xxvii]

*

"Was there any difference in the sound of the reports you heard?" Henderson asked Waygood.

"No."

"Did one sound duller?" prompted Campbell.

"No, one report was not duller then the other two!"

"What time was that again, that you handed over your tram?" quizzed Henderson.

"That was at eight forty-eight."

"And who did you hand over to?"

"A regular motorman."

"What was the name of the motorman?"

"I don't know!"

"Do you remember the number of the tram?"

"No, the conductor takes the number."

"Who was the conductor?"

"I don't recall who the conductor was, listen I'm trying to help you guys, why are you quizzing me?"

"You would understand Mr. Waygood," explained Henderson, "that we need to track down all possible leads, they might be able to tell us more, is there anything you remember about that tram."

"It was a full route tram, Ipswich Road to Clayfield, that's about it."

"Thanks for your information, Mr. Waygood," said Henderson, "if you think of anything else please get in contact with C.I. Branch."[xxviii]

-o-

By now in my research I had come to the conclusion that the veracity of each witness would need to be tested. I searched for each of them amongst electoral roll records and newspapers. Did anyone have a secret past that was not considered during the investigation?

*

I imagined the conversation between Henderson and Campbell as they returned to their motor-car.

"What do you think?" Campbell would have asked.

"I'll come clean," said Henderson, "I did a background check on Mr. Waygood before we left C.I. Branch."

"What did that reveal?"

"Well, he did serve in the A.I.F., first time he joined up in the August of 1914, he was working as a theatre usher down in Sydney, did six months as a private up in Rabual."

"In the Battle of Bita Paka?"

"Possibly," said Henderson, "Then he joined up again in February 1918, from here in Brisbane, said he was working as a clerk. I don't know how much action he saw in Rabual but when he joined the second time, he was covered in scars. At that time, he was deployed to Moascar in Egypt where he worked in the cookhouse."

"So his story pans out then."

"Well, I am still concerned about his reliability as a witness," said Henderson, "do you recall a house fire in Zillmere about four years ago."

"Was that the one where the owner's husband insured the property for £500 when a contractor said he could have built it for £300?"

"Yes, and the water tanks were empty at the time as it was claimed that they needed to be cleaned out."

"Oh, didn't he also work as an inspector for the Insurance Company," said Campbell, "Fire and Accident, wasn't it?"

"That's the one," said Henderson, "would you be

surprised that the Inspector, the husband of the property owner, was one Mr. Francis Beauchamp Waygood."

"Fair dinkum?"

Henderson nodded.

"Didn't one of our chaps investigate coming to the conclusion that the fire had not been accidental?"

"Yes," replied Henderson, "young Constable Fahey from Sandgate, but in the end, no charges were laid."[xxix]

10 TWO SHOTS OR THREE

Henderson and Campbell continued their inquiries at the Returned Soldiers Garage, trying to locate the taxi driver that Stanley Cumming had said had picked him up after he had left Miss Clutterbuck. Eventually they located a driver with the Yellow Cab Company, Robert Carius. Mr. Carius told them he was proceeding along Stanley Street in South Brisbane, in the direction of Woolloongabba at about midnight on the night in question. He had a fare, a ship's officer dressed in uniform. He was taking him over to his boat at Musgrave Wharf when just past the garage they were now in, a young man hailed him. He told him that if he would get on the running board of the car he could have the car as soon as it was disengaged by the officer.

"What did he do when you told him this?" asked Campbell.

"He got on the running board," replied Carius.

"What did you do then?"

"I dropped the ship's officer and then this other gentleman engaged the cab."

"Where did you take him?"

"I drove him up as far as the intersection of Stanley

Street and Annerley Road, at what is known as Clarence Corner."

"Is that where you left him."

"Yes, we had caught up with a tram which was proceeding towards Woolloongabba, and the man asked me to pull up, he said he would catch the tram."

"What then?"

"He paid his fare."

"Could you describe his appearance please," asked Henderson.

"He was a slight built man, tall, dressed in a navy blue suit, clean shaven. I would take him to be somewhere between twenty-eight or thirty years of age. But it was dark so I cannot say if I could identify him if I saw him again."

"Thank you Mr. Carius," said Henderson, "could you tell us your address, should we have further questions."

"I reside at Clyde Street in Annerley."[xxx]

*

Henderson and Campbell made their way to George Street in the city to speak to the manager of the City Cash Store, Mr. Robert Adamson. Mr. Adamson had been mentioned by Miss Clutterbuck as having seen her and Stanley Cumming on the night in question. He told them he had been proceeding along Queen Street at about eight o'clock when he met Josephine Clutterbuck outside the shop of Poulsen the Photographer.

"How do you know Miss Clutterbuck?" asked Campbell.

"As far as I know she is employed at Melican's boarding house, I know her from going to Melican's, Mrs. Melican is a relation of mine by marriage."

"What did you do when you met Miss Clutterbuck?"

"We had a conversation for a few minutes, then I noticed a young man come up to us from the direction of Costa's Cigar Store, lighting a cigar."

"Did he speak to you, this man?"

"Yes, he said 'Good night' and I said 'Good Night' and then we both walked off."

"What did Miss Clutterbuck do?"

"She left me and joined the young man, I went across and caught a tram."

"Did you know the young man?"

"No, but I would recognise him if I saw him again."[xxxi]

*

Henderson and Campbell returned to C.I. Branch and caught up with Detective Burns. Burns had been sent to the Empire Theatre to speak to the girl at the ticket window to see if she remembered seeing Stanley and Miss Clutterbuck. Burns relayed to them how the girl could not remember swapping downstairs tickets for dress circle, but it is a common thing. He had shown her the ticket butts obtained from Miss Clutterbuck and the girl at the ticket desk confirmed that she had sold the tickets, from the window, on that night. Burns also checked the seats in the theatre and they were as described by both Stanley and Miss Clutterbuck. He had also confirmed that once the tickets had been purchased they were torn in half by the door-keeper, the butts then being handed to the usher, the usher shows the purchaser to the seat and returns the butt to them. The other half, kept by the door-keeper, is put into a locked box and sent to the Sydney head office for audit purposes. He also interviewed the usher and he couldn't recollect who occupied the seats, but confirmed he did not wear a uniform, that he was in standard evening attire.

-o-

The public interest in the case must have been heightened by the daily updates reported in the newspapers. This must have been a point of frustration for Meldon. Critical information was being leaked to the reporters from his office. It was the newspaper reports that prompted Stanley Crane, a master painter resident of Brunswick Street in Fortitude Valley, to come forward. Crane called C.I. Branch and informed them he had some information that may assist them in the inquiries, he had seen two people acting suspiciously on the night of the crime. Henderson and Campbell where dispatched to interview Crane. The detectives introduced themselves to Crane and asked him to elaborate on what he had told C.I. Branch.

*

"On the night of the shootings," said Crane, "I was proceeding in a motor car along Annerley Road from Yeronga, going in the direction of the city, when I got within about fifty yards of the Railway Bridge, on the Dutton Park side, when I saw one man running across the road in the direction of Tillot Street, from the right hand side of Annerley Road that is the Gaol side. He came from the footpath about ten yards from the railway bridge, that is the overhead bridge, and he crossed Annerley Road, and ran in the direction of Tillot Street, which is on the opposite side of the road from the Gaol."

"We know where that is," said Campbell, "what had this man done to make you suspicious?"

"While he was crossing the road he was looking over

his left shoulder, I should say repeatedly, until he got within fifteen yards of Tillot Street. He then got on the footpath and proceeded to walk to Tillot Street, he seemed to get a hitch onto his trousers and he pulled his trousers up, and straightened his coat by catching hold of it near the lapels. I saw him reach Tillot Street and immediately on reaching it he turned and ran down the right hand side of Tillot Street, then I lost sight of him."

"How was he dressed?" asked Henderson.

"He was dressed in a dark suit, just coat and trousers, he had no waist coat, he did not appear to be wearing braces as he had to pull up his trousers."

"Was he wearing a hat?"

"Now, I'm not sure if he had a hat or not."

"How was his demeanour?" asked Campbell.

"He appeared to be excited."

"Can you describe this man for us," quizzed Henderson.

"He was tall, and slightly built, about six feet high, slight build."

"Did you see his face?"

"Yes, my head lights were on and there were lights about, so I had a fairly clear view of him, enough to distinguish countenance and features, he was clean shaven but he appeared to have a certain amount of growth on his face, and he had a sallow complexion."

"Did he have a collar?"

"No, well, I could not say, hang on, no he was not wearing a stand up collar, but he may have been wearing a turned down collar, the collar of his shirt, but no tie."

"What did you think at the time?" asked Campbell.

"He gave me the impression that he was escaping from the Gaol."

"You told C.I. Branch that you saw two people, is that

correct?" asked Henderson.

"Yes, when I got to within ten yards of the Railway Bridge, the overhead bridge, I noticed a man peering across the road from where the other man had come from, and he was approximately ten yards from the Railway Bridge on the Tillot Street side of Annerley Road, and was peering from the direction that I had seen the other man coming from, and he appeared to me to be watching to see if there was anyone watching the other man. I was going slowly at the time and I passed him and went on."

"Could you describe this man?"

"The second man was about five feet three inches in height, very slightly built, and he wore a dark suit, which appeared to be much too large for him. He was wearing a vest, and he had a very clean white shirt, and the collar was much too big for him, and a dark coloured tie, oh, and he had a grey felt hat, very clean shaven, and he had a very thin face."

"Do you recall anything else about this person?"

"No, nothing else."

"What did he do after this?"

"Well I continued on my way, so I didn't see in what direction he went."

"What time was this?"

"About ten minutes past nine."

"How can you be so sure?"

"I looked at my watch shortly after passing and it was twelve past nine, and it was about two minutes before that that I saw them."

"How's your watch for keeping time?"

"I don't know, it might have been minutes either way, it might have been a bit fast or slow."

"Could you identify these two again if you saw them?"

"I don't think so."

"Do you remember anything else?"

"The clothes on the smaller man were much too big for him, and his hat, well the rim of his hat was turned up, all the way round."

"What did you do then?"

"I then went home and got there about nine forty that night."

"When did you hear of the murders?" asked Henderson.

"The next day, and what I had seen, struck me as a coincidence."

"Did you hear any shots fired that night, or any reports like shots."

"No, no I didn't."

"Do you know the place where the murders occurred?"

"I know the back of the Gaol, the reserve there, that was the direction that I saw the first man coming from."

"How old do you think these men were?" asked Campbell.

"I would say the first man I saw was about thirty-five years of age, and the second, I should say would be about thirty."

"Would you appreciate," asked Henderson, "the difference between five feet nine inches and six feet?"

"I am a good judge of height, as my business teaches me to be accurate with height. I would appreciate that difference, and the difference between five feet three inches and five feet six inches!"

"How close did you get to the second man?"

"At the nearest distance I passed to him would have been two yards, I had a good look at him."

"But you don't think you could identify them again."

"No, not with any degree of certainty."

"If you had to judge how much the first of the men

weighed what would you say?"

"He would have been about eight stone, so somewhere between seven and nine stone."

"Did the second man see you at all?"

"No, I don't think so, he looked straight across the road all the time, and he didn't look at me while I was looking at him."

"Do you have any reason to suspect that the smaller of the two you saw was not a man?"

"What, a woman, no, no, I wouldn't have thought so," said Crane.

"What were you doing out on that night?"

"An employee of mine, Edward Dymond, had left his tools on the job and he had to go out to collect them from the house, I can't remember who the tenants were, but they saw me leaving."

"Did you speak to them?" asked Henderson.

"There was no remark passed, that I know of, when we were leaving."

"Edward Dymond was travelling with you then?"

"Yes."

"Did anyone see you arrive home?"

"I don't think so, except that Ted was with me."[xxxii]

"Thank you Mr. Crane, we'll be in touch if we need further information," concluded Campbell

*

Detectives were dispatched from C.I. Branch to the homes of people residing in the vicinity of the shootings to clarify if two or three shots were fired. However, they found the process of extracting the barest of information very difficult. A 'hush' attitude had been taken up, if the murderer was willing to 'hit' a copper then what might the cove do to ordinary folk. They checked with wardens on duty at the Gaol and the statement made by Frank Waygood, the tramway man, was collaborated as regards the number of shots although the exact time was slightly out. However, both sources agree that the shooting was in the vicinity of nine fifteen.

*

The workload of C.I. Branch was increasing as several women had written quite openly to the office declaring that Cumming, while at South Brisbane, had included them in the distribution of his amours. Some of these seemed to have been sparked by a desire to seek notoriety. Some of the writers were married, yet others were known to police and were said to be far from having much claim to respectability. But as the police discreetly and tactfully interviewed such husbands as they could, they either refrained from comment or appeared quite indifferent to their wives' liaisons. The police wanted to focus on the letters found in Cumming's locker but identification was difficult as some used merely the signatures of 'Jessie', 'Marie' or 'Vera'.

-o-

At one stage I entertained the thought that the letter signed 'Vera' may have been from Vera Meskell, the object of Spider Raper's affections. Spider and Vera had lived together as man and wife in Spring Hill, until Vera left him for the more sanitary surroundings of Highgate Hill. Early in December however, Spider had convinced the tenants of 'Wattan' in Blakeney Street to allow him to stay. Spider was a powerful man said to have the brute strength of three men when he reached the boiling point of rage. On the night of his death Spider, Vera, and the other tenants of the house had been out drinking. They returned to 'Wattan' with a few of Spider's mates and continued drinking, transforming the evening into a party. Spider, however, had become fractious and quarrelsome demanding money from Vera. The others tried to intervene but Spider had convinced himself that he was competing for her affections with another tenant, George Ward, newly arrived from the country. Spider had asked Vera to accompany him outside as he wanted to speak to her in private. Ward had queried, 'Spider, are you going to touch her?' 'No,' Spider had replied 'everything will be alright'. With that, Vera and Spider went out the front door closing it behind them. Not one minute had passed before they heard the woman screaming. Ward rushed out and beheld Spider with his hands around Vera's throat. He leapt over the fence hearing Vera's dress tear as he did so. Ward extracted Spider from the woman. Then Spider closed in on Ward, tearing the shirt off his back, letting go, then ripped a paling off the fence and with a few blows Ward had been felled. This allowed Spider to 'put the boot in' with all the savagery his passion could excite. The other tenants arrived and Spider's mates lugged him off down the street. Another tenant, Howard, dragged Vera and Ward into the house and locked the door. But Spider broke free from his captors and rushed back to the house, exclaiming 'I'll clean the blanky lot up!' arming himself with another fence paling he besieged the front door which yielded to his ferocious cracks finally succumbing to a bombardment of flower pots. Ward went for his revolver and fired the weapon from behind the breakfast room door, down the corridor towards the front door. Ward didn't want to find out what had become of the missiles he had launched down the corridor, throwing himself out the back window. One of the bullets had found it's mark and Spider staggered into the street, he threw his hands wildly towards the heavens, uttered a despairing cry, then fell dead in the street right in front of his mates.[xxxiii]

If Spider hadn't died five days earlier, he would have been a prime suspect in the murders of Cumming and Walsh. George Ward, Spider's killer, may also have been considered, save for the fact that at noon the next day he had walked up to Detective Mullaley and announced 'I am the man who shot Spider Raper'.

I am certain the detectives were glad they didn't have to take inquiries to Spring Hill, for it had an unenviable reputation as the happy hunting grounds for gangs of ruffians. It was known that six gangs, or 'mobs', operated there. Although there had been calls to clean up the area, the gangs were so well organised and the legislation so inept that the police felt powerless. It had long been the favoured haunt of the likes of 'Spider Raper', 'Long Larry' and 'Tommy the Hound'. For years, respectable local residents had called for a police station in the vicinity but the Home Secretary held the view that the establishment of a police station would not provide a remedy. The newspapers reported it an extraordinary thing that 'a systematic attempt had not been made to drive these desperadoes from their dens'.

Spring Hill's dark side streets were known to be full of crooks that lived predatory lives, who clustered together to form the unsavoury underworld of the city. In any street were to be found the 'tank-opener', 'safe-blower', 'hold-up men', 'burglars' and common 'thugs'. Their woman and female associates were used as bait to 'shepherd a joker' or lure an unsuspecting ordinary person down these side streets where they would 'go through' them for their 'roll'.

A place were sly grog flowed when the front doors of the hotels were closed, and 'angi' could be snorted. As the police said of this quarter, 'the men do the trade, the women are too busy fucking'.[xxxiv]

The public was concerned that Spring Hill had the potential to develop into an underworld on a scale similar to Sydney and Melbourne. There the geniuses of crime were to be found, the thinkers and directors who worked on large scales, but Brisbane didn't offer the scope of opportunity afforded to such brainy crooks from the South. But Brisbane was progressing and Spring Hill was developing into a regular hotbed of highly organised crime.

The press noticed this sudden increase in crimes of violence and attributed this to the wholesale transfer of senior men from the C.I.B.

Senior men such as O'Hara, Farrell, McCarthy, Jessen, and Sullivan had been sent up country.[xxxv] It was as if someone wanted to remove as much practical knowledge and experience as possible from within C.I. Branch.

11 LETTERS TO ONLY LOVE

Detective Elford had returned from Mount Morgan and delivered a report to Sub-Inspector Meldon. Included in the report was the correspondence he had collected. These constituted letters received by a woman who had been identified as the mother of Cumming's illegitimate child. They were reported as being from Cumming himself.

*

Queensland
(Sunday) 5-12-26

To Only Love & Darling Boy

Dearest I presume my Dear Love & Baby you will begin to think I have wiped you off the map but as I had but little or no news to write about I presumed it advisable to hold back. However Dear Love I received both yours and must say without exaggeration your previous letter I think was one without doubt the sweetest and most loving letter I ever received from you or anyone throughout life.

Never did I realise such tried & sweet love imbedded before & must say overjoyed to think Dearself & Baby Love was so well. Same here only tried to sleep on that after the night work & dependent on receipt of bad news from my father. I got a call out at 1am and had to go over about 5 miles as he had a very bad turn The Dr was called & he advised he was suffering from a leakage from a valve & the head causing the blood to flow to travel quick to the head. I stopped with him till 3:30 am (Sunday) & at that time his severe pain eased off & he was inclined to sleep & as he is a big age, it will come hard on him 85 in April next so up to time of writing I cannot say Love how he will fair but we must hope for the best.

By your last Love I was sorry to hear you were worrying. Why I hope not because I went to that 'Picnic' Now look Love if I don't go out somewhere I will be only fit for the scrap heap. One thing that keeps my spirits up is your most loving long & interesting letters. Ask yourself one question without them What would my life be? I sorely wish I could screen half that goes on in my home & present it before you. I think you would not believe it. Another principal item my four children. They do their utmost to make me happy however Dear Love as soon as rain comes I am putting in for holidays as a change from household worries will do me the world of good. So I hope Love you will always send me lovely letters. Remember Love your loving and true hearted Boy is putting up wonderful trials & inconvenience for <u>Your Dearself & Baby Love</u> I do it all with a smile. I consider I have won the fights all the same. I get hell morning noon & night & I do smile & that is what hurts her. I told my T she is not game to go too far as she would only be hanging herself with her own rope. She would never get anyone else to work like me & give her the same money. I only wish Dear

Love you were here to handle it. I had some very long burst since I finished N.D. I was on special on Saturday night & did not get home till 12 midnight & was called out again at 1 am & got back home at 4:30 and walked about 5 miles done it in about 65 minutes I will have to write all my relations in reference to my father's illness. I don't know what this letter will be like Love as I am awfully tired & will have to be on duty at 6 am tomorrow morning. The Trocadero is closing on 16th of next month as the ground is resumed to widen the street. Very few of the Dance halls is doing any 'Biz' most of the people goes to Speedway over 30,000 spectators. I have not been out but I believe it is most exciting. The drought is awful & if it keeps up much longer it will put up the cost of living considerably. Well Dear Love I don't feel in the humour to write I presume Love you will get me nothing for myself for keeping you so long waiting for a letter. So please Dear Love excuse me for this time I know you will. If I had you on this bed for five minutes I know you would & some of the finery would be displaced & frills displaced. I feel about 100 and four in the shade. My T is still doing penance & likely to I am afraid & I will have to have a cold shower after this. Well Dear Love I am enclosing a P.N. for 5/- for our Dear Baby Love

Now as I have no more news I close good bye bye
With heaps of love and kisses
From your ever loving boy M.
xxxxxxxxxxxxxxxxxxxx[xxxvi]

-o-

When I first read this letter it didn't seem to fit at all with the letter reported to have been found in the Acting Sergeant's locker. I thought there must have been some reconciliation, then read the following letter.

*

Queensland
12/12/26

My Only Love & Darling Baby
Dearest, I received your most loving long and
interesting letter a few days ago and pleased to hear your
Dearself and Baby Love was progressing so favourably as
this leaves your Dear Old Boy same. Things in general is
about the same as when I wrote last hence I have not been
out to any amusements since I wrote last with the
exception when I finished work at 10pm Consb James & I
went down last Thursday night to view Sundry Band very
nice for those that likes a cameal music. I did not care for
it. 10/6 Tickets at the 'Trocadero' very large crowd there. I
was pleased to get such a lovely hello from you & so long
however do you do it. You don't know the comfort that
letter is to me. My heart simply sings when I read yours
especially when I find you & Baby Love is well and happy.
I was so pleased you did not go to church as I don't like
you meeting 'B' I never doubt you but his past actions you
told me was quite enough to arrest him. I don't think Love
if I ever met him I could speak civil to him. Fancy meeting
T.D. Yes I think he is fond of the hops a lot chews it &
dirty at that. One that I pride in keeping my clean Love. As
a rule two showers and a shave every day Last night I got
home 10:30 & under the shower I went & into clean
clothes & took my rug and pillow & slept on the verandah
to daylight but so if you were there Love. What say you.
This is a thing all my mates cannot understand it does not
matter how hot it is I can stand out on the points or

anywhere & into middle of the day take off my socks & they are as dry as when I put them on, my Father is exactly the same way very hard feet in fact I could wear a pair for a week & you would not know hardly I had them on I also wear calves underpants much cleaner. I am awfully particular about my clothes. I have 5 suits & everytime I wear them I brush and clean them & put them away. I feel very queer Love when I read in yours that I would probably lose my mind when I see your panties. Are you sure you have not made a mistake & meant I might lose something else I am afraid this will be such a brief up I will be about running over top of them. I had a good laugh at your dream. You must of felt queer Did anything happen I presume you were feeling about to see if I was anywhere close. When you mentioned the Drill Hall Do you remember the night I had to go fishing with the wire for its 'practice' I often laugh when I think of that I only wish you were here now. Something doing have you mentioned in your last 'Love'. Well I blame you for our love no that was to be & will always last on my part & I have nothing to doubt it will be always the same with you. I will never forget the day I typed that little note to you to meet me I thought over it many times before I posted same thinking I may offend you & the hours from the time I posted it till your arrival with your loving & smiling face entered the office Don't you think Love I looked excited if I did not I felt that way in fact words cannot express my feelings Love & you remember all that followed. All the same Love I was frightened to trespass too far thinking I might offend you. Then when it came to the meet on that bridge & not seeing you. I am sure if I had of not any duty to perform there would have been troubled waters. Then the second my job came and I night & we went down to that old tree on the river opposite the railway station. This will no doubt bring

back fond & loving memories Yes my only 'Love' I am
nervously longing & praying for to be long side of your
Dearself. I did not put in for my holidays yet Love I am
anxiously waiting to know if you will be able to come with
me If not I will have to give you a holiday later. I don't
wish to go Love till rain comes but I am afraid Love I wont
be able to hold out much longer. There is a great change in
the weather today I am afraid Love if rain don't come soon
several people will lose everything. On the land Love is not
all sunshine. Tonight, Sunday, I am relieving a man to give
him his Sunday off next Sunday will be my day off. There is
two of our men transferred, viz. McCulloch (Plain Clothes)
to CI Branch & Sgt Davis to Barcaldine. I am grateful the
latter is gone awful liar & a skite he will find out he wont
have all his way among the 'Shearers'. The Trocadero lost
their appeal in the full court Re 'sly grog selling' They are
closing on the 16th of next month. The court has resumed
the ground for street undeniably. Some nice new buildings
for business has been erected in Melbourne Street from
Hanley St to Grey Street and they look very nice. Brisbane
is going ahead fast. You remember I mentioned that two
houses being built in front of mine. There is a nice new one
erected on one and the other the allotment was sold by
auction yesterday for £250 Thirty two perches so you see
Love property is valuable here you cannot go wrong with
City property. Well my love my Mrs. & I is not playing
trains & not likely to either. Whatever love there was, if
any, is as the song says, Love & lost. It is an awful pity
Love we did not meet earlier in life. Just look at my life, on
good wages & a home & no comfort except my four
children. The old lad is still here & I told my T. he best
pack up at the end of the year & get out failing this I will
feel it my duty to place all of his things on the street. It
appears to me he wants to run the show & is always

interfering with the other children. I never speak to him. He always can find plenty of money for motoring but can find but very little to put into this home. He had a good trial outside & found it was not a pleasure so he wants to brief on me but I will see he wont. I have plenty to do – look after the others. Another thing Love I notice if he goes out of a Sunday she wont cook a hot dinner just puts down a few scraps of cold meat & we get to make the best of it. I will make a big change next Sunday. I shouldn't tell you this Love because I know it will make you worry. Never mind 'Love' I am always happy and can smile through it all as long as your sweet love will always stick to me. I know it will. I am amorously looking forward to be back to see your loving & smiling face once again. (It will be a real honeymoon wont it Love xxxx) I always found you so nice and clean & loving in your ways, so different to most. I laughed Love when you mentioned they were going to wear that undergarment I wonder will they be open for inspection. I give so Love there would by some signs to. Anyhow Love we will lived our own inspections What say you. Well Love I will go out for the day make a day out with my pal (he is a train driver) I don't like going about on my own. I only wish I was a little closer to you Love as we are covering a lot of ground or I should say a lot of pleasant moments. I have not put that new suit on waiting to put it on when I take you out. I forgot to mention Love my father is on the mend & expect he will about in a few days. I was pleased to learn Love our lad the Darling was so bright & contented I would love to see him & I just think it will be long now. Now Dearest Love I will pay my bye with one longing of love & kisses of joy,

From your most loving & true hearted Boy M[xxxvii]

-o-

On first reading I was again taken by the difference in tone to the letter reported sent from her. On subsequent readings I noticed some irregularities. Cumming had five children. The letter states there are four. Did he not include Stanley? But then he mentions Stanley as 'the old lad', who was to be told to 'pack up' and failing that, his things would be placed in the street. I came to the conclusion that the Cumming home was not a happy one, and it appeared that Stanley was still a point of frustration for the Acting Sergeant.

*

The next letter had been typed out and the sign off had been hand written.

Wednesday
21/12/26

To My Only Love & Darling Baby Love

I received your most loving letter a few days ago but was too busy to answer same, so please Love excuse me for this time as we are awfully busy two shooting cases this week. First Love I wish to express my sincere sympathy in your sad bereavement. It is hard to think a person in the prime of life should be cut down so sudden and hard for those that is left behind. I also wish to ask you Dear Love to pardon me for not sending you and Baby Love a Christmas present as I am too busy to select something nice; however Dear Love I am enclosing £1 so you can get some little article for both that you would like. I will bring you something nice when I go up & that will be on or about 1st of February and I am putting in this week. Please let me know if this will suit you. Now Dear Love I must close as I have another urgent message to go up and see my Father as he is seriously ill.

So Bye Bye & heaps of Love &

Kisses to your Dearself & Baby Love & Sybil

Also a very Merry Christmas 'n Prosperous New Year

From Your Very Loving Boy M.

Kiss right here Love

X xxxviii

-o-

This apparent discrepancy between the tone of the letter from the locker and these gnawed at me. I thought they may have been written by another woman yet the margin had been appended with the initials F.A.D. Francis Annie Doak. Her sister in-law, Elizabeth Carroll Mee nee Doak, had passed away suddenly on the 16th December from blood poisoning at the age of 40 years.xxxix Yet, there was no mention of being classed in the low set nor of anything that I thought would be construed as insulting. Due to my suspicions I had a closer look. The letter was dated just two days before the murders. That's when it struck me, I checked the date again. The 21st December 1926 was a Tuesday.

*

With the letters was additional information that had been collected from the woman in Mt. Morgan. The information stated that she claimed that she had received another letter, that she had destroyed, but in it she claims that Cumming had written that should he ever be killed, it would be his wife and son that would be behind it.

I can just image how Meldon would have bellowed for Henderson and Campbell to get into his office.

"Have you heard from that bloody solicitor McGrath?"

Campbell and Henderson would have just shook their heads.

"Get back out there and chase him up! We need to talk to Mrs. Cumming and her son!"

*

Henderson and Campbell returned to the office of W.J. McGrath to again be informed he was not in. Henderson requested to speak to W.J. McGrath himself. He told that gent what he had come to find out, if Gerald McGrath had provided advice that Mrs. Cumming and her son Stanley were not to give any information to Police or answer any of their questions.

"I'll look up the books," recalls Henderson of W.J. McGrath saying as he flicked through three separate journals before entering the office of Gerald McGrath and bringing out a further book.

"I'm sorry," W.J. McGrath had said, "there is no record of it in my books. I think you may have come to the wrong office, I am sorry I can't give you any information."

Henderson and Campbell would have been reluctant to return to C.I. Branch, having to inform Meldon of what they had learnt at the solicitors office. Meldon must have calmed down and taken the time to think through his next move in the absence of the detectives.

Meldon wanted to 'flush them out' and appears to have called the editor of the 'Truth' newspaper. The newspaper was very thankful for the exclusive and reported the vital information that Meldon had passed on in the next edition.

'It is now more likely than ever that Cumming was done to death by someone who had a reason to resent his gay Lothario habits, someone who had cause to bitterly deplore the Sergeant's guilty relations and attentions to certain women, or a certain woman. It is known that Cumming wore a wide regulation belt around his waist while in uniform and attached to this belt were a pair of keys, the keys belonging to a box in which he kept papers of a private nature. There was one distinctive theory that presents itself. Whoever committed the murders knew of the existence of the keys and was keenly desirous of gaining access to some closed secret to which the keys were the open sesame. Or did the keys open some other secret of which the world is yet ignorant. His transfer to another centre removed him from the influence of pouting lips and trim ankles in Mount Morgan, but his Don Juan notions were with him wherever he went and his reputation as a man of many loves followed him about. Cumming was wearing his belt with handcuffs and keys on the night of the murders as far as C.I. Branch is concerned the murderer crept upon the guilty pair, after the Acting Sergeant had removed his belt, and fired the revolver bullets into them. Then, with the two dead bodies at his or her feet, the murderer, whether a man or a woman, seems to have stooped and picked up the belt before a hasty, stealthy get-away was effected. The importance of the whereabouts of the keys is therefore, patent. The keys are hidden somewhere and their discovery would immensely raise the hopes of the investigators who are trying to bring about the arrest of a murderer. The hunt for the keys is on.'

*

The next day Henderson was at C.I. Branch in his

office when he was told that there was someone at the counter for him. According to Henderson the following conversation took place.[xl]

"Can I help you?" said Henderson.

"I'm Gerald McGrath, I am acting for Mrs. Cumming and her son and I have come down to see if I could get a look at some documents that you took from her house on Christmas Eve. I want to get some particulars from them."

"You're Gerald McGrath?" asked Henderson.

"Yes."

"Mrs. Cumming told me that you were acting for her and she said that you had advised her, and her son, not to answer any questions that were asked of them by any of the Police, did you tell her that?"

"Certainly not, I wouldn't do that!"

"Well about the documents," said Henderson, "you will have to see Sub Inspector Meldon because he is the person to decide whether you can see them or not. If you will come this way, I'll show you to his office."

Henderson led McGrath to the muster room as Meldon's office adjoins that room and motioned for him to stand still while he knocked at the door. A call of 'Yes' signified Henderson could open the door and he cracked it just enough to get his head around to speak to Meldon, letting him know that McGrath was there to see him.

"Bring him in!" said Meldon and Henderson motioned for McGrath to enter as he fully opened the door.

"Sub Inspector Meldon, I am Gerald McGrath acting for Mrs. Cumming and her son and I desire to get some particulars from certain documents that the Police have obtained and I have been told you are the one to decide such things."

"Are you aware, McGrath," said Meldon, "that Mrs. Cumming and her son have informed the detectives that she will not come to C.I. Branch to answer any further questions or make a statement in respect of the murder of her husband and the woman Walsh, stating that you advised her not to do so, is that correct?"

"No, I never gave her that advice."

12 FOR THE RECORD

Sub-Inspector Meldon requested Henderson and Campbell to formally interview the members of the police force that had been on duty at South Brisbane Station on the night of the tragedy. He wanted to ensure they had everything documented 'for the record'.

According to documents the detectives first spoke to Senior Sergeant Caulfield who was in charge of the South Brisbane Police Station. He knew both Cumming and Mrs. Walsh. He explained to the detectives that at two p.m. on the day in question Cumming had paraded before him, to take charge of the second relief, which would operate from two in the afternoon until ten that evening. He had under his supervision four constables, namely Rawlings, Baker, Griffiths, and Cunneen.

"Did they have their cuffs and other appointments?" queried Campbell.

"Of cause the Constables did," replied Caulfield, "they have to show them on parade before going out, but you know that."

"Yes," said Henderson, "but Meldon wants it all formally recorded. What about Cumming? Did he have his cuffs?"

"Alright," acknowledged Caulfield, "I didn't see Cumming's handcuffs as he was the Non Commissioned Officer in charge of the relief and it is not customary for the Non Commissioned Officer to do so."

"So did he have his cuffs?" asked Campbell.

"I could not say if at that particular time he had his cuffs or not. He should have had them, I know his key to the handcuffs were found on the body."

"And you're sure that that key was for his cuffs?"

"Yes, that key was number fifteen, and those handcuffs, number fifteen, had been issued to him at the Police Depot on his transfer to South Brisbane."

"Did you see Cumming again after you paraded him?"

"No, that was the last time I saw him."

"How was he?"

"He seemed to be in good health and spirits."

"Did you give any specific instructions for duty on that day?" asked Henderson.

"Yes," responded Caulfield, "I gave him instructions to be in the vicinity of Victoria Place, at the south end of Victoria Bridge at about eight o'clock when the hotels would be closing and to assist his men generally if they required it, as a lot of people were coming in for Christmas and there was generally a fairly rowdy crowd in that vicinity of Victoria Place and the Railway Station."

"For the record," said Henderson, "could you describe the boundary between the South Brisbane and Woolloongabba Police Divisions."

"For the record," said Caulfield a little annoyed, "the boundary commences at the York Hotel, being the corner of Annerley Road and Stanley Street and works on the right hand side from the York Hotel up to the junction of Gladstone Road and Annerley Road near the South

Brisbane Cemetery. We also patrol the South Brisbane Cemetery and Dutton Park. On the other side of Annerley Road, including the Gaol, is in the Woolloongabba Police Division."

"Do you know the scene of the tragedy?"

"Yes, and that is in the Woolloongabba Police Division. Cumming in the ordinary course of duty would not attend to anything on the Gaol side or on that side of Annerley Road."

"What about complaints regarding the Lock Hospital?"

"No, those complaints are attended to by the Woolloongabba Police."

"Did anything happen that afternoon that would have necessitated Cumming going over to the place where his body was found?"

"No."

"We believe you examined the records of the relief tickets issued in South Brisbane, what did you learn from those records?" asked Henderson.

"I discovered that on the twelfth, nineteenth, and twenty-sixth of January 1926 the records, initialled by Cumming, show that he signed relief tickets on those dates for Eileen Gladys Walsh."

"Why would he sign for them?"

"As on those dates he was second in charge at South Brisbane between five in the afternoon until eleven at night, and the second in charge issues relief tickets."

"What can you tell us about his belt and keys," said Henderson.

"Cumming usually wore a leather belt on duty and attached to the belt was a bunch of keys on a little leather strap which he fastened on to the belt on the right-hand side. As far as I can remember there were probably about nine or ten keys on the leather strap, and a trinket of a lady's shoe. And there were leather loops on the back of the belt where the handcuffs would fit in."

"And on the day you paraded him, would you say he had them on him?" asked Campbell.

"On that day, when I paraded him for duty, I could not say whether he had the belt, handcuffs, or a bunch of keys. I have caused search and inquiries to be made but can get no trace of them. Without actually seeing them it is most likely that he had them on that night."

"Why do you say that?"

"From my supervision of him I know he was very particular about these articles and he would be unlikely to forget the whole lot of them."

"Do you recall when Cumming joined South Brisbane?" asked Henderson.

"Yes, it was the Second of August 1923, I was then second in charge, then I was transferred to Roma Street, that would have been the 22nd of October 1924, and I remained there until I was transferred permanently in charge of South Brisbane on the, 10th February 1926. I have been here ever since."

"What about Cumming?" asked Campbell.

"He was at South Brisbane the whole time, since his arrival from Mt. Morgan."

"What would you say of Cumming, as a police officer?" asked Henderson.

"I would say during the time he was under my supervision, he was very punctual in coming on duty. And he was of very temperate habits."[xli]

"Thank you Senior Sergeant," said Henderson, "could you tell me please are any of the constables that were under Cumming that night around at the moment?"

"Constable Baker is on the counter at the moment," replied Caulfield, "I'll introduce you."

Caulfield escorted the Detectives to the front counter of the South Brisbane Police Station on the Corners of Grey and Glenelg Streets. Caulfield remained with them as they questioned Baker.

Henderson and Campbell explained to Baker their need to formally record his evidence. Baker reported that he knew Cumming but not Mrs. Walsh. He further stated that he was on duty with the second relief on the night in question and that Cumming was in charge of the relief.

"Did you see Cumming after you paraded?" asked Campbell.

"He visited me several times during the afternoon of that relief."

"What duty were you on that day?"

"From instructions from Cumming, I did beat duty from Victoria Place along Stanley Street to Russell Street thence Grey Street to Melbourne Street, and back to Victoria Place. It was a busy night."

"When did he last visit you?" asked Henderson.

"At Victoria Place at about seven forty-five."

"And that was the last time you saw him?" asked Henderson.

Baker looked at Caulfield before responding.

"No, I saw him later at five minutes past eight, he arrived on the front of an outbound tram, proceeding along Stanley Street in the direction of Woolloongabba."

"Where were you?"

"I was at the intersection of Stanley and Russell Street."

"What was the number of the tram?" asked Henderson.

"Where was the tram going?" asked Campbell.

"I could not say what tram car it was, or its destination."

"What could you make of his disposition at that time?"

"He appeared to be in good health and spirits, that was

the last time I saw him, and he was sober."

"Did he have his cuffs and other appointments?"

"I could not say if he had his belt, handcuffs, or keys with him then."

"Did you know of his having entanglements with woman?"

"No, I did not know anything about his private life."

"How long had you known Cumming?" asked Henderson.

"About a year."

"Did Cumming speak to you at the Palace Hotel Corner?"

"I don't remember."

"Do you know of any other police that may have been there that night?"

"There was a constable on traffic duty there, at Victoria Place, and there was another constable there on duty also, as far as I know I was the last to see him that night."

"How do you know that?" asked Campbell.

"I have ascertained that by speaking to the other police on that relief."

"Would that be a normal thing," asked Henderson, "that that would be the last time you would see him."

"In the ordinary course he would visit me just before we finished at ten o'clock, unless something occurred in his duty that took him away."[xlii]

-o-

I mulled over Constable Baker's statement. I needed to review the Refidex Street Directory from 1926 and flicked between Maps numbered twenty-nine and thirty.[9] In his

---

[9] Figure 4 – Refidex Directory 1926 Map 30

statement Baker says he was on beat from Victoria Place, down Stanley Street to Russell Street, then proceeded up Russell Street to Grey Street, Grey to Melbourne, then Melbourne back to Victoria Place. A clockwise beat.

Yet a tram outbound to Woolloongabba down Stanley Street would have approached Baker from behind. How did he see Cumming on the front of it I asked myself.

I shrugged it off. So he turned around. Besides he says that was at five past eight, contradicting what Stanley Cumming had told the detectives about seeing his father outside the Palace Hotel and he was looking suspicious by not completing his statement.

I had to work through the timeline of the sequence of events that led up to the murders to make sense of the various witness accounts.

Cumming arrived home at Wilton Street for tea at six thirty, without an exact time for when he left, I worked backwards from the earliest sighting.

That was seven forty-five at Victoria Place, according to Constable Baker. From Wilton Street to the Fiveways would be about a five minute walk. It would be logical to think that he would not have been waiting long for a tram as that was a major interconnector for three tram lines running down Stanley Street. Assuming he waited ten minutes, any of the trams passing through there would have taken him directly to Victoria Place. A tram would take about five minutes from the Fiveways to Victoria Place without stops. Allowing ten minutes for the journey with stops would make it seven twenty-five that he left home, at the latest.

Then I asked myself what if he walked? He could have walked from Wilton Street to Victoria Place in just over half an hour, and based on Baker's account, I assume that Cumming visited others before him, so I think we can be confident that he left home sometime just after seven, but no later than seven twenty-five.

Baker says he saw Cumming on an outbound tram heading to Woolloongabba at the corner of Stanley and Russell Streets, but Stanley Cumming and Miss Clutterbuck say they saw the Acting-Sergeant outside the Palace Hotel.

It is about a five minute walk from where Melican's was to the hotel. He could not have been in both places at the same time. Either someone had their times wrong, or, someone lied.

The next person to see Cumming is the witness Witt, who claims to have seen the Acting-Sergeant around eight thirty outside his Mother's shop in Annerley Road.

If we assume that Cumming caught a tram to Clarence Corner and walked up to Annerley Road and past the shop, and the time is accurate, then, allowing five minutes to walk there, ten minutes for the tram, he would have left the vicinity of the Palace Hotel around quarter past eight, tying in with what Stanley Cumming said.

Constable Baker's statement did not seem to fit.

The next sighting is by James Jamieson, who states that he saw Cumming and the woman Walsh walking down Annerley Road from Gladstone Road at about nine thirty an hour after Witt saw him. This would have given them enough time to walk up the hill and return in the direction Jamieson states he saw them.

Yet Jamieson did not see either of them when he alighted from his tram, nor did he mention having seen them in Gladstone Road as the tram he was in approached his stop. I concluded he might have been reading the paper, or looking out the other side.

Then how do these sightings reconcile with the times given for the shots being heard.

Witt says he heard two shots at about nine thirty, the

last one duller than the first, Jamieson who heard two shots at quarter to ten, Waygood heard three shots, all the same, at five past nine, and Leonard Johns states that between nine fifteen and ten he heard two sharp reports, like revolver shots, and then a duller report afterwards. The wardens at the Gaol collaborate the number of shots with Waygood but more likely to be quarter past nine.

So who do we believe?

Was it faulty memory, faulty hearing, or was there something else? I was suspicious of Waygood due to his apparent insurance fraud. I looked into Jamieson.

I found a newspaper report naming a James Jamieson as being committed for trial on charges of false pretences and stealing. Jamieson also used the alias Thomas Page. The name Page leapt out at me. The woman that Mrs. Cumming and Stanley reported seeing her husband with in a café in Edward Street was Mrs. Page. The 1915 newspaper article stated that James Jamieson alias Thomas Page was 26 years of age.[xliii]

Was the James Jamieson born in 1889 the same James Jamieson residing in Annerley Road in 1926? He should have been about 37 years old. A little more research and it appeared that these were two different men although I was unable to rule it out conclusively.

I then factored in Eileen's movements on that night. According to the family's evidence she left home around eight o'clock to go to a pillar box. There are two possibilities, one on Annerley Road and another at the Gloucester Street Station, about the same distance from the Christie residence in Stephens Road, about a ten minute walk there and back. If she left home around, eight twenty, eight twenty-five, she would have been at the Pillar Box as Cumming was passing Mrs. Witt's shop, a chance meeting, that fits in with what the family told detectives, she rarely went out at night, had her ordinary house dress on and asked her niece to accompany her.

But that left an hour before Jamieson claims to have seen them up on Gladstone Road. I checked the distance from the pillar box to the reserve. Estimating it would take about fifteen to twenty minutes to walk there. With twenty minutes walking, then twenty minutes canoodling, that brings the time up to about five past nine, corresponding to when Waygood says he heard the shots.

According to Stanley Crane he nearly ran over a suspicious duo at about ten minutes past nine near the Railway Bridge. It would only be five minutes from the scene to where he saw them.

I needed to construct a table with the details of the various witness accounts.

Witness	Number of Shots	Time Heard
Frank Waygood	3	9:10 – 9:15
Boggo Road Warders	3	9:15
Leonard Johns	3	9:15 – 10:00
William Witt	2	9:30
James Jamison	2	9:45 – 10:00

A general consensus would suggest that three shots were fired at nine fifteen. The one that stood out for me was the account of James Jamieson. I was already suspicious of him due to the Thomas Page alias I had uncovered. I found an aerial photograph of Boggo Road Gaol from 1929 and considered Jamieson's evidence. He stated that he saw Eileen and Cumming walk down Annerley Road then turning into the Gaol Lane that leads to Burke Street. This was not possible. Due to the bend in

Annerley Road he could not have had a clear sight of the Gaol Lane.[10] I immediately considered what Jamieson might have to gain if he was lying. What purpose would it serve to conceal the number of shots fired and the time that they were heard? I checked the records again, he was a waterside worker, but appears to have been apprenticed as a printer. If he had nothing to gain had he been put up to it? By whom?

I went back to Eileen's past, was there something that connected the victims together. Was there something that connected them to Jamieson? Both Eileen's husband and mother stated she was not in receipt of relief payments. Yet Sergeant Caulfield stated he found some from January that were initialled by Cumming.

I reviewed the statements about the detectives pursuit of the Page woman's husband. They'd heard back from interstate inquiries regarding his movements on that night and it had been established beyond doubt that he was not in Queensland at the time, and for some time previous, and hasn't been since. Again it appeared as though there was no connection between James Jamieson and Mrs. Page.

I went back to the list of women that Cumming was associated with, to make sure all the husbands were accounted for. There was one that the newspapers reported that caught my eye, Soppy.[xliv] Could it have been a misinterpretation of Stoppy?

*

The newspapers caught Walsh in a melancholy frame

---

[10] Figure 2 - Aerial view of Boggo Road Gaol, Brisbane, 1929

of mind and he told them his story. He was born in Maryborough some thirty-six years prior and brought to Brisbane in his early school years. He had lived at South Brisbane and that was when he first got to know young Eileen Gladys Christie, who was still a girl in pinafore and plaits. They 'virtually grew up together' spending much time in each other's company. When the war broke out his devotion to her had reached somewhere beyond the friendship stage. Walsh described how he had enlisted in the November of 1915 and soon afterward he was sent across to Egypt with the 17th reinforcements to the 15th Battalion. From Egypt he went with his company to France where he served twelve months at the front line until on the Eleventh of April 1917 he was wounded at Bullecourt and made a prisoner of war by the Germans. He explained to Campbell that he remained a prisoner of war until the end of the conflict being compelled to assist in the digging of gun pits for enemy artillery, and the spreading of barbed wire, and the multitude of other jobs that his captives forced him to do. The food, what little he was given, was polluted and the constant grind of solid work had sapped his stamina such that he spent several months in a German Hospital the result of exposure and emaciation.

"Throughout those dreary days," said Walsh, "I never forgot that little girl in Brisbane. Any time the opportunity was made open to me I wrote her. And finally when the big stoush ended the first thing I did was cable Eileen, telling her that I was safe and on my way back home."

He continued his story relaying how he arrived back in Brisbane in the May of 1919, and that evening he met Eileen at Clarence Corner. Walsh spoke softly now with hesitant words under the sway of memory's emotion as his elevated ideas about the girl were to receive a staggering shock. Eileen had confessed to him that she had slipped from the path of virtue, and that, before very many months would pass, she would become a mother. When her daughter was born he was one of those that went to comfort her, he could not let her face a world alone with what a satirical society would call a love-child. It was no easy job for her and her pitiful sight reawakened the devotion that he held for her. But the babe lived only a short few months before it died, and the unhappy mother laid it to rest in the Catholic portion of the South Brisbane Cemetery. Not far from where she herself had been interned.

"Months passed, we began to see more of each other and then we agreed that the past could be forgotten and we directed our hope and purposes towards a brighter future together, so that at the end of 1920 we were secretly married. Secretly because our families did not look upon our union favourably. She was a Catholic and I'm a Protestant, and the divergence of our religious views were reckoned to be a bar to happiness."

"So we were married by the Reverend John Marshall Sands at the Congregational Manse in Vulture Street. Then one month later a baby boy came into the world, and we christened him James Frederick Walsh. Then two and a half years later and we were blessed again with the arrival of another boy, Ronald Samuel."

"That's when the trouble commenced in earnest!" stated Walsh, "interference from outside fuelled her discontent, influences which turned her against me, because of my religion!"

"In July of 1924," continued Walsh, "she went into the Mater Hospital for an operation and while she was there, I had to address my letters to her through someone else, so that her people would not know that I was still keeping in touch with her."

"I wrote her at least three times to come back to me from her mother's and although she told me she wanted to come back to me she said she did not know what to do, because if she did come back she would antagonise her people. She came out of hospital and lived with me for a while, then one day, she walked out of the place. We never lived together again."

"The two boys were left with me for some time, the youngest was still just a baby, just twelve months old, then one day I received a message that an accident had occurred up the street, and that one of Eileen's family was involved.

I hurried up the street to see what had happened, but, I could not locate any accident. When I returned the older boy had been taken away."

"It was just impracticable for me to look after the youngest so I conceded his custody to my wife."

"I'd like to get my kiddies back," Walsh told reporters, "I could bring them back under my care and place them in the charge of my mother and married sister."

The reporters suggested to Walsh that this may not occur as there had been accusations that he had, in the past, submitted too much to the desire for drink.

"I roundly condemn such talk as specious falsehoods! There is not a single instance where I have lost a job through drink! The fact I was out of work sometimes made things hard, but that was no fault of mine. If there was slackness in the boot-making trade I could not help it! I did my best to keep in work, and the few drinks I took caused no injury to anyone, though Eileen did not like me to drink at all."

"Whatever failing my wife had," continued Walsh, "she was a good wife to me. Left alone we would have been unceasingly happy. She was a good mother to our boys, so I was content for her to keep them with her. Now that she is gone, I want my children and, before God, I am going to have them!"[xlv]

-o-

The detectives must have asked Walsh if he know the father of the child that passed away. If they were to exhaust all avenues of enquiry. Eileen named the little girl Gladys Delacour Christie, so I took that to confirm that the father was James Delacour.

*

After the newspaper story I assume that the detectives must have arrived at the Delacour residence in Cornwall Street just off Logan Road. If they had stopped to check some facts before setting out to the home they would have learnt that James Delacour had been reported as a missing person four years earlier.

I assume that after they had agreed that none of them had any news on the whereabouts of James Delacour, a line of questioning would have occurred of his wife Mary Delacour. They would have discretely inquired, 'did she know Eileen Walsh or possibly know of the woman by her maiden name, Eileen Christie', 'was she aware if her husband knew Eileen'.

Mary Delacour would have responded she did not.

Although James was born in Maryborough, she had met him in Bundaberg and that was where they were married when he was twenty-five years of age. Their first three children had been born there, their youngest had been born in Brisbane after they moved to Coorparoo around ten years earlier. James was a labourer and they had moved to Brisbane to improve his employment prospects.

Shortly after arriving James had tried to enlist for the war but was rejected due to an inguinal hernia and chronic rheumatism. When asked if anything out of the ordinary happened recently she confirmed that since she had reported James missing to police early in 1921, she had received about three letters in a woman's handwriting requesting to know the whereabouts of her husband. The letters were not signed but the return address was listed as Annerley Road South Brisbane. The letters expressed some degree of urgency to locate him. She no longer had the letters, they had been destroyed.

At first I thought it a bit odd, both Walsh and Delacour being born in Maryborough. Then I discarded the idea as another one of those coincidences that I had cautioned myself about.

13 CUMMING V'S CHRISTIE

From the evidence it is suggested that Henderson and Campbell spent the next few days running out leads. Predominately this meant discrete conversations with at least a dozen women and their husbands recording their movements on the night of the tragedy. Even more 'bushie types' would be taken to C.I. Branch for questioning, but all could account for their movements on the night. No one however, could be linked to the purchase of the automatic pistol reportedly sold by Hawgood the pawnbroker.

The detectives were tired, they had been working the case hard spending long hours both in the office and chasing possible leads. They presumably were seated in the case room in mid-January 1927, going back over the information collected so far, when a constable announced that they had a visitor at the front counter. Henderson must have been taken aback as he took in the scene at the front counter. Mrs. Cumming stood there. Detective Henderson escorted Mrs. Cumming to an interview room and got her comfortable before commencing his questioning. He read aloud her previous incomplete statement as recorded by Detective Campbell.

According to Henderson the following conversation ensued,

"Why have you decided to complete your statement?" he asked.

"Well, I am sorry now that I had taken up the attitude I did, I was badly advised and I have now come to make a statement and answer any questions I am asked."

"When you last spoke to Campbell," said the Detective, "you stated that on the night of your husband's murder, you left home and went to see your mother, tell me about that please."

"Stanley left home between seven and seven thirty and I left sometime between seven fifteen and eight o'clock. I took the tram and went to visit my mother."

"Did you go alone?"

"Yes"

"Did you change trams?"

"No, I took the one tram to the Valley."

"Why did you go to the Valley?"

"To see my mother, she resides at Constance Street, in the Valley."

"When did you get there?"

"I got there about eight o'clock or a little sooner."

"What was your mother doing?"

"She is an old lady, eighty-five years of age, what do you mean 'what was she doing'?"

"I mean had she already retired for the night?"

"No, I don't think she was in bed when I arrived."

"Why did you go there?"

"To see if there was anything she required and that she would like for Christmas."

"How long were you there for?"

"I remained with my mother for over an hour."

"Please continue," said Henderson.

"I left my mother's place at about nine fifteen and I walked up to the Valley and had a look at some of the shop windows, and then I caught an Ipswich Road tram at the Valley Junction, and returned home by that car."

"What time was this?"

"Well, as we passed through Stanley Street I noticed that it was nine forty-five according to the South Brisbane Town Hall clock. I got home at five minutes past ten and all the children were then in bed and all was quiet."

"All the children were in bed?" questioned Henderson.

"All were in bed, with the exception of Stanley."

"So what did you do?"

"As usual I prepared my husband's supper, and then I got a book and started to read, until about eleven-thirty, expecting my husband to come home anytime as usual."

"Precisely what did you do then," asked Henderson.

"I went to my room, at eleven thirty, and switched on the light, I had not undressed at this time, and I walked onto the verandah. I had a look down the street thinking that I might see my husband, and just as I was about to go back into my room I noticed two Policeman in uniform walking up the street and I thought one of them was my husband. I waited till the Policemen came up to the gate, I was rather disappointed to see that my husband was not one of them. One of them spoke to me, he said, 'Is this where Cumming lives?' and he then said 'Is the boss home?' and I said 'No.' I told him I was disappointed that I thought he was my husband coming up the road. He then entered into a conversation with me and asked me if a house was for sale further along the street, and I told him the house had been taken by another constable that was coming there to reside. He then said 'Well tell the boss I was asking about the place'. Then they left."

"Did they tell you your husband was missing?"

"No, they did not say anything about my husband, that he was missing or anything like that."

"What did you do then?"

"I went to my room, and went to bed after undressing, I must have dozed off as the next thing I recall was being awoken by a knock at the door. I answered the door and discovered it was Sub-Inspector Bergin, and he asked me if my husband was at home and I said 'No' and then he said, 'have you any idea where he is?' and I again answered 'No' and that he had not returned home after duty. Sub Inspector Bergin then said to me, 'Mrs. Cumming your husband has not reported off shift, don't get alarmed as he may have been called away somewhere, do you think he has gone up to see his father?' His father had taken bad turns before that and my husband had to go up there before. I said to Sub-Inspector Bergin that my husband would not leave the station without making some arrangement, that is if he was going up to see his father. Then he asked me if my son was home and I replied 'No' and then he said 'What time does he come home?' and I said 'If he is out to any enjoyment he generally catches the last tram home'. He then said he would make inquiries at Red Hill, where my husband's father lives, to see if my husband had gone there and that he would let me know later on. The way he spoke to me he gave me the feeling not to worry, not to look at the black side of things. I did feel more relieved after Sub Inspector Bergin spoke to me. It would have been another twenty minutes or half an hour that my son came home, that is the boy known as Stanley."

"Where were you when Stanley arrived home?"

"I was in my room, Stanley came in the back way as is usual for him, and I went out and told him about Sub Inspector Bergin calling, and I told him what he had told me, and that he would let me know the result of his inquiries. He then went to bed, that is my son, and I went to bed but I did not sleep, and Stanley went to his room, he said to call him if he was asleep if I got any word."

"And did you, get word?" asked Henderson.

"A Policeman came later on about two in the morning, or maybe between two and three, and he said the word had come through that there had been no trace of my husband at Red Hill."

"What did you do then?"

"My son and I spoke to the Policeman on the verandah. I had a bad turn then, and the Policeman took my son down to a hotel at the corner of the Gabba and got me some brandy. Stanley returned later on alone."

"What happened then?"

"I had a coat over my gown when I was speaking to the Policeman so I got dressed after that, that is while Stanley went down with the Policeman to the hotel. When Stanley came home he gave me some brandy and I went to sleep after that."

"What time did you stir from your sleep?"

"I was up again at four thirty and my husband had not returned. I then came to the conclusion that something had happened, and then I lay down, as it was too early to go anywhere as the trams had not started to run then. I waited until the first tram in the morning, that being about five thirty, and I went to the South Brisbane Police Station, and I saw a constable there, and I told him that I had come down to see if Mr. Cumming had been there."

"What was the constable's name?"

"I don't know, I gave the constable to understand that I would wait there to see if my husband had turned up, and he told me that there was no trace of my husband then, and that if they got any word that they would let me know. I then left the Police Station and went to Tribune Street in South Brisbane and met some of the Police coming off night duty and I inquired of them if they had seen my husband, and they said they had been searching everywhere but they could not get a trace on him."

"What did you do then?"

"I caught a tram home, when I got home all the family was there, and I told Stanley what I had done, and that there were no tidings of my husband."

"Did Stanley tell you where he was going the night before?"

"No."

"What did he do after you told him there had been no tidings of your husband?"

"Stanley said to me, 'Mother, will I go to work or stay home, or what will I do?' and I think I told Stanley to go to work as it was Christmas Eve and they would be busy."

"What did you do then?"

"I then went on with my household duties and then at about eleven o'clock Constable O'Sullivan called to see me and he said 'Your husband has been found shot behind Boggo Road Gaol'. I then lost control of myself and became upset. Some of my neighbours then came in, and later Detective Corbett and two other detectives came, and I think it was Detective Corbett that said, 'You may as well tell her the lot' and then they told me that there was a woman found shot with him."

"What did the Detectives do?"

"They stayed there talking to me, and they looked around, and Mr. Corbett said to me 'did he carry a revolver with him?' and I told him that he did not carry one on the early shift. Detective Corbett looked at a brown bag there of my husband's and he discovered my husband's revolver there, and he said it was fully loaded and then he unloaded it."

"When did you next see Stanley?"

"I got a telephone message sent to Stanley telling him to come home, and he did, and after he came home I got word that I was wanted to go to the Morgue, and Stanley and I went to the Morgue, and there I saw the dead body of my husband, which I identified, and I also saw the dead body of a woman, but I did not know the woman, and I was informed that was the body of the woman that was found near the dead body of my husband."

"What did you and Stanley do then?"

"My son and I then went down to the Valley and told my mother what had happened, so far as I knew, and I went to my brother and then to Smith's the undertaker for the funeral. Mr. Smith sent away certain wires for us to the relatives. After that I came to C.I. Branch with Stanley, and I saw Detective Campbell and some other Detectives and I returned to the Morgue again with some of the detectives."

"Hadn't you already seen the bodies?"

"What? No, the first time I went to the Morgue I did not see the bodies. I returned about four thirty and it was then that I saw the dead bodies of my husband and the woman."

"What did you say while there?"

"I don't remember saying anything at the Morgue."

"After attending at the Morgue, do you recall returning home with Stanley and Detective Campbell?" asked Henderson.

"No, I do not recollect that."

"Don't you remember me taking possession of an automatic pistol and some bullets from Stanley, at your place?"

"Oh, yes, I remember that."

"Do you recall," Henderson checked the notes

Campbell had provided him with, "saying at the Morgue 'it's terrible I have often told him that he would meet with a sudden end, he took no notice of me'."

"I don't remember saying that at the Morgue!"

"Didn't you also say 'Oh Daddy, Daddy, I knew it would come to this, I have warned you that you would meet a terrible end'."

"I did not say anything of the sort!" said Mrs. Cumming with indignation.

"Did you or did you not kiss your husband on the forehead and say 'Daddy, God forgive you?"

"Yes, I kissed the body on the forehead but I do not recollect saying anything at the Morgue," said Mrs. Cumming becoming very agitated.

"Don't be alarmed Mrs. Cumming," said Henderson, "remember if you answer truthfully it will help us find your husband's murderer. Please tell me what you did on the afternoon of Christmas Day."

Mrs. Cumming sat blinking.

"You visited the home of Mary Christie didn't you?"

"Yes."

"Tell me about that please."

"I visited her house after lunch, sometime between one and three in the afternoon."

"Was anyone with you?"

"My daughter Tessie."

"Tell me," said Henderson, "what did you do after lunch and why did you visit the home of Mary Christie."

"After lunch Tessie and I were at home alone and I said to Tessie we'll go down to Smith's the undertaker in Wickham Street with the intention of seeing my husband again, as that is where his corpse had been taken, it was removed from the morgue. I met one of the men at Smith's and I told him what I had come down for, and he said I couldn't see the body. He said 'on account of the body having to be kept till Monday it had to go through a process' and that it would be better not to see it."

"What did you do then?"

"After the conversation with Mr. Barstow we left, and I said to Tessie, 'I don't feel inclined to go home, I'd like to go to the spot where the tragedy had been committed."

"Why?"

"That being really to satisfy myself that anyone that lived in the neighbourhood could have heard the shots."

"Continue please," said Henderson, "how did you get there?"

"We caught an Ipswich Road tram and proceeded to Vulture Street South Brisbane, where we alighted, and from there we went along to Stephens Road and I remarked to my daughter that I would call and give my sympathy to the mother of this woman. We walked along Stephens Road and I located the house as being the one that appeared in the newspapers. We went there and I saw Mrs. Christie, she being on the verandah at the time, she then being leant over the verandah railing. I leaned over the fence and I said 'are you Mrs. Christie' and she said 'Yes' and I told her I was Mrs. Cumming."

"Had you met her before that moment?"

"No I had never met her and she did not know me."

"What did you talk about?"

"I said 'I came to offer you my sympathy' and she replied, 'You have mine' or 'You have ours'. Just then another woman came through the house, whom I now know was Mrs. Jones, and she said to me 'sit down'. I told her where I had come from and I mentioned to her that I was having my husband buried on the Monday. But I don't know whether she, or the mother of Mrs. Jones, said to me 'We had Mrs. Walsh buried yesterday' that being the Friday afternoon. I then spoke to Mrs. Jones saying 'Did you ever see my husband here?' and she said 'No, the only time I have met him was at South Brisbane Police Station through business transactions'. The mother, Mrs. Christie, then spoke and said, 'my daughter had hard times with her husband' and she was in receipt of Government rations, and also went out working, and although she did she never seemed to have any money. She said 'when my daughter went out to post a letter that night we had to give her the money to buy the stamp', she said, 'I did not think she had any appointment to meet anyone that night, because on leaving the house she left a candle lit in the bedroom, which looked as if she did not intend staying long'. And her mother remarked 'my daughter had only her working clothes on and no hat' and she added 'the pillar box she was going to was in Annerley Road'. That was all that was said. Then I left."

"So nothing else was said?"

"Well as I was leaving I said 'It's a sad affair for all of us'. That was all that took place."

"So your daughter didn't speak."

"Oh yes, Tessie spoke to Mrs Jones and said 'I have seen you before, up at St. Ita's Church', and she said 'yes, I attend there'. That was all that was passed."

Henderson read through the notes he had just taken, cross referencing them to his notes from when he spoke to Mrs. Christie.

"When you offered your sympathy to Mrs. Christie did you also say 'I don't know if you will accept it or not'?"

"I deny saying that."

"Did Mrs. Christie reply 'I accept the sympathy and I am awfully sorry for you'?"

"No she did not reply saying that."

"Do you remember Mrs. Christie asking 'did you know

my daughter' and you replying 'No'."

"I don't remember that."

"Did you say 'where is the body' and did Mrs. Christie respond 'it was buried the previous afternoon'."

"No, most certainly not! Mrs. Christie told me that herself about my inquiries."

"Did you say 'You got rid of her quick didn't you'."

"I never mentioned those words."

"Did you ask 'has my husband ever been here drinking or playing cards here'? and did Mrs. Christie respond 'Never'."

"I did not say that, I said to Mrs Jones 'has my husband ever been here' and Mrs Jones said 'No'."

"Did you say, 'if not here it must be at a place further down the street'."

"No, I did not say that."

"Did you ask Mrs. Christie how long she had lived there, and did Mrs. Christie respond sixteen years?"

"No, but Mrs Christie told me that herself, that she had been living there sixteen years, she volunteered that, I had no need to ask her that question."

"Did you say to her 'if it's not you it must be someone else'."

"I did not say that."

"Did you say 'I have always warned my husband that this would be his end, but he only laughed and said it will be a good man that will get me'."

"Such a thing was never mentioned!"

"What would you say if I told you that Mrs. Christie said that you said, 'he was always so fond of beautiful women and girls, but let him look at them lying at the Morgue twenty-four hours afterwards with the paint and powder off'."

"It is a deliberate falsehood!"

"And if I also told you that Mrs. Christie states that you said 'it is a strange coincidence that was the only night that he went out without his revolver, and he left it on the table'."

"That is another deliberate falsehood! He did not leave the revolver on the table at home, it was where the detectives found it, in his bag."

"Do you recall saying to Mrs. Christie, 'are you aware that his belt, handcuffs, and keys were missing."

"I may have said that, I could have said that, but I do not remember saying that, but it is quite natural that I would say that, as they were missing."

"Did Mrs. Christie say to you 'have you got any idea who murdered my daughter and your husband'."

"I don't remember her asking that, she could have said that to me, but I don't remember."

"Did you say to Mrs. Christie 'don't you think the husband did it'."

"I am positive I never said that, I never passed such a remark."

"Did Mrs. Christie respond 'No' and did you reply 'or did he pay someone else to do it'."

"No, no I did not, I did not pass such a remark."

"Did Mrs. Christie respond 'he had no money to pay anyone to do such a terrible crime'."

"I did not hear her say that. I was not there long enough for all this to have passed."

Henderson continued to pose questions around the interview that he had had with Mrs. Christie and Mrs. Cumming continued to deny having said any of it, or not remembering what was said. Finally Henderson asked what she had done when she left the Christie residence.

"I went to the scene of the tragedy and then I went home."

"Have you forgotten what you said to Mrs. Christie that day?"

"No I have not."

"Why do you think she would say that you said those things?"

"The only reason that I can assign for Mrs. Christie fabricating this evidence is on account of my husband bringing her daughter to that, the fact of her daughter being found in the position she was with my husband, and I would do the same thing. She would naturally blame my husband."

"What do you mean you would do the same thing?"

"I mean that she blamed my husband for what happened to her daughter, and I blame the woman for what happened to my husband. I can give no other reason for Mrs. Christie fabricating her evidence."

"So when you say you 'would do the same thing' do you mean fabricate evidence?"

"No I do not!"

"What do you think happened to your husband and Mrs. Walsh?"

"Well, the person that did it was very callous and I don't believe my husband had his clothes disarranged or the woman had her clothes disarranged as they were when he was found."

"What do you mean?"

"The person who did it exposed them like that to put that as a motive. I consider that the clothes were disarranged as they were after the tragedy happened and before they were found."

"Did Mrs. Christie suggest to you that your husband was the cause of her daughter's death?"

"No, she did not say at any time or suggest to me in any way that my husband was the cause of her daughter's death."

"Thank you Mrs. Cumming," said Henderson, "you have been very helpful today, I think we can leave it there for now and continue again tomorrow, if that suits you." "Yes, that would be splendid," said Mrs. Cumming.

"And when do you think might Stanley come and speak to us?"

"Stanley has said everything he knows, he will not be in."

-o-

Now I desperately wanted to see Stanley's statement. What would his recollection of the conversation at the Morgue be? Why did Mrs. Cumming suggest that Mrs. Christie had fabricated evidence? Was her theory of what happened to her husband and Eileen, that their clothes were disarranged, purely to deflect attention away from her family? Why was Stanley holding out on answering questions? Did his mother know more? Had Mrs. Cumming received a visit from someone that had given her this information. Did that same person warn her off talking to police accounting for her earlier stance?

14 THE TROCADERO INCIDENT

The detectives made their way to the Trocadero Dance Hall in Melbourne Street in South Brisbane. Campbell related how he had made some inquiries into the movements of Acting-Sergeant Cumming during the week leading up to his death and learnt that Cumming had been at the Trocadero the night before he was killed. The Manager, Joseph Lionel Herbert had told Campbell he had some interesting information that may have a bearing on the case.

The Detectives were escorted to the office of Mr. Herbert. There they saw Joe Herbert, a man of dark complexion with brown hair and eyes. He looked up from his paperwork when alerted to the detectives presence and stood to shake their hands. Henderson placed him at five foot five and a half inches tall and eleven stone. Herbert directed the detectives to take a seat.

"How long have you been here Mr. Herbert?" asked Campbell.

"Coming up to four years now, I've been the Managing Director of the Trocadero Dansant."

"We hear you know Acting Sergeant Marquis

Cumming," said Henderson, "is that correct?"

"Yes that is correct?"

"Do you know this woman?" asked Campbell handing Herbert the postcard bearing Eileen's photograph.

"No, I have never seen the woman whose photo is on this postcard, alive."

"Do you know Mrs. Cumming?" asked Henderson.

"Only by sight," responded Herbert.

"How did you know the Acting-Sergeant?"

"Up until about eighteen months ago he patrolled special duty at the Trocadero on different occasions."

"You said you had some information for us Mr. Herbert, what might that be?"

"Well, I remember an occasion about eighteen months ago, Cumming and Constable Dwyer were on special duty, I was in my office at about eleven o'clock on this particular night when I heard a disturbance inside the vestibule hall, so I went upstairs, and I saw Cumming and I spoke to him."

"Why was that, that you spoke to him?"

"I was told that he was having an argument with his wife upstairs."

"Did you know his wife?"

"Not at that time. I spoke to Cumming and told him he was employed there to stop any argument or trouble and it was out of place for him to be the cause of an argument, and therefore, would he kindly take his arguments outside. If I remember rightly he said 'Alright Mr. Herbert it is only the wife and I will see that she gets out of this place'. There was no more disturbances that night."

"And why was that so remarkable?" questioned Henderson.

"Well, on the following morning Mrs. Cumming came to my office at the Trocadero and she told me who she was, saying 'I'm Mrs. Cumming, Mr. Herbert I want to speak to you, I am very sorry for what happened last night' and she went on to tell me of her trouble at home with Mr. Cumming, and I said to her 'how can I help you in that matter, I think the proper thing you can go about is to approach the authorities in charge of him and make your complaints to them'. No doubt Mrs. Cumming was greatly upset, she was crying half the time when she was telling me."

"What did she say to your suggestion?"

"She said she would go to the Commissioner of Police, and get him dismissed, and I said 'I would not do that as it is his living'."

"Did she mention what trouble she was having at home?"

"She told me of the trouble she had with him on account of his always going out with girls, and after she finished, she said 'what do you think of him?' and I said 'Well I can't help you in that' and she said 'don't you think he ought to be shot!' and I said 'I am not a judge for that, but don't you do it, the best advice I can give you is to go up to the Senior Sergeant and put your complaint because I am myself going to complain to the Senior to send me other men instead of Cumming and Dwyer, as they did not come on for duty but just to look at girls dancing."

"How do you mean?"

"Instead of going about their duty and walking about the place they used to get into corners and talk to different girls."

"What did you do?"

"I complained to the Senior Sergeant, and he ceased sending them to me."

"What else did Mrs. Cumming say?"

"She said her husband was a disgrace and did not

support her. From what she told me and what I saw of him while he was at the dance hall, I consider she had good grounds for complaining, as a wife."

"And this is what you told the Senior Sergeant?"

"I made the complaint to the Senior Sergeant on those grounds yes."

"So Cumming did not do special duty at the Trocadero after that?"

"After I had the conversation with Senior Sergeant Casey the only time he did special duty at the dance hall was on Wednesday the 22nd of December last, starting at eight and finishing at eleven."

"Thank you Mr. Herbert," said Campbell, "your information has been very insightful."

-o-

There was no denying the fact that Herbert's evidence provides the motive for Mrs. Cumming to be suspected. The conflicting accounts of what happened at the morgue and the encounter with Mrs. Christie heighten that suspicion. Yet there were other factors that bothered me about Herbert's evidence. Cumming had not been assigned to special duty at the Trocadero for eighteen months. Then the evening after his return, he is shot dead.

I researched Herbert to see if there was anything in his past that may have prompted his evidence. From newspaper articles I learnt that he was convicted of selling sly-grog only the month before. So I went deeper.

Joe Herbert had been born in Montreal in Canada and been in Australia for over ten years. He had served with the Australian Imperial Forces in the Great War but hadn't distinguished himself. He had been found guilty of wilful disobedience and then, at a Court Martial, he was charged with intent to defraud and receive a bribe, and for receiving a bribe in Cairo. His twelve month sentence of imprisonment with hard labour was suspended after six months and he was sent to re-join his unit. After fifteen months of railway construction in Egypt he spent four months in hospital after a freak accident with a boulder that fractured his right femur, tibia, and fibula.[xlvi]

Since his return Herbert had been under surveillance by the Commonwealth Investigation Branch (today known as ASIO), suspected as a Communist sympathiser and subscriber to funds.[xlvii]

The Trocadero property was resumed by the council to enable it to widen Melbourne Street. A confidential report of the resumptions committee adopted by the council on December 14, 1926 stated that a letter had been received from Messrs. Tully and Wilson, solicitors for the Trocadero Dansant, Ltd., advising their willingness to accept £15,000 in full settlement of their claim. The committee recommended that a settlement should be arrived at that figure.

This was cause for concern. Joe Herbert did not appear to be a reliable witness. I asked myself the same question I had asked of Jamieson. If he was lying, what was in it for him?

*

Detectives went through the papers found in the locked box at the Cumming's residence. From those papers it appeared that the Acting Sergeant was a prosperous man, he owned the property at Wilton Street outright, and that was valued at between seven and eight hundred pounds. There was a bank deposit book with a very healthy balance. There were also a number of chits for the sale of cattle. The papers also indicated that he may have made some money venturing into possum skin trading.

To confirm this information I searched for his will. The Acting-Sergeant died intestate. His wife applied to be Adminstratrix of his estate but was unable to raise the surety bond required. The duty fell to the Public Curator. The documents held by the State Archives reveal however that his estate was worth £1,745 including the unencumbered property at Woolloongabba as well as three separate fixed term deposits. His accounts held £78 in Mount Morgan, £210 at Rockhampton and £420 at South Brisbane. He was also due an amount of £127 from the proceeds of the sale of cattle.[xlviii]

I thought that this was enough information for me to suspend my theory that Cumming was murdered after he had made a blackmail attempt against one of his paramours or their husbands. His accounts did not support a theory that he was hard-up. Was this really a case where the obvious answer was the correct answer? I needed to know more about Cumming the man.

-o-

I ventured to the Queensland State Archives to review the Acting-Sergeant's police personnel file. At first I was disappointed to be told that Item ID 566416 Police Service File Cumming Marquis, was not available for public access until the 24th July 2046. Then I was told that portions of the file were not restricted and I would be allowed to view that portion. From the information I was given I learnt that Cumming had been sworn in during March 1900. He was a month shy of his twenty-first birthday and had been working as a farm labourer. His education was described as fair.

This record sheet revealed an unremarkable career in

the beginning, he was reprimanded in 1903 for carelessness on leaving a drunken Kanaka chained up unguarded, in consequence of which the prisoner escaped. Then in December of 1907 he was again reprimanded when on interviewing a witness he had requested him to give false evidence at an inquiry. The first positive record of his service was dated July 1913 when he received a reward payment of £2 for the zeal and intelligence shown in connection with the arrest and conviction of Joseph Emanuel for cattle stealing.

The file contained correspondence relating to the 1922 audit of the aboriginal banking accounts and agreement books held at the Mount Morgan Police Station. The auditor found irregularities in the account of an aboriginal half-caste girl named Maudie. Inspector Quinn of Rockhampton requested clarification of the Chief Protector of Aboriginals as to the minimum wage that should be paid to an aboriginal domestic. The response left little doubt.

Protector of Aboriginals
Mount Morgan
Re: Your Report 160/1923 of the 20th instant.

The minimum wages laid down in the regulations of June 6th 1919 governing Aboriginal employment provide that an aboriginal domestic of the class of this girl is stated to be must receive eight shillings per week and clothing or fourteen shillings weekly and find her own, this rate should be enforced immediately. I would be glad of a report as to why this woman had been so long on the ridiculous wage of three shillings six pence per week and who is the Protector responsible.

Re: Withdrawals

In the case in question there should be very little need for withdrawals seeing she is provided with clothes by the employer consequently it would be difficult to define the amount or period of such but care should be taken that such money would not be used to purchase clothes.

Copy of Regulations of June 6th 1910 enclosed for your guidance,

Chief Protector of Aboriginals.[xlix]

Police Sergeant P. O'Grady, Mount Morgan Protector of Aboriginals responded on the 9th April 1923 where he confirmed that the aboriginal agreement book at the Mount Morgan Police Station showed that agreements for the years 1922 and 1923 were made by Acting Sergeant Cumming, husband of the Aboriginal's then, and present, employer. He also confirmed that the agreements had been refreshed by Cumming while O'Grady was on annual leave. He also noted that withdrawals had been made when the Acting Sergeant was temporarily in charge of the office. Quinn reported that he had questioned Cumming and that he had stated that the same was drawn to purchase clothing for the Aboriginal, although he admitted that according to the Agreement her Employer was compelled to find her clothing.

I tried to reconcile the information I had. At the time of Cumming's death he had a healthy bank deposit balance and owned his own home, but four years prior, he had been found making improper withdrawals from the bank account of a twenty year old aboriginal girl in the employ of his wife.

I continued to review the personnel file and found that at the same time that the irregularities in the bank account were found he had also been charged with disobedience of orders, that between the 12th January and the 16th February 1923, in not having a patrol made weekly to Mount Usher, vide instructions to him by Inspector Quinn on the 8th January 1923.

An inquiry was held by Inspector Quinn with him as reporting officer and the witnesses including Sergeant O'Grady, Constable J.A. Condrick, and Constable Elford. The Commissioner of Police found Cumming guilty and the Acting-Sergeant was reprimanded at the beginning of June.

I felt that Cumming's presence must have created tension within the police station, given that his fellow officers had provided evidence against him. Later in June he must have had enough as he requested a transfer from Mount Morgan. I speculated that there may have been some disturbance within the home for him to behave the way he had. His son, Hamill Sylvester, passed away in July. Yet this had not been a prolonged illness, Hamill had died from acute septic endocarditis causing cardiac failure. Hamill was a month shy of his sixteenth birthday.

Inspector Quinn forwarded the transfer request to the Commissioner of Police remarking, 'Should you consider this application, I would recommend that this man, from what I know of him since I have been here, is certainly not fit to hold his present rank, be transferred to some centre such as Brisbane or Mackay where he would be under constant supervision of an Officer. He is utterly useless where he is, and a continual air of discontent is over the place which he is undoubtedly responsible for.'[1]

I pondered if Cumming really was a deficient officer or if he was persecuted by Quinn and O'Grady for another, yet to be revealed, indiscretion. Then I considered how did Cumming go from pilfering the account of his Aboriginal servant, to being comfortably well off in just over four years. I suspected he may have been 'on the take'. I grew to dislike him. Why was Eileen with this man?

The file also indicated that Cumming had applied for

ten days sick leave required to recuperate from an operation. This request was certified to be correct by the Government Medical Officer, Dr Joseph Espie Dods.

*

Mrs. Cumming presented at C.I. Branch the following day to continue giving her statement to the detectives. Sub Inspector Meldon had passed onto them the letters he had been sent from Mt. Morgan with strict instructions not to show them to anyone. I suspect Henderson would have got straight to the point.

"Mrs. Cumming, we are in possession of certain letters written by your husband that indicate his home life was not a happy one, would that surprise you?"

"Yes, it would surprise me."

"Would you say you quarrelled often?"

"No."

"Mrs. Cumming, do you know Mr. Herbert the Manager of the Trocadero?"

"I may have spoken to him once, yes."

"Well, we have spoken to him recently," said Henderson, "and he informs us of a quarrel between your husband and yourself at the Dance Hall, would that be correct?"

"If he means the New Year's Eve of 1925, that is the 31st December 1924, then yes."

"What was the quarrel about?"

"Earlier that day my husband said he was going to the Trocadero and I said 'what about taking me there after you have finished work, we can spend an hour or two there'.

He did not agree to that, as he said he was going to spend the evening with a party of friends."

"What shift was he working?"

"That evening?"

Henderson nodded before Mrs. Cumming continued.

"He was on the second relief due to finish at ten o'clock. So I went to the Cremorne Theatre which came out at about ten thirty, and then I went to the Trocadero. I went upstairs and watched the dancing."

"Did your husband know you were going to be there?"

"I told him I intended going there, yes, I told him some time that evening."

"Please continue Mrs. Cumming."

"While at the Trocadero I saw my husband crossing the floor and go and join a party of ladies at an alcove, and men there too. I saw my husband have a drink there, and I got up and walked towards the alcove and met him coming out and I said to him, 'Well I have got you there'. He was then cross and he said to me 'You have no right here, you ought to go home!' He was annoyed. I said to him 'I have as much right to be here as you have. I said to him 'You have no right to be here in uniform, if you want to be here you ought to have taken that off.' Then Mr. Herbert, the Manager of the Trocadero was at the door. My husband got cross as I would not go out, and I said to Mr. Herbert, my husband had been sneaking about this place for some time, and of course he never mentioned that I should go there at all, he was against me going there, and I have come on my own account. Then my husband said to me 'If you don't go out and go home I will have you put out!' Stanley was at the Trocadero but he didn't know I was there. After those words with my husband I went upstairs and stayed for a while there, and Stanley came up to me, and I told Stanley what had happened, and Stanley and I then went home."

"Where was your husband?"

"My husband was not at home when we got home, but

he did come home later, but I don't know what time he came home. I did not hear him come home."

"You didn't hear him come to bed?"

"My husband and I always occupied separate quarters."

"Did you speak to Mr. Herbert again?"

"The next day I went to see Mr. Herbert, of the Trocadero, and I apologised to him for what had happened the previous night. I then saw Senior Sergeant Casey who was in charge of the South Brisbane Police Station."

"Did you tell Mr. Herbert that your husband was a disgrace to you?"

"No I did not!"

"What if I told you that Mr. Herbert said you did?"

"If Mr. Herbert said I said that to him that would not be correct."

"Did you tell Mr. Herbert that your husband did not support you?"

"No!"

"Did you say to Mr. Herbert, and I quote," Henderson referred to his memorandum pad, "the way he is carrying on he should be shot."

"What? No. No I did not say that!"

"Did you say to Mr. Herbert that you had complained to Senior Sergeant Casey?"

"I may have said that, but I do not recollect if I said that or not."

"What did you say to Senior Sergeant Casey?"

"I said that I had a good mind to see the Commissioner of Police to get my husband transferred from South Brisbane, as I did not like it."

"Why did you say that?"

"The reason I said that was because I desired myself to get away from South Brisbane, and also because my husband was going out a good deal at night time, and day time, but he did extra duty."

"Might he have been in civilian clothes to undertake extra duty?"

Mrs. Cumming was thoughtful for a moment before responding.

"When he was dressed in his civilian clothes he did not tell me that he was going on duty, but I did not approve of his going out so much alone."

"Do you remember any other incidents when he went out alone?"

"I remember one incident, when my husband had dressed, that he was going out, and I suspected that he was going out but he did not tell me where, and I sent my son Reg, who would have been nine years of age then, and I sent him to where my husband went to, and Reggie came back and he said that his father said to him 'Did your mother send you to follow me?' and Reggie said to his father, 'Yes' and that his father had said to him 'Go home at once or I will kick your behind!' From then on my husband went out at night when off duty, on his own, frequently, and he did not tell me where he was going."

"Any other occasions?"

"About three months ago my husband put on his uniform at seven p.m. but he was not due on duty until ten and I asked him why he could not wait and have some music with the children and he told me that he had a lot of writing to do before going on duty, and that he was going straight to the Police Station. More than an hour after that I became suspicious and I rang the Police Station and I inquired if my husband was there, and they said he was not, but that he would be due there at about nine fifty. I then got a tram and went down to the South Brisbane Police Station, getting there about nine thirty and I remained there for about ten minutes and I saw him coming down from

Vulture Street down Grey Street. At this time I was standing on the front steps of the Police Station. I said to my husband 'This is a pleasant surprise to me' and he then passed on and walked into the Police Station. I went into the Police Station after him and I said to him 'I just came down to see if you were telling me the truth, and I am not satisfied that what you told me is all lies. He told me to go home."

"Did you mention this to anyone?"

"I complained to Sergeant Casey about my husband misleading me as to when he had to go to work. I was very annoyed about that."

"Were you annoyed at the Trocadero?"

"I felt a little peeved seeing my husband there enjoying himself and me not being there."

"So you were unhappy?"

"Any unhappiness would fade out and we would continue to live out a happy life again."

"Were you agitated when you went to see Mr. Herbert?"

"No, I was not agitated when I saw him the next morning, I was quite calm."

"Do you know why your husband was at the Trocadero the night before the tragedy?"

"Was he? I had no idea, but it doesn't surprise me."

"Do you frequently follow your husband at night, Mrs. Cumming?" asked Henderson.

"No, I followed him once at night, that being the night he went to a place at Annerley Road on a Sunday night, I told you about that didn't I?"

"About your husband sitting on a bed with a man and a woman?"

"Yes that was it, that was the only time."

"What about when you found him with Mrs. Page?"

"I did not follow him, I was going out on other business, and I went to the pictures after I had finished."

"Are there any other occasions when you followed your husband?"

"No, none."

"Could you have forgotten about other occasions?"

"No, there were no other occasions that I may have forgotten."

"Have you ever caused your husband to be watched by anyone?"

"No."

"Did you hire an inquiry agent?"

"No, I did not!"

"Tell me about Stanley," said Henderson, "this letter suggests that Stanley was to leave the family home, was that correct?"

No doubt Mrs. Cumming had shifted uncomfortably in her chair.

"Well?" said Henderson.

"My husband may have said something like that."

"When was this?"

"The morning after Stanley came across my husband and that Page woman in the street at South Brisbane."

"The next morning you spoke to your husband?" queried Henderson.

"Yes," replied Mrs. Cumming, "the morning after I said to my husband 'How are things?' and he said 'Not too bad' and I said 'You had a bit of excitement on your own side, Stanley saw you again with this woman, why did you chase him across the street?' and he replied, 'He had no right to follow me!' and then I said, 'He was not following you, he only came upon you by chance'. Then my husband said 'I am going to make new rules around here, Stanley will have to get out by the First of January!'"

"How was your husband when he said that?"

"He was annoyed at that time. I said 'Stanley will not go he has done nothing wrong, it's you that has done wrong, and you ought to be ashamed of yourself to mention such a thing'."

"Was Stanley aware of his father's wish?"

"I don't know, but that was the last incident in which there was a difference between us."

"Do you know what firearms were in the house on the night of the tragedy?"

"No."

"Did you know your son had an automatic pistol?"

"Yes, I know that, but I don't know where it was on that night."

"You know the detectives collected firearms from your home."

"Yes, the next day, they took possession of a revolver belonging to my husband."

"Did you know Stanley had an automatic pistol in the house?"

"Yes, he has had it for some time."

"Are you aware that he also had cartridges for that pistol."

"No, I didn't know that."

"You warned your husband about other woman, didn't you?"

"Yes, I have at times warned my husband of the dangers he was running by carrying on with other woman in the position he held, and he has said to me that it would take a smart man to catch him."

-o-

I wondered if the detectives considered Stanley as a

smart man.

*

"How did your husband receive his mail?"

"He used to get private mail addressed to him at the Police Station, and some used to come to the house."

"Did Stanley have his automatic pistol on his person on the night of the tragedy?"

"As far as I know he did not carry the firearm with him that night or any night."

"Do you know the whereabouts of your husband's belt, handcuffs, and keys?"

"The detectives and myself have searched our home and there is no trace of those items."

"What can you tell us about their disappearance?"

"I cannot explain anything about their disappearance, as far as I know he should have had them on him."

"A word of advice," said Henderson, "if I were you I'd be telling Stanley to come and speak to us."

"That is up to my son."

15 THE MOUNT MORGAN INCIDENT

Days became weeks as detectives traced through the list of names they had acquired that were known associates of Acting Sergeant Cumming. Many of the women were contacted and discrete inquiries made as to their husband's whereabouts on the night of the tragedy. Each one in turn another dead end. They were also side-tracked at times such as when their investigations led them to a particular woman who they established was a bigamist, a woman that had caused friction in the Cumming household that was a wife three times over. Still the pistol, the murder weapon, eluded them. As did the belt, handcuffs, and keys.

*

On the morning of the 19th January I imaged Meldon was in his office reading the newspaper when he bellowed for Henderson and Campbell to get into his office.

"What have you pair been fucking about with for the last three weeks?" Meldon demanded to know.

"What do you mean Sub-Inspector?" Henderson would have queried.

"If there is any truth in this fucking newspaper report,

then I should be hiring their reporters to get to the bottom of this case, instead of you pair of bloody galahs!" Meldon may have snorted before throwing the newspaper at Campbell.

"Don't just fucking stand there," said Meldon, "get down to that paper and get the name of their source, and I don't care if you have to tear the place apart to get it, do your fucking job for a change!"

Campbell was immersed in the newspaper article as the detectives made their way back to their office. He began to sit down when Henderson took up his coat in the crook of his arm placing his hat on his head before taking Campbell by the elbow.

"You can read it on the way," he said.

*

The reporters at 'Smith's Weekly' didn't need much convincing to hand over the name of Jessie Cumming to the detectives, the possible threat of prosecution for perverting the course of justice may have been enough incentive. They had the scoop. There was little more to be gained by holding on to the information.

Jessie Black was nineteen when she married Sydney Cumming, cousin of the Acting Sergeant, in 1903. Three months later she gave birth to her first daughter. Her second child was born the following year. Sydney Cumming would describe his wife as 'unsettled for some years', after he had arrived home from work in 1925 to find she had left him without a word. Jessie had previously left him for a period of four years, but he had induced her to return.[li]

The detectives worked quickly to secure her statement and hauled the Acting Sergeant's wife back to C.I. Branch for questioning.

*

Mrs. Cumming took her seat behind the desk clutching tightly at the straps of her handbag resting in her lap. Her hat was pulled down low on the back of her neck and forehead, resting on the top of her spectacles.

"Thank you for coming in to speak with us again," started Henderson, "we would like you to clear up something for us."

Mrs. Cumming nodded in acknowledgement.

"We have spoken to Jessie Cumming and she has told us of the incident that occurred, in Mt. Morgan, on the night you 'accidently' caused a heavy canvas to fall on your husband's head. Would you like to tell us what occurred after your husband's return."

"My husband returned that night, no later than about eight or nine o'clock, I was still upset over the earlier incident, and I turned to Jessie and said, 'I will give him a devil of a fright', and knowing that his revolver was in a chest of drawers in our room, I got it, that being before he came home, and we were standing on the verandah when he returned."

"And what did you do?" asked Henderson, "and remember Mrs. Cumming, Jessie Cumming has made a sworn statement about the incident."

"He came to the front gate, my husband, but I can't recollect of any words that passed then, and...."

"Yes Mrs. Cumming," urged Henderson.

"And I fired into the garden bed in that position on the verandah, but I did not fire at my husband, but at his side, into the garden bed, after doing that I got the revolver and threw it across me."

"What did your husband do?"

"He came in, and he walked across and picked up the revolver, and then after that he came onto the steps on the verandah."

"Where was he when you fired the shot?"

"He was standing at the front gate, out on the footpath, outside the gate."

"What did you do with the revolver, after you fired the shot?"

"I threw it across me, from the left to the right of me."

"What did your husband do?"

"He came up the steps, with the revolver in his hand, and he said to me, 'I could have you up for using firearms in the public street'."

"So you were still agitated from the earlier incident," said Campbell.

"I was not agitated."

"You were upset."

"I was not upset!"

"You tried to shoot your husband."

"I fired the shot but I did not intend to shoot him."

"What did your husband say, about you trying to shoot him?"

"He did not say anything about the incident as he knew that it was not done to shoot him."

"Did Jessie Cumming try to stop you?"

"No, she did not make any attempt to take the revolver from me prior to my firing the shot. She was enjoying the joke as well as I was."

"Did Jessie Cumming ever touch the revolver?" asked Henderson.

"No, she had nothing to do with the revolver."

"What happened to the revolver after you fired it?"

"My husband brought the revolver inside again."

"Did you load the revolver?" asked Campbell.

"It was always loaded, and it was then."

"Had you loaded the revolver before then?"

"No, I did not load the revolver before then."

"What did your husband say about the incident after that night?" asked Henderson.

"That ended it that night."

"Did you say to Mrs. Jessie Cumming," said Campbell aggressively, "that you 'will not let him come in the gate alive'."

"NO, I never said that."

"Had you fired a shot before that?" continued Campbell.

"No."

"Or since?"

"No, I never took the revolver before or since to fire a shot."

"Did you speak to your husband later about the incident?" asked Henderson.

"I apologised the next day, that I fired the shot, for doing it."

"How did you know your husband had been out to see another woman?"

"At that time I had a black girl named Maudie in my employ. When my husband left I asked Maudie to see which way he went and what she told me suggested to me that that was where he was headed."

"Was Maudie there on that night?"

"I could not say where she was on the night of the incident."

"Was your son at home?"

"I can't remember if Stanley was there or not."

"Did your husband threaten you with a firearm after that incident?"

"My husband never threatened me with any firearms."
"Did you have other quarrels about women while in Mt. Morgan?" asked Campbell.
"No, there were no other quarrels."
"You had a row though about trying to shoot your husband!"
"I did not try to shoot my husband! There were no rows about it in our home!"

-O-

It appeared as though the police were of the strong opinion that it was either the wife or the son, or both in cahoots that killed the pair. Some conjectured that the shooting showed unwanted accuracy and skill, the handiwork of some practiced shot. Others discounted this being of the view that the shots were fired at close range, in the darkness, with each shot doing its work instantaneously.

The detectives considered the fatal wounds. The bullet that slew Cumming entered by the shoulder blade, traversed the neck muscle, severed the spinal cord, passed through the brain, and lodged in the crown of the skull. Mrs. Walsh was shot below the right eye, the ball passing out at the base of the skull after traversing the brain. They surmised that whoever did the deed must have crept on hands and knees with snake-like stealth until right alongside the unsuspecting pair. That death came upon both with awful suddenness is shown by the fact that not a sign of kicking movement was found beneath Mrs. Walsh's shoes, while all that gave any indication of movement by Cumming was a slight dustiness on his left boot. It was obvious that Mrs. Cumming was not a woman with snake-like stealth.

Stanley however, owned a revolver and was reportedly an accomplished shot. His whereabouts on the night were collaborated, but, both he and Miss Clutterbuck seemed to remember very little of the entertainment that evening. Detectives considered if they could have snuck out at some stage.

With Stanley taking the stance not to answer the questions of the police, they had to pursue other lines of inquiry. They undertook the task of discretely contacting all those implicated through the letters found in the Acting-Sergeant's locker.

As Meldon had told the papers, 'From the highest to the lowest the police ranks firmly and insistently affirm that there is no 'dead end' factor in our investigations, far from that he most sanguinely asserts, that time, our most faithful ally, will tell'.

-o-

A week later and Mr. Kirwan, the Minister for Works, announced that he would retire from the supervision of the Golden Casket drawings. In the five years that Mr. Kirwan had supervised the Golden Casket from when the Government had assumed control, the Casket had moved from taking six months to fill to now closing in ten days. The total receipts during that period had amounted to over £4m of which more than £2.1m had been paid out in prizes with just under £1.2m being paid to the Home Department fund for hospitals, motherhood and child welfare, including maternity homes and baby clinics. Mr. Kirwan also announced that he would be succeeded as supervisor of the drawings by Mr. Mackay, chief clerk in the Home Department, who would be assisted by Mr. Bradbury, accountant of the department.[lii]

Michael Joseph (Mick) Kirwan entered a bootmaking

apprenticeship before transferring to the Railway Department as a porter based in Brisbane. Mick was an active member of the Australian Railways Union who was sacked from his position after the general strike of 1912 who then attempted the seemingly hopeless task of wrestling the seat of Brisbane from the long-term sitting member. That year however there had been a sense of disquiet with the Government and Kirwan won the seat by a slender majority.

*

Mary Christie had made a report to South Brisbane Station that someone was acting suspiciously around the family home in Stephens Road. Campbell and a couple of uniformed constables went to speak to her.

Mary Christie described how someone was prowling about her place, she had seen him on three occasions.

"The first night I came onto the verandah and he was standing directly opposite my door, in Stephens Road, in the middle of the road, that is opposite my front door of my house, and I went down to the front gate, and when he saw me coming he went towards Annerley Road, and there was a motor car coming up the street and he then turned his back so that the light would not show his face."

"How did he walk?" asked Campbell.

"He walked pretty smart."

"And the next occasion?"

"The next time I saw him he was in white, and he had a biggish sort of hat on, pulled down over his eyes, and I went down and locked the gate, and he walked past the gate, and he went towards Glen Street, a side Street off Stephens Road. That was the last time I saw him."

"How tall was this man?"

"The prowler was of medium height."

"Do you know who he was?"

"I have no idea who he was, and I do not know what the man's purpose was."

"Right," said Campbell closing his memorandum pad, "I shouldn't be too worried if I was you Mrs. Christie, we have had reports of fowls being stolen in this locality."

"What, round here?" asked Mary.

"Yes," replied Campbell.

"But it's only St. Lawrence School across the road, why would anyone be looking for fowls around here?"

"Please don't worry yourself," pleaded Campbell, "I am certain your prowler is just our fowl thief, but please let me know immediately if you see this man again."

-o-

I then read about the stroke of luck for a young chap from Mount Morgan. When the Mount Cornish holdings expired and were thrown up for ballot, Mr. Albert Edward Delary Smith was successful in drawing a thirty thousand acre block, after which he won the Golden Casket.

On the 27th December 1926 the newspaper heralded an Engagement Notice, Smith – Stopford. 'The engagement is announced of Mr. A.E.D. Smith, Mount Morgan, second son of Mr. and Mrs. Smith, Maryland, W.A. to Miss Mary Stopford, only daughter of the Hon. James and Mrs. Stopford, Rose Street, Annerley.'[liii]

The Member for Mount Morgan, Mr. James Stopford as Home Secretary, was the minister responsible for the administration of the Golden Casket.'[liv]

What if Cumming had stumbled across something in connection with the Golden Casket and he had to be kept quiet. Then another coincidence.

James Stopford's younger brother, Joseph Henry Stopford, had been employed at the Golden Casket Office since 1924 often officiating at the Golden Casket drawings. Prior to joining the Golden Casket Office he had been employed as a moulder at the Mount Morgan mine.[lv]

In my mind this was enough to develop a conspiracy theory centred on the Golden Casket. I started to believe that winning Golden Casket tickets were used as a means of distributing payments for illegal activity and money laundering. It was common practice for purchasers to use nom de plumes to buy tickets, ensuring their anonymity.

Was Cumming's inclusion of a Casket Ticket with his letter to F.A.D. really just a gesture of good faith, or, did he want to establish the quality of a counterfeit ticket?

But how did Eileen fit in? I could only conclude that she was just collateral damage, or a case of mistaken identity.

16 REWARD FOR INFORMATION

Weeks were now becoming months and Henderson and Campbell had all but extinguished their lines of inquiry. The strongest motives they had, still rested with Mrs. Cumming and her son Stanley. Mrs. Cumming had voluntarily come forward to complete her statement, yet Stanley had not. They had hoped that they had placed enough pressure on Mrs. Cumming for her to convince Stanley to also come forward, but this had still not eventuated by the Easter weekend. The newspapers had begun to reflect public sentiment that asked why a felon had not been brought to justice. In fact it was suggested that a very large and responsible section of the community, held the opinion that those in authority did not want the murderers brought to justice. They argued that while this view may not be justified it was certainly present in the minds of the public and it should be expected that the Government, aware of this, should take steps to silence the cynics. This prompted the Home Secretary, Mr. J. Stopford, to respond when questioned on the subject of a reward, to comment, 'Cabinet has not considered the question of offering a reward for information that will lead to the apprehension of the person or persons who murdered Acting Sergeant Cumming and Mrs. Walsh at South Brisbane in December last'. He also indicated that it was unlikely that the Government would offer a reward.

The Government was considered implicit in this failure to secure a culprit. In view of the lack of information it was considered unsurprising that the police had failed, yet the Government, instead of coming forward with the offer of a reward for information, had calmly announced that it hadn't considered the matter and that it didn't think it would offer a reward anyhow.

Why? The public began to question. Was it so sure of the identity of the culprit that it considered it futile to offer a reward, or was it that public opinion was right, that the authorities preferred to cloak as far as possible the extensive amours of the policeman that flaunted his uniform. Was the Government protecting the force against any loss of prestige as a result of revelations that might result from a criminal trial. The newspapers argued that public safety and public peace of mind demanded that some effort should be made to clear up the mystery surrounding the double murder. Further it argued that the fact that a jury might not feel justified in recording an adverse verdict against the culprit was beside the point.

The newspapers reported that if the Government didn't feel inclined to offer a reward, that it might consider the advisability of holding a public inquiry concerning the happening, rather than the poor satisfaction of learning that the murderer had died of old age.[lvi]

Meldon would have been agitated on reading these comments in the 'Truth' newspaper. Had he been given instructs not to provide any particulars of the case to the press in any circumstance? The stance that had been taken was seen by the public as there not being any serious effort made to bring the murderer to justice. Did Meldon have considered it a grave suspicion while recognising it existed nevertheless?

It hadn't escaped the reporters that the remarkable feature of the crime was that Cumming's belt, handcuffs, and keys were missing, and no effort as yet on the part of investigators had led to the discovery of the articles. The keys, the press concluded without any doubt, were taken to gain access to the destruction of some of the policeman's private property. But what that property was or who would be most anxious to destroy it after the murder were questions that they felt had not been satisfactorily answered, as far as the public was concerned.

Meldon must have been feeling the pressure, through the press, to bring forward a culprit, but he had not been able to secure vital physical evidence, the murder weapon, or the policeman's effects, or Mrs. Walsh's wedding ring. Without those he had been told that a conviction would not be able to be secured. Something had to break, and soon.

*

Mrs. Cumming read the same newspaper article and spoke to Stanley again. Stanley agree to consult his mother's solicitor, Mr. W.T. King, for a second opinion as to his best course of action. Mr. King's advice to Stanley was that he 'always tell everything'. With that, Stanley accompanied his solicitor to C.I. Branch.

*

Stanley and his solicitor, Mr. King, were escorted to an interview room before being joined by Detectives

Campbell and Henderson. The Detectives had been taken aback to hear that Stanley Cumming had decided to present himself to make a statement.

"Why have you come here today Stanley?" asked Henderson.

"I have decided to answer any question put to me on the advice of my solicitor," said Stanley indicating that Mr. King was his newly appointed legal representative.

"Your mother told us of an incident when she discovered a letter that indicated that Acting Sergeant Cumming had a child to another woman, could you tell us about that please," said Henderson.

Stanley looked at Mr. King and waited for his nod before proceeding.

"I remember, several years ago, my mother telling me about a letter that she found belonging to my father, in a woman's handwriting and with certain initials thereon."

"When was this?" quizzed Campbell.

"This being somewhere about the latter end of 1924."

"Go on please Stanley," said Henderson.

"I decided to trace out whose initials were on the letter. After looking through the electoral roll I came upon a name that I thought might be the one whose initials I had seen. I then traced out who that person was, and I subsequently interviewed that person, who was a woman, and I obtained from her a written statement admitting that he was the father of her illegitimate child. That statement I subsequently gave to my mother and I understand she destroyed it or had it destroyed."

"Did your father know of this statement?"

"It was mentioned to my father, about the particulars I got in that statement, and I got the admission from that particular woman that she did write that particular letter to my father."

"Did you discuss it at all with your father, Acting Sergeant Cumming?"

"On one occasion at home I discussed the matter with my father, mentioning to him that accusation that was made against him was a fact, that being that he was the father of another woman's child."

"Did you tell your father you had obtained a statement?" asked Campbell.

"No, I did not tell my father that I had got a statement but I told him that I had found out."

"What did he say?"

"He said that any man might make a mistake once, and that he hoped that I would overlook it."

"Did you?"

Stanley looked towards Mr. King seeking reassurance before answering.

"I told him that I decided to."

"When did this happen?" asked Campbell.

"While we were living at Gladstone Road, South Brisbane."

"Tell me Stanley," said Henderson, "do you remember how you told your father, what you said, about overlooking it?"

"I told him that I would overlook it and that I hoped that he would mend his ways."

"Anything else?" asked Campbell.

"Nothing further was said."

"When was this?"

"It would have been in the earlier part of June 1925, that I came back from Mt. Morgan with the statement, so it would have been sometime in 1925 after June, but I cannot say what month or date."

"Did this cause trouble between you and your father?" asked Campbell.

"After he gave me that assurance everything was alright for a while."

"For a while?" quizzed Henderson.

"I had a second discussion with my father about the latter part of 1925, when my father came home one night and he had taken liquor, but he knew what he was doing."

"So he was drunk then," stated Campbell.

"I would not say he was drunk."

"What did he say Stanley?" asked Henderson.

"He said, 'If I like I could shoot the both of you' and he put his hand to his hip pocket, I ran out of the room and my mother also left the room."

"Why did you run away?" asked Campbell.

"He had just come off duty at the time and I thought he might have his revolver with him."

-o-

This was the second time I had learnt that Stanley had ran away from his father. I wondered if he was frightened of him?

*

"What did you do Stanley?" he asked instead.

"As far as I remember I then went to the Roma Street Police Station intending to tell them all about him, but by the time I got there I changed my mind about what I was going to do."

"So you didn't go in and tell them?" asked Campbell.

"Yes, No," said Stanley, "I went into the station and they wanted to know what I wanted, and I said to someone there, but I do not know of what rank, that my father threatened to use firearms. I think I told them that he was a policeman, but I am not certain if I told them who my father was."

"What did the policeman you spoke to say?"

"He said, 'Oh, he is only bluffing, you had better go along home' and as far as I remember that ended that episode."

"Why did your father threaten you?" asked Henderson.

"Through the information that I gained at Mt. Morgan, that was the cause of his making that threat."

"We have learned that you left home after that Stanley, is that correct?"

"I left home and went to live at Stephens Road in South Brisbane."

-o-

Another coincidence. Stanley moved into the same Street that Eileen and her family lived.

*

"Because of the trouble at home," stated Campbell.

"I left home for no reason of any domestic trouble but because I desired a change, a change of surroundings."

"How was it different Stanley?" asked Henderson.

"The place I went, the surroundings were different to my own home."

"How was that Stanley?"

"They were older people there, the place I intended going was a boarding house where there were older people, and I preferred to be amongst them instead of being at my home. I became accustomed to strangers and I got more pleasure out of their company than I got at home."

"How long were you there Stanley," asked Henderson.

"I only remained about a month away."

"Were you seeing Miss Clutterbuck then?" asked Campbell.

"I had no girlfriend in particular at that time."

"Why did you return?"

"My mother said that she thought that I should be at home, and then I decided to go back, which I did, and where I remained."

"Doesn't sound particularly convincing to me," said Campbell.

"They are the true facts," said Stanley.

"Didn't your father tell you he intended for you to leave the home?"

"My father has not told me directly to get out of my home, but he told my mother that I would have to get out, that being previous to Christmas 1926."

"When did your mother tell you this?"

"As far as I remember about a month prior to the 23rd December 1926."

"What reason did your mother tell you that your father gave for wanting you out?" asked Campbell.

"I don't recollect whether my mother told me the reason why my father said I would have to get out of the home."

"Do you know why your mother was upset with your father?"

Stanley again looked for a nod of reassurance from Mr. King before speaking.

"My father used to go out a good deal and not take my mother out and not tell where he was going. His conduct seemed to annoy my mother a good bit, and she accused him of paying attention to other woman, and he denied that."

"When last we spoke Stanley," said Henderson, "you mentioned a Mrs. Page, do you remember what you told us?"

"Yes."

"Do you remember pointing out to Detective Campbell where you last saw that woman?"

"Yes."

"I found that woman," said Campbell flicking through his memorandum pad, "and she told me you accosted her at Annerley Road and she states you said to her, 'I thought you said you lived at Dutton Park', and she replied 'This is a very mean thing for you to do, your mother told me you had got all you wanted from me, and yet you are dogging me up'."

"I don't recollect that being said."

"Do you remember saying to her 'What are you coming this way for if you live at Dutton Park'."

"I don't deny that I said that."

"Did she reply, 'I came this way to get something for supper, it's just as close to where I live coming this way as it is coming Dutton Park way'."

"I deny she said that."

"Did you say to this woman, 'I don't know if what you told me is right, I am going to go with you, and get you to show me the house'."

"I did not say that!"

"Didn't she ask you to leave her!"

"She requested me to leave her several times, she said the neighbours might see me coming home with her."

"Did you put it to her to show you the house where she lived!"

"No, I decided not to speak, but look, which is what I did."

"So you didn't say to the woman 'I am going to get you to show me the house'."

"No."

"Do you recall crossing the overbridge, going over the Railway line?"

"Yes."

"Didn't she tell you it was the third house from the corner?"

"No, I believe that just before we got to the overbridge she said 'don't come any further it is not very far now'."

"Are you aware that you can see the Gaol when on top of the bridge?"

"Well, one might be in view of the Gaol when on top of the bridge."

"Didn't you say to this woman at that location 'My father is no bloody good he has been causing a lot of trouble at home, a man ought to bloody well do time for him'. Well did you?"

"No, I did not say that."

Campbell slapped his memorandum pad onto the desk.

"Alright Campbell," said Henderson, "Stanley, do you remember telling us how you met this woman on another occasion?"

"Yes."

"Could you tell us please about that occasion, your father had asked if you were following him, and he rushed at you, and you went home and told your mother about it."

"The next morning my mother spoke to my father about it, I think I was in my room and they were in the kitchen, and I heard my mother say, 'What did you chase Stanley for last night?' and my father said, 'He shouldn't follow me' and my mother said, 'He did not follow you'."

"What did you do after you heard that Stanley?"

"I came into the kitchen where my father was having his breakfast, and had mine also."

"What did your father say to you?"

"He did not say anything to me."

"Didn't he say," said Campbell, "I am going to make new rules here, and Stanley will have to get out on the 1st of January!"

"I did not hear my father say that."

"But you knew that was what he wanted!"

"Yes, my mother told me afterwards."

"This caused tension between you and your father didn't it!" stated Campbell.

"Nothing further happened from that date onwards to my knowledge."

"Your father told you to get out of the house!"

"My father did not tell me directly that I would have to get out of the house, my mother told me afterwards."

"Stanley," said Henderson calmly, "would you have a look at something for me?"

Henderson waited for a nodded response from Stanley before sliding the letter of the 12th December 1926 in front of him.

"Do you recognize the handwriting Stanley?"

"I recognise the handwriting as that of my father."

"Could you read this section for me please Stanley, starting at the line 'Just look at my life' down to 'I will make a big change next Sunday'."

Stanley left the letter on the desk and ran his finger along the lines as he read the words. Mr. King lent in so that he could also read the letter.

"What do you say Stanley?" asked Henderson.

"I take it from this that he is alluding to me, that I will have to get out, and refers to me, but that is lies, from start to finish. As a matter of fact I have always paid my way since I started work, as well as I could, and since I started work I paid my wages to my mother, and when I got sufficient money I clothed myself, and paid my way as well."

"What do you think your father meant when he wrote that?"

"It would appear that he intended that I should leave home in the near future."

"Why did you move to Stephens Street?" asked Campbell.

"As I said, I left home because I wanted a change of surroundings."

"House not up to scratch?" queried Campbell.

"I was well fed at home, and had a clean home to go to, but besides that I preferred company."

"Didn't you leave home on account of domestic troubles!"

"I deny that. I used to visit my home about once a week, I was away for only about a month, the boarding house suited me for a month or thereabouts, I was quite satisfied with it, and content."

"Why did you go back then?"

"My mother thought I should be at home, she enticed me to come home."

"So your mother tells you what to do then," said Campbell.

"No, she could not induce me to remain in the first instance!"

"So you spoke about it then."

"There was no discussion about it."

Henderson picked up the letter from the table.

"Could I read this to you Stanley for your thoughts, 'He had a good trial outside, and found that it was not a success, so he wants to loaf off me, but I will see he won't'."

Stanley took out a handkerchief and wiped his brow.

"It appears as though my father is referring to me, and the time I left home and went to the boarding house."

"So your father's actions drove you out of the house," said Campbell.

"No, they did not, I would not have gone back if that was the reason, nor would I have gone near the place!"

"Thank you Stanley," said Henderson.

"When did you last fire your pistol before we took possession of it?" asked Campbell.

"Previous to that date I fired one shot, at Scarborough."

"What did you fire at?"

"Nothing in particular, I just fired out into the sea."

"What did you do with the pistol afterwards?"

"I cleaned it and put it back in my box."

"And it remained there?"

"I took it out of my box about a week before the 23rd December 1926."

-o-

Inexplicably at this crucial stage in the investigations, Henderson was granted 20 days leave.

*

James Walsh also had cause to seek a solicitor as he wished to apply to the courts for a variation of an order in respect of his two children. He had been ordered to pay 8/ a week each for their support and the amount was paid to the Clerk of Petty Sessions. However, when the order was made Eileen had been alive, and she and her two boys were living with her mother. She had died without leaving a will and the Court of Petty Sessions did not know what to do with the £4 that James Walsh had paid to date. Walsh did not want to have the order over his head and wanted instead to pay the funds directly to his mother-in-law.

Walsh had written to Mary Christie stating that he wanted his children and if she refused he was willing to apply for a writ of 'habeas corpus'[11]. A compromise had been reached however and Walsh had agreed to allow his children to live with her for a year. The children were greatly attached to Eileen's sister and Walsh did not think that a separation at that time would do any good. Walsh's solicitor, Mr. W.J. Kennedy, stated in the Summons Court that the position requested was to have the order varied so that it could be wiped out.[lvii]

*

The reporters of the 'Truth' newspaper continued their outrage at the persistent delay of a public inquiry. They insisted that an inquiry must be held if no other reason than to prevent the establishment of a very dangerous precedent. It considered that if any evidence is adduced almost half a year after the event would throw fresh light on the mystery it would be a surprise. The paper contended that there could be a no more damaging illustration of Queensland's lackadaisical criminal system than the fact that such a period had been casually allowed to elapse without a public inquiry not having been instituted.

Henderson presumable read the article knowing Meldon would again be agitated by the report charging the authorities with implicitly ignoring the case.

'Was it, or is it the authorities intention to let the whole matter be quietly forgotten in the dust of some official

---

[11] The means by which a person can report an unlawful detention or imprisonment to a court to bring the prisoner to court, to determine if the detention is lawful.

pigeon-hole? The facts suggest that this is a course which would suit some people – but not the public.'[lviii]

The 'Truth' reporters approached the Minister concerned, the Home Secretary Mr. Stopford, to ask what steps if any had been taken to hold a public inquiry to which Stoppy had replied he didn't know that any had been taken or were proposed to be taken. The newspaper charged that he was in fact, doubtlessly burdened with many Ministerial duties, so that he seemed hardly to appreciate the point that an inquiry was necessary. He did intimate to the reporter that if a request were made to him for an inquiry into the Cumming-Walsh murders he would see that one was held.

The reporter published that he was astounded and that it was extraordinary that the Department of its own accord should not have considered a public probing of the crime strictly necessary long before this, but such was the position.

The reporter pressed his concerns and at his request the Minister undertook to obtain from the Commissioner of Police any reasons there might be for a delay in the institution of a magisterial inquiry in open court.

By the time the reporter approached Meldon the Sub-Inspector had made up his mind to inform them that application had already been made to the Clerk of Petty Sessions to arrange a date when a magistrate would be available to begin hearing the evidence the police had collected and deign to put before the public.

Meldon had told the reporter that he could not forecast a date. "That," he said, "would be fixed by the Clerk of Petty Sessions, who, I understand, has the matter in hand."

Meldon had made the reporter aware that the detectives entrusted with the job of investigating the mystery have, without exception, done their work well.

However, Meldon had not considered that the reporter would seek to verify his statement. Henderson thought how that was high praise but saw it more as publicity than a true reflection of the Sub-Inspector's opinion.

The newspaper article also reported that on definite authority it could state that the Department of the Clerk of Petty Sessions had NOT received any request to arrange a date for any inquiry into the murders. The newspaper report went further.

'The hesitation of the authorities to hold an inquiry, their apparent anxiety to let as much time elapse between the murders and the inquest, the fact that the 'Truth' was informed in one quarter that a public investigation was to be held and in another that nothing whatever was known of such an intention – these are points which must strengthen the public's opinion that the whole business is fishy, and very fishy indeed!'[lix]

Henderson was probably glad he did not have to report to C.I. Branch the next morning. Meldon would no doubt have been livid with the newspaper article as it carried the Sub-Inspector's photograph in the middle of the paragraph.

*

A week later at the Brisbane City Council meeting held on May 31, 1927, a report from the Special Resumptions Committee, comprising the Mayor (Alderman W. A. Jolly, C.M.G., chairman), Aldermen A. Watson, R. W. H. Long, and E. Barstow, was presented to the council stating that the sale of the property known as lots 5/11 Trocadero had been negotiated with Mr. Herbert, of the Trocadero Dansant Ltd.

The terms of the loan would allow Mr. Herbert to pay off the debt to Council over a five year period with interest payable only if the scheduled repayments were missed. Mr. Herbert negotiated that he, as purchaser, be allowed to take down the front of the building now upon the resumption, and re-erect same on the new alignment of a similar structure and condition to that in which it is now, notwithstanding any existing by-law to the contrary. The council would be responsible to fill in the 20ft. in depth along the whole frontage of the property after re-erecting the new frontage. The council to open a lane from Grey Street to Hope Street to abut on the rear of the Trocadero premises. Further, Council would extent an amount of £6000 for the expenditure to set back the building and erect up-to-date shops on the frontage, improvements and extension of the dance-hall and the installation of a sewerage system.

The council meeting was informed by Chair of the Special Resumptions Committee that 'The committee has gone carefully into the proposal of Herbert's solicitors, and whilst not approving of the principle generally, considers that owing to the circumstances in the case the council would be well advised to agree to same'.[lx]

-o-

In 1924, the Queensland State Parliament passed the City of Brisbane Act to set up a single local government in Brisbane. Before this, the Brisbane area had been divided up into 20 local authorities and joint boards. The act reduced the number of aldermen for the Brisbane area from more than 200 down to 20. The newly elected Council, headed by Brisbane's first Lord Mayor, William Jolly, took over the local administration on the 1st October 1925. Mr. James Stopford as Home Secretary, was the author of the City of Brisbane Act, the Minister who steered it through Parliament.[lxi]

Why was it that a man convicted of sly-grog selling and who had his dance hall resumed by council, suddenly find it returned to him? With interest free payment terms and to be given the funds to undertake the set back of the property to allow the road to be widen! Why did council agree to open a laneway to the back of the property? Why did council agree to the installation of a sewerage system. What were the 'circumstances' that led council to agree to these terms? Was it purely a coincidence that the proprietor of the dance hall, Joseph Herbert, had provided incriminating evidence against Mrs. Cumming?

*

Two weeks later a magisterial inquiry began under Magistrate Staines.

17 LET THE INQUIRY BEGIN

Arthur Staines, Esquire, J.P. and Magisterial Inquiries Officer was assigned to hear the evidence to be collected under oath from witnesses brought forward by the police. For the purpose of inquiring into circumstances surrounding the deaths of Marquis Cumming and Eileen Gladys Walsh who were found dead in the Railway Reserve, Annerley Road, South Brisbane on the morning of the 24th December 1926. Arthur Staines was a fifty-one year old career public servant having joined in Mackay in 1894. He had been appointed the Brisbane Magisterial Inquiries Officer in 1925 from his previous role as the Clerk of Petty Sessions for Gatton, Helidon, and Laidley. He was a small man of thin build with a balding scalp and thick moustache.

Sub-Inspector Meldon, Chief of the Criminal Investigation Branch would conduct the inquiry. Henderson had been called back from leave and sat in the public gallery with a large contingent of the press and interested members of the public. At the opening of the inquiry on Thursday the Twenty-Sixth day of May 1927 he made a statement before calling for evidence.

"The delay of this inquiry has not been undue, and no attempt was made to deceive the press. We have had to follow many avenues of investigation, some of them demanding the greatest tact and delicacy."

"It is only right," responded Staines, "that complete investigation should be made before an inquiry was held, otherwise the object of the inquiry would be defeated. It is a privilege of anyone to ask for an inquiry by giving notice via a requisition. An inquiry cannot be withheld. It is my custom to admit to these inquiries, parties or representatives involved, so long as they are not suspected of the deed. Is anyone, being called to provide evidence at this inquiry, under suspicion?"

Meldon responded, "No."[lxii]

Appearing in the interests of Theresa Jane Cumming and Marquis D. J. Stanley Cumming was Mr. W.T. King of Messrs. Delaney and King Solicitors, and on behalf of Mr. J.S. Walsh, Mr. W.J. Kennedy, Solicitor. They were there to examine the witnesses along with Meldon and Staines. The court was open to the public and the gallery was filled with newspaper reporters and members of the general public. Amongst them were the witnesses to be called upon to give evidence.

The first witness sworn in under oath was Acting Sergeant of Police, William Gilbert Bonas of South Brisbane Police Station. Bonas described in great detail how he had found the bodies. He was handed a photograph by Meldon and confirmed it as 'a photograph of' how he found, and the position in which he found, 'the bodies'. The photograph was admitted as Exhibit 1.

As he gave his evidence Bonas produced the physical evidence to have it admitted. The two spent cartridge shells were tendered as evidence and they were admitted and marked as Exhibit 2. The bullet that had been extracted from Cumming's skull, Exhibit 3. The tunic worn by Cumming entered as Exhibit 4. Cumming's Shirt, Exhibit 5. Cumming's Flannel, Exhibit 6. Eileen Walsh's hat, was also tendered, admitted, and marked Exhibit 7 and was placed before the court. It is stated that Stanley Cumming turned ashen faced when the blood stained garments of his father were presented, he diverted his gaze to the floor.

Next to be called to the stand was Dr. Espie Dods, G.M.O. who swore under oath that he was a duly qualified Medical Practitioner and Government Medical Officer that did not know the deceased Acting Sergeant Cumming nor the deceased Eileen Gladys Walsh.

-o-

To this point I had had no reason to doubt the intentions of the G.M.O. Yet, he swore under oath that he did not know Cumming. I had subsequently learnt through the Acting-Sergeant's police service file that Dods was the medical examiner that cleared Cumming as fit for duty after his operation. This led me to be suspicious of his evidence.

*

Dods began to describe in detail the position of the bodies and the results of the post mortem. As he began to speak Mrs. Cumming rose to her feet and hastened to leave the courtroom. She would wait until she was called before re-entering the courtroom. Sub-Inspector Meldon began to examine the witness.[lxiii]

"Would death be instantaneous in both cases?" he asked.

"Yes," replied the Doctor.

"What position would you say Cumming was in when he was shot!"

"Lying down on his face."

"Would the person who fired the shot be in close proximity?"

"Standing nearby," replied Dods, "Mrs. Walsh, I think, was probably shot when she was sitting up. It all depends on the position of the person who fired. Assuming that the person who shot Cumming was standing up at the back of Cumming when he was shot, then to shoot Mrs. Walsh, she must have been sitting up."

"From what you have seen on examination, what position would you consider Cumming and Mrs. Walsh were in when he was shot?"

"They were embracing."

"Would the position in which you saw the bodies at the scene be natural in the circumstances?"

"They were consistent."

"Was there anything that would indicate that there was any skill necessary in shooting the couple?"

"No."

"How did you come to that conclusion?"

"They were close together. The fact that the two shells were found in a line about 10 feet and 14 feet away would indicate that the two shots were fired by the one person from the same position. If Cumming had been shot where I saw him the cartridges would probably be ejected to the right front of the automatic, or the person who would have fired the shot assuming he were at Cumming's feet. I don't think the shooting of Cumming was self-inflicted."

The magistrate asked Mr. King and Mr. Kennedy in turn if they had any questions for the witness, neither did. Sub-Inspector Meldon requested permission to re-examine and this was granted.

"Could you explain again please about the wound being self-inflicted."

"Cumming's wound was not self-inflected, but it was possible that a wound such as Mrs. Walsh's could have been self-inflicted but Cumming's could not have been."

"Does the position of the wound lead you to that conclusion?" asked Staines.

"The position of the wound would vary according to the position of the person that fired the shot."

"Explain to the court please," said Meldon, "your thoughts on the position they were found."

"I think that Cumming was shot while in the position of having connection with Mrs. Walsh."

"Do you think you missed anything?"

"Deaths will always bring about an omission."

"Could you say who was shot first?" asked Staines.

"By the assumption that I formed that Cumming was on top of Walsh I would say that Cumming was shot first."

Outside the court, in a corridor, Theresa Jane Cumming sat apart from the other witnesses. She was a lonely figure, dressed from head to toe in black denoting grief, but to some, her manner and alertness appeared suspiciously devoid of grief.

The next witness to be called was William Thomas Taylor, the Queensland Railways fireman, that raised the alarm of the tragedy. He described the scene and left the witness box without questioning from Mr. King or Mr. Kennedy.

-o-

In his evidence the fireman that first discovered the bodies reported that the clothing of the deceased, about the neck and shoulders, were saturated in blood. I considered the photograph taken shortly after the police arrived. The blood about Cumming's neck had soaked the front of his shirt. To a position where his chin might of reached if he strained his neck to touch his chest. If he had been shot from behind and instantaneously been thrown onto his back, why was there so much blood on the front of the shirt? Surely gravity would have forced the blood to have pooled at the back of the neck? And the G.M.O. reported that he had found a bullet wound with powder marks on the back of the deceased, but Cumming's was found dressed in tunic, shirt and undershirt. How did he get powder wounds on the skin?

I then considered the position of the bodies. Dods had reported that the bullet that killed Cumming had severed his spinal cord, yet he had also stated that Cumming must have lurched upwards before succumbing to the injury to fall some two feet away from Mrs. Walsh. Wouldn't he have been paralysed? The bullet didn't have enough force to penetrate the skull so it did not seem as though the force of the bullet alone could have moved a body of that weight the distance it would have travelled to reach its final resting place. The trajectory of the bullet that killed him had been from left of his spinal cord to the base of the skull. Whereas the body had been thrown in the opposite direction to the bullet's trajectory.

The GMO reported powder marks on both victims. For the powder to have marked the skin of the policemen through his tunic the assailant would have needed to be in very close proximity when the shot was fired. Closer than standing at the victims feet as the GMO concluded. I found myself agreeing with Mrs. Cumming, that their assailant arranged the bodies and clothing as they were found.

Dr. Espie Dods further gave evidence that he found spermatozoa on Mrs Walsh's person and that it was 'recent'. He was not questioned as to what he meant by recent but we can assume that he meant that the sperm was still live when he examined it. We now know that a woman's cervical fluid provides the sperm with the nutrients they need to survive during their journey to the ovum. The typical lifespan of sperm in a woman's body while fertile cervical fluid is present is three days, but in the right conditions sperm can even live up to five days. In the absence of cervical fluid, sperm have a brief lifespan of a mere few hours. The only inference that can be drawn then is that Eileen was close to ovulating and had sexual relations sometime during the five days leading up to her death.

*

Meldon then called Mrs. Cumming to the witness box, and she was duly sworn in under oath. On taking the stand she said her husband was on good terms with herself and their family at the time of his death. Meldon asked her to tell the court of her actions on the afternoon of her husband's death. She recounted the story she had given earlier, of spending time shopping for Christmas presents, of her husband's arrival home for tea, and gifts being presented. After she told the court of how she had received the news of her husband's death Meldon began to ask more direct questions.

"Do you remember saying anything at the morgue?"

"No, I don't."

"Detective Campbell called on you several times?"

"Yes."

"Do you recollect Detective Campbell taking charge of an automatic pistol and some cartridges from a room at your home?"

"Yes."

"Do you remember saying to Campbell at the morgue, 'It is terrible. I have often told him that he would meet a sudden end'!'"

Mrs. Cumming hesitated.

"You then commenced to cry. Do you remember anything like that taking place? He was a man of very daring disposition."

"On this occasion," suggested Mr. King.

"On this occasion," said Meldon, "do you remember saying it?"

"You either do or you don't," offered Mr. King.

"Did you say," said Meldon raising his voice, "'It is terrible. I have often told him that he would meet a sudden end. I knew it would come to this. I have warned him that he would meet a terrible end'!'"

"I don't remember saying that."

"Might you have said it?"

"I don't know."

"This was at the morgue?" queried Magistrate Staines.

"Yes," responded Meldon annoyed by the interruption, "Did you turn to the body Mrs. Cumming and say, 'Daddy I knew it would come to this. I have warned you that you would meet a terrible end'?"

"No."

"Do you remember kissing the body, on the forehead?"

"Yes."

"Did you say, 'Daddy, God forgive you'?"

"No, I did not say that."

Meldon paced before the witness box and exhaled loudly before continuing.

"Where was your husband stationed before he came to South Brisbane?"

"Mareeba, Capella, Emerald, Mt. Morgan, North Rockhampton, Marmor Westward."

"When did he come to Brisbane?"

"About four years ago."

"You had some trouble, domestic trouble, some years ago?"

"Where?"

"Anywhere!"

"The first trouble was at Mt. Morgan."

"At all other places your life was comparatively happy?"

"Very Happy."

"The first sign of any domestic trouble was at Mt. Morgan?"

"Yes."

"When was that?"

"About five years ago."

"He was in charge at Mt. Morgan for about six months and he was instructed to live in the senior sergeant's quarters?" asked Meldon.

"Yes."

"And he desired not to?"

"Yes."

"Did any friction crop up there?"

"I can't say."

"Do you know this woman," said Meldon, "If your worship pleases I will submit this name on a piece of paper."

Magistrate Staines nodded, he had been made aware of the sensitive nature of the names of female associates of Acting-Sergeant Cumming and had agreed that their anonymity would be maintained.

Meldon passed the piece of paper to Mrs. Cumming.

"Yes, I knew her."

"Was this particular woman sending vegetables and things up to your house?"

"Yes."

"What happened?"

"At first she denied it," replied Mrs. Cumming, "then she said she had sent them in return for kindnesses he had done for her."

"At another time you found something at home?"

"Yes."

"The same woman?"

"Another one."

"Where?"

"Mt. Morgan."

"What was it?"

"He got a letter one morning, and left it when he went out."

"You suspected he was intriguing with some woman?"

Mrs. Cumming hesitated.

"Don't say so if you did not," said Meldon, turning to the court he added, "I would not condemn him."

Mr. King now addressed Mrs. Cumming.

"At this particular time did you suspect that he was going out with women?" he said.

"Yes, I did. But all the same, when he came home he used to say he was with men friends."

"Did you suspect him?" quizzed Meldon.

"Yes."

"Do you remember a woman, related to your husband by marriage, staying at your house there for a while?"

"Yes."

"An unpleasant thing happened?"

"I remonstrated with him about going out. The relative suggested having some music and we agreed but my husband was all dressed to go out. I said to him 'Dadda are you going out?' and he said yes. I asked him, 'Won't you stay with us this evening?' but he said 'No, I am going out'.

With that he went downstairs. There was a piece of canvas over the top of the stairs, I leaned over the balustrade to speak to him, and it hit him on the head. He must have thought I did it purposely. He was a very quick tempered man and rushing up the stairs he grabbed me by the shoulders and pushed me against the wall. Our visitor said, 'Oh, Mark, don't hit Tottie'. Tottie meant me. He then let me go and went out."

At this point Meldon requested an adjournment of the inquiry to the next day. Magistrate Staines granted the request.

*

The next morning Mrs. Cumming was re-sworn on oath to continue in the witness box. Meldon continued his questioning.

"Yesterday, you told us of an unpleasantness at the home in Mt. Morgan. You had a visitor. Your husband was going out. Tell us what happened when he returned."

"I was upset, by the incident that evening, I turned to our visitor and said 'I will give him a devil of a fright' and knowing that his revolver was in a chest of drawers in our room, I got it, that being just before he came home, we stood on the verandah when he returned."

"How did your husband return? Did you speak to him?"

"He came to the front gate, but I don't recollect any words that passed then."

"And you fired a shot at your husband!"

The court erupted with chatter. Staines tapped his gable.

"Order," said Staines, "Order in the court."

"I fired into the garden bed," said Mrs. Cumming, "I

did not fire at my husband, but at his side, into the garden bed."

"What did you do with the revolver?"

"I threw it across me."

"What did your husband do, after you fired a shot at him?"

"I fired into the garden bed!"

"Take your time," said Mr. King in an attempt to have his client regain her composure.

"My husband came in and he walked across and picked up the revolver, after that he came onto the steps on the verandah."

"Where was your husband when you fired the shot?" asked Meldon.

"He was standing at the front gate, out on the footpath, outside the gate."

"How did you dispose of the weapon?"

"I threw it from the left of me to the right of me."

"What did your husband do, after the shot was fired?"

"He came up the steps with the revolver in his hand, and he said to me, 'I could have you up for using firearms in the public street'."

"And you were agitated."

"No, I was not agitated at the time."

"You were upset then."

"I was not upset!"

"So you were calm when you tried to shoot your husband?"

"I fired the shot but I did not intend to shoot him!"

"What did your husband say, about the incident."

"He did not say anything regarding it, he knew that it was not done to shoot him."

"Did your visitor try to take the revolver away from you?"

"No, she made no attempt prior to my firing the shot, she was enjoying the joke as well as I was."

"Did you load the revolver or was it already loaded?"

"It was always loaded, I don't know anything about revolvers."

"Did you say to your visitor 'I will not let him in alive'?"

"No!"

"Did any other quarrels crop up in Mount Morgan, about other woman?"

"No. The things I have already referred to did not cause rows in my home!"

"But you were upset?"

"Yes. I am very sorry to have to mention them, for he was a good man."

Mrs. Cumming's burst into tears but quickly regained herself and blew her nose.

"When did you come to Brisbane?"

"About three years ago. My husband came down first, I did not come down till about three months afterwards, I sold the house at Mt. Morgan in the meantime."

"You told us about an incident here in Brisbane about a letter, could you repeat what you told the Detectives?"

"While in Brisbane I remember my husband coming home from work, he took some letters from his pocket."

"When was this?" asked the Magistrate.

"We came down in October of 1923, so somewhere about the following July the incident took place about the letters."

"Thank you," said Staines, "continue please."

Mrs. Cumming recalled how her husband had placed the letters on the table and she could see that one was in a woman's handwriting and how her husband had subsequently locked the letters away in his box for personal papers. She had opened the box and took the letter with the woman's handwriting, the letter had been signed in certain initials and she discovered from it that her husband was the father of another woman's child.

"Where was the letter from?" asked Staines.

"From Mount Morgan."

"What did you do with it?"

"I kept it."

Mrs. Cumming then told how she had told her husband that she had opened his box with his own key.

"His own key?" questioned Meldon.

"Yes, he left his keys there, hanging on his bed."

"Didn't you tell the Detectives you used the key from the duchess?"

"I tried the key of the duchess, but that key would not open it. I remember now that I opened the box with his own key and not the key of the duchess as I had previously told the Detective."

"What did you say to your husband?"

"I said to him 'I have found out all your secrets now, if I had waited for twenty years, I could not have learnt more'."

"What did your husband say?"

"He demanded the letter from me, and I refused to give it to him."

"Did anyone else see this letter?"

"I believe I showed Stanley that letter when he came home and Stanley made some inquiries about the initials and he located a name, and he wrote a letter to that address."

"He wrote about your husband being the father of another woman's child?" asked Magistrate Staines.

"That letter was about another matter altogether, but written to obtain the initials of this man's wife so as to identify the letter which I had taken possession of from that party."

"How did that make you feel?" asked Mr. King.

"I was very annoyed about this matter and I told my husband that I would make arrangements for a judicial separation and I consulted a solicitor."

"Was that the end of the matter?" prompted Mr. King.

"No, some months later Stanley went to Mt. Morgan in course of his occupation, and on his return he told me that he had seen this particular woman and he had got from her a signed statement admitting that my husband was the father of her child, and he gave me that statement and I destroyed it."

"Did your husband know of this statement?"

"I told my husband what Stanley had obtained and my husband got annoyed, with this information that Stanley had obtained, and he came home one night and appeared to have had some drink, and he came into the room where Stanley and I were and said 'I could shoot the two of you if I liked', and he placed his hand towards his hip pocket where he usually carried his revolver, and I said 'Oh Dadda there is no need for that'."

"How did that make you feel?"

"That upset me."

"Continue please," said Mr. King.

"The following night he came home and had a quarrel with Stanley, and in consequence Stanley left home and went to reside in Stephens Road."

"How long was Stanley away Mrs. Cumming?"

"He was away some weeks and he eventually came home."

"Did this create bitterness between you and your husband?"

"After the incident my husband and I made it up."

"Why?"

"I consulted a friend of mine and they advised me for the sake of the children to forgive him."

Mr. King continued to ask questions regarding Mrs. Cumming's suspicions of her husband, the incident when she found him sitting on the end of a bed with a man and woman, the time she sent her younger son to follow him when her husband had said 'Go home at once or I'll kick your behind', the time he went to work early and her not believing what she was told and confronting him outside the Police Station.

"So you were annoyed with him?" quizzed Meldon.

"I was naturally annoyed with him."

"Do you remember New Year's Eve, that is, the 31st of December 1924 when your husband went to the Trocadero?"

"Yes."

"Could you tell the court please what happened that night."

Mrs. Cumming repeated the story of how she had also gone to the Trocadero that evening and on seeing her husband in the company of a group of men and women she had said, 'Well I have got you there', and her husband had become very annoyed with her and told her to leave.

Then Mr. Herbert had approached her husband and after she told him about her husband sneaking about, her husband had become very cross and threatened to have her put out. She had left him and after a while Stanley approached her and he took her home.

"The next day I went to see Mr. Herbert of the Trocadero and apologized to him for what had happened the previous night. I then went to see Senior Sergeant Casey who was in charge of the South Brisbane Police Station."

"Did you tell Mr. Herbert that your husband was a disgrace to you?" quizzed Meldon.

"No I did not."

"What if I told you that Mr. Herbert said you did?"

"If Mr. Herbert said I said that to him that would not be correct."

"What if I told you that Mr. Herbert said you told him that your husband did not support you."

"I did not tell that to Mr. Herbert."

"What of Mr. Herbert's assertion that you said, 'the way he is carrying on he ought to be shot!'"

"I did not say that."

"Did you say to Mr. Herbert that you would complain to Senior Sergeant Casey?"

"I may have said that I was going to complain, but I don't recollect if I did or did not."

"What did you say to Senior Sergeant Casey Mrs. Cumming?" asked Staines.

"I said I had a good mind to tell the Commissioner of Police to get my husband transferred from South Brisbane as I did not like it."

"Why did you say that?"

"I desired myself to get away from South Brisbane, and also because my husband was going out a good deal at night time, and I did not approve of his going out so much alone."

"Might he have been doing extra duty?" asked King.

"When he was dressed in his civilian clothes he did not tell me he was going on duty."

"Let's try your memory on something else," said Meldon.

"Do you remember about two months prior to your husband's death, your husband, after being on night duty got up hurriedly about mid-day one day, and refusing lunch went out?"

"Yes, and in civilian clothes."

"Did you go out later yourself?"

"Yes."

"Why?"

"On business, but I was also suspicious."

"About where your husband had gone and with whom?"

"Yes, I went down near His Majesty's."

"After being there for a short while did you see your husband come out of the dress circle entrance?"

"Yes, and he glanced back over his shoulder and he was joined by a woman who was following him."

"You got Stanley from his work, and you saw your husband and the woman together in a café in Edward Street."

"Yes."

"Did you walk up to the woman and say do you know who you are with?"

"Yes. The woman said 'No'."

"At that you said, 'this man is my husband' and she got up and walked out?"

"Yes. I followed her out and left my husband in the café. She told me she had never seen him in the pictures. He asked her to have afternoon tea with him."

"Did the woman say don't make any fuss about it because of my crippled child?"

"Yes."

"Did you say I am as pleased as if I got a fiver to have caught him out with a woman, as he is telling me that he was out with men pals?"

Mrs. Cumming hesitated for a moment appearing to refresh her memory before stating, "Yes, I said that."

"Your son followed the woman to a street at Dutton

Park but lost sight of her?"

"Yes. My husband always told me that he had been going out with gentlemen friends, but now I could see that he had been telling me an untruth. He said he only met the woman by accident in the pictures, but I did not believe him."

"Some Saturday night later did Stanley tell you that he had seen your husband with the same woman in Melbourne Street?"

"Yes."

"And the woman had two children with her?"

"Yes."

"His father saw him getting a good look at them and saying 'Are you following me?' he made a run at him?"

"Yes."

"The next morning did your husband say 'I'm going to make new rules here, Stanley will have to get out by January First' and he was annoyed."

"Yes."

"What did you say?" asked Mr. King.

"I said Stanley would not go. He had done nothing wrong, and he ought to be ashamed of himself to mention such a thing."

"Was this the last incident where you had a quarrel or difference with your husband prior to his death?" quizzed Meldon.

"Yes."

"At your home on the night of the tragedy there were two revolvers?"

"I did not know if there were any revolvers."

"You knew your son had an automatic pistol?"

"Yes."

"Have you at times warned your husband of the danger he was running by carrying on with women in his position."

"I have warned him."

"He said to you, 'It would take a smart man to catch me'?"

"Yes."

"There has been no trace found of your husband's handcuffs, keys, and belt?"

"No."

"Did you ever say that your husband got what he deserved?"

"No, I did not," said Mrs. Cumming in a subdued tone.

"To Detective Henderson?"

"No, I did not."

"To any of the Detectives?"

"I do not remember saying that to any of the detectives."

"Did you tell anyone that you locked your husband out at night?"

"I never told anyone I locked my husband out at night!"

"You locked your husband out at night?" asked Mr. King.

"I never locked my husband out at night. If my husband is supposed to have told anyone that I locked him out at night, that is not correct."

Meldon had lost his momentum, he returned to his chair, slumping into it as he did so. He looked at Staines and the Magistrate referred to his notes.

"In regards to the letter from Mount Morgan," said Staines, "what did you do with it?"

"I took copies and I took that letter to solicitors at the time that I anticipated judicial separations, but I destroyed the original letter."

"Did you speak of the letter to anyone?"

"I did not expose my knowledge of this woman in reference to my husband to anyone outside my family and my solicitor, that is the identity of that woman."

Staines made a notation before he lent back into his chair.

"I think we need a recess," he said, "court is adjourned for one hour."

*

Sub-Inspector Meldon approached Magistrate Staines during the recess. He wished to present in evidence a number of letters but doing so would expose names which he had been directed could not be made public. When the court was reconvened Staines addressed the courtroom.

"Let the record show that by request of the Bench and on their own initiative the press will abstain from publishing any locality or names or other matter that would tend to identification of any person mentioned in the letters that will be tendered as Exhibits. This request is made by Sub-Inspector Meldon."

Mrs. Cumming was re-sworn on oath and returned to the witness box.

Meldon walked towards the witness box with a number of letters in his hands. He passed the first of them to Mrs. Cumming.

"Can you identify this?" asked Meldon.

"That is a copy made by me from the original letter which was received by my husband on or about July 1924."

"I submit this letter into evidence," said Meldon.

"Copy of letter tendered, admitted, and marked as Exhibit 8," said Staines.

-o-

The letter from the 'Conceit Bitch', which seemed to indicate that Cumming had corresponded with the mother of his illegitimate child in unflattering terms, was a copy made by Mrs. Cumming. Was it possible that Mrs. Cumming had constructed her own version of the letter? And if so, for what purpose?

*

Meldon handing Mrs. Cumming a letter dated Fifth December 1926.

"That is in the handwriting of my husband, with the exception of the initials in the margin."

"I submit this letter into evidence," said Meldon.

"Copy of letter tendered, admitted, and marked as Exhibit 9,"[12] said Staines.

"And this?" said Meldon handing Mrs. Cumming a letter dated Twelfth December 1926.

"I recognize that writing as the handwriting of my late husband, with the exception of the initials in the margin."

In the margin the letter bore the initials F.A.D.

"I submit this letter into evidence," said Meldon.

"Copy of letter tendered, admitted, and marked as Exhibit 10," said Staines.

"And this letter dated the Twenty-First of December 1926?" said Meldon handing it to Mrs. Cumming.

"It's a typed letter, but the handwriting on the bottom thereof I recognize as the handwriting of my late husband, but the initials on the margin is not the handwriting of my husband."

Again, in the margin the letter bore the initials F.A.D.

"I submit this letter into evidence," said Meldon.

"Copy of letter tendered, admitted, and marked as

---

[12] Figure 8 - Letter presented to Inquiry as written by Marquis Cumming.

Exhibit 11," said Staines.

"Mrs. Cumming," said Meldon addressing the witness, "What can you tell the court about the contents of this letter?"

Meldon passed the letter dated the Fifth of December 1926 to her. Mrs. Cumming adjusted her spectacles on her nose and mumbled to herself as she spoke each word under her breath. When she had finished reading it she looked up at Meldon and passed the letter back to him.

"Anything in that letter," said Mrs. Cumming pointing at it, "referring to my husband's home life is not correct, a tissue of falsehood."

"And this one," said Meldon passing her the letter dated the Twelfth of December 1926.

Again Mrs. Cumming adjusted her glasses, holding the paper in both hands and tilting it towards the light. Again she mumbled under her breath as she read the words. She dropped her hands to the table, rolling her eyes to the ceiling, she exclaimed, "Oh my stars," before being induced by Meldon to finish reading the letter.

"What say you on the contents of that letter," said Meldon.

"Respecting anything in that which refers to the deceased's home life is not true."

"What do these letters tell you about your husband?"

"By those letters I could see that his home life was not happy. I can't understand why my husband could have put pen to paper to this woman, or anyone, being lies about his own wife."

"What reason did you give your husband to write like that?" said Meldon with his back to Mrs. Cumming facing the gallery.

"I did not give my husband any reason to write like that about his home life. It was quite a surprise to me when I was told by detectives after the death of my husband that such letters were written."

Meldon spun around quickly and held onto the front of the witness box.

"Do you know who shot your husband?" he said directly.

"I only wish I did."

"Or the deceased Mrs. Walsh."

"She was a perfect stranger to me."

"You do not know who shot your husband?"

"I do not know who did, or who shot the deceased Mrs. Walsh."

"Have you any reason to suspect any person or persons of having shot your husband or Mrs. Walsh?"

"I have not."

"To return to the Trocadero incident, are you sure that you did not say to the manager that your husband ought to be shot for the way he was carrying on?"

"I did not say it."

"Please yourself whether you answer this or not. Did you have anything to do with the cause of your husband's death?"

"Nothing whatever."

"Can you give any more information or throw any light on the cause of the death of the deceased?"

"Nothing whatever."

"Did you love your husband?" asked Mr. King.

"Notwithstanding my husband's failings I had an affectionate regard for him up to the time of his death. At the time my husband last left home all was happiness and all past events had been forgotten and forgiven, and a true spirit of Christmas time was prevailing in our house at the time he left home. He seemed very pleased indeed with the present I gave him, it was always a customary thing for me, to give him a Christmas gift. The greater part of our married life was a life of happiness."

"Did you ever get annoyed by the things you heard about him?"

"Yes, things I heard at times used to annoy me, but they had been eliminated on the night of the 23rd December 1926."

"Would you say you were skilled in the use of firearms?"

"No, not at all, I have only had to do with firearms on the occasion that I mentioned."

"Do you know if your husband had his keys on him on the night in question?"

"They may have been on him and they may have been off him."

"Did you assist the police with their inquiries?"

"I gave the Police every assistance in endeavouring to solve this mystery."

"Every assistance!" said Meldon loudly, spinning in his seat as he did so.

"I gave the Police every assistance, with the exception that I refused to go down to the Police Station as I got legal advice. Apart from that I gave every assistance to the detectives that I could."

"Why did you change your mind?" asked Mr. King.

"I have realised since that it was necessary that myself and any members of my family should be closely questioned."

"Did your family give you advice?"

"My brother-in-law gave me some advice, that is the brother of the deceased, told me to abide by the advice given by the solicitor."

"Mr. Walsh, any questions for the witness?" asked Mr. Staines.

Mr. Walsh shook his head.

"Mr. King?"

"Mrs. Cumming could you tell the court of your husband's will?" asked Mr. King.

"My husband did not leave any will."

Magistrate Staines broke the moments silence in the courtroom.

"Mrs. Cumming you are excused for now, Sub-Inspector Meldon, would you like to call your next witness."

"I'd like to call Stanley Cumming to the witness box," said Meldon.

Marquis David James Stanley Cumming, the dead policeman's eldest child made his way to the stand. Stanley, as he preferred to be known, wore a dark overcoat over his grey suit. His hair stood almost vertical from the top of his head exposing his male pattern baldness, or 'Widow's Peak'. He had inherited the large nasal features of his mother. He was described as a tall, slightly built, young man by those that saw him.

Stanley reported to the court the details of his whereabouts on the night his father was murdered, how he had spent the night in the company of a young lady before making his way home arriving a little after quarter past twelve.

18 FORENSIC EVIDENCE

That weekend the newspapers attempted to outdo each other with salacious reports and daring headlines. Headlines such as, 'Kissed the Forehead of her Dead Husband', 'When Mrs. Cumming Visited Morgue', 'Daddy! God Forgive You, I Knew It Would Come To This!', 'Widow Tells Of Affairs That Aroused Her Suspicions' and 'Love Letters Sealed With Sighs, Tears and Kisses' appeared in the 'Truth'. They also published the letters that had been presented in evidence, taking care to obscure the names and locations as directed by the court. 'The Daily Standard' had run the headlines 'Mrs. Cumming Tells of Dramatic Denouement of Deceased Husband', 'Used Revolver Once To Frighten Him', and, 'Poignant Evidence At Inquiry'. 'The Brisbane Courier' had decided on the simpler approach of 'Double Murder', 'No One Suspected'.

On the Monday morning Sub-Inspector Meldon called Stanley Cumming back to the stand and he was again sworn under oath.

"When detectives first questioned you Stanley," said Meldon, "you were only too anxious to inform the C.I. men all about your father's affairs with various women.

Why was that?"

"I was rather keen on supplying that information to the police."

"But a remarkable change came over you though didn't it Stanley. You had partly completed a frank statement to detectives, but when later asked to continue it, you refused to do so. The detectives considered this to be a very queer stand for you to adopt. Why were you not frank about the matter and keep your word to give the police every possible assistance?"

"I had legal advice."

"Did your mother, in the presence of detectives, say, 'I won't go near your office or make any statement. I have told you all I know on the matter. You won't find the murderer here'."

"I don't recollect that."

"Well then, do you recollect yourself saying to Detective Henderson, 'I've just come to my senses. I'm not going to say any more. I'm sorry I told you so much'."

"No, I don't recollect that."

Sub-Inspector Meldon continued to question Stanley and Stanley continued to reply that he could not recollect any of the statements Meldon attributed to others that they had either heard Stanley say, or that had been said in front of Stanley. It became clear to those in the gallery that the youth suffered from a faulty memory. Meldon persisted with his barrage of questions.

"Do you remember your mother saying 'He', meaning your father, 'has got his just desserts and I will say no more. I don't want Stanley to go to your office again. You had him for over ten hours on Sunday and I have had legal advice and will say no more. It appears you are inclined to make us out guilty."

"No, I don't recollect that."

"Do you deny that your mother said this?"

"I do not deny that, she may have said it, but I don't recollect it being said."

"Then, did your Uncle say that they and you had been advised to keep away from the Detective Office?"

"I do not remember."

"You refused to answer any questions yourself?"

"Yes."

Meldon was taken aback, he had expected that Stanley would have responded with a faulty memory again.

"That was very unsatisfactory. Did you not realise that it was absolutely necessary that the detectives should question you in order to clear up the mystery of the murders?"

"I realise that now."

"And you are giving the court frank answers to the questions?"

"Yes, before I thought I had told the detectives all I could."

"You were not the one investigating. It was proper for you to answer any reasonable question put to you."

"He was only carrying out his solicitor's advice," said Mr. King.

"Ain't you his solicitor?" asked Staines.

Mr. King then went to great pains to explain to the court that he was not the solicitor who advised the Cumming family to adopt a policy of passive obstruction to the police.

Meldon then asked Stanley to relay the story of how he came about obtaining a statement from a woman at Mount Morgan. Stanley obliged and went into detail about how he had traced the woman he suspected his father was carrying on with. He said he discovered her identity by a ruse and then directly taxed her with having engaged in an affair with his father. He described how he had succeeded in getting a signed confession from this woman that his father was the father of her illegitimate child.

"Where is the confession now?"

"I do not know, I understand it was destroyed."

"Did you speak to your father about this woman?"

"Yes. He said 'Any man can make a mistake once, I hope you'll overlook it'."

"Did you?"

"I said I would, I said, 'I have decided to overlook it but I hope you'll mend your ways'. He said he would."

"But your father hadn't forgotten it, had he Stanley? You claim he came home one night and putting his hand to his hip pocket he said to you and your mother, 'I could shoot the two of you if I liked'. You state that you were frightened by this. Then you went to live in a boarding house in Stephens Road. Why?"

"I wanted a change."

"What was wrong with your home?"

"Nothing, I preferred the company of strangers for a while."

"You didn't leave because of domestic trouble or through rows with your father?"

"No."

"So you mean to say then that your mother is incorrect when she has sworn on oath that the reason for your leaving home was due to trouble with your father over what you had found in connection with the woman at Mount Morgan?"

"It is incorrect."

"Who induced you to come back? Did you get sick so quickly of you preference for the company of strangers?"

"My mother induced me back."

"So she could induce you to come back but not induce

you to stay at home in the first place? Did your father ever tell you to leave the house."

"No, he told my mother, but I don't remember if she told me what reasons he gave for wanting me to get out."

"And you persist in saying that you left home of your own accord and not because of family strife?"

"Yes."

"If the court pleases," said Meldon, "I would like to get the witness's impression of Exhibit 10, the letter dated the Twelfth of December 1926."

"The court will allow it," said Staines.

Meldon handed the letter to Stanley.

"So Stanley, this letter written by your father announces his intention to eject you from the family home in the New Year."

"It is just a tissue of lies," responded Stanley.

Meldon then quizzed Stanley on the incident involving Mrs. Page, when his mother had come to him one afternoon while he was at work. Stanley described how he had approached her and followed her to Dutton Park.

"Did you say to this woman," said Meldon, "My father is no bloody good. He is causing a lot of trouble at home and a man ought to bloody well do for him?"

"I did not say that Inspector, it is a lie."

Meldon asked Stanley to state his version for the court which he did.

"Didn't you come across this woman again, in the street, with your father. Didn't your father demand to know if you were following him and chased you across the street?"

"Yes."

"Yet in view of all this you still maintain that you did not leave home because of trouble with your father, and that you were on good terms with him?"

"Yes," said Stanley.

"It appears to me you are not telling the truth," said Meldon spinning around suddenly and looking Stanley hard in the eyes, "Do you know who shot your father?"

"I do not, I wish I did know."

"Or Eileen Walsh?"

"No."

"Do you have any reason to suspect anyone who would shoot them?"

"I don't know of anyone who would, I came to the conclusion that someone connected with the woman or women or that someone who had a fancy for the woman who was shot, must have done it."

"The matter of fancy," said Meldon drily, "cuts both ways. Have you told us everything you know?"

Mrs. Cumming who was sitting in the courtroom during her son's testimony began to weep and she never looked up from the table when these direct questions were being asked and answered.

"I've told you everything I know, as far as I know my father had no enemies."

"How often did you follow your father?"

"I have never followed my father!" protested Stanley.

"What about your mother, how often did she follow your father?"

"To my knowledge the only time she followed him was on the occasion when she found him with the woman in the café in Edward Street."

"Did you," said Meldon, "either directly or indirectly have anything to do with causing the deaths of your father or Eileen Walsh?"

"No."

"If the court pleases I would like to present as evidence the automatic pistol taken from the Cumming home, the property of Stanley Cumming."

"Stanley is this your firearm?"

"Yes."

"Automatic pistol property of Stanley Cumming, tendered, admitted, and marked as Exhibit 12," said Staines.

"Are these your cartridges?"

"Yes."

"Cartridges for automatic pistol property of Stanley Cumming, tendered, admitted, and marked as Exhibit 13," said Staines.

Meldon handed Stanley a revolver.

"Can you identify this for the court?"

"That is my father's revolver. Detective Campbell took possession of that revolver at our home."

"Revolver property of Acting-Sergeant Cumming, tendered, admitted, and marked as Exhibit 13," said Staines.

"No further questions your honour."

"Mr. King?" queried Staines of Stanley's solicitor.

"Yes, I do have questions your honour."

"Why do you own a pistol Stanley?"

"I bought the pistol for my own personal protection. I was working for Finney's and my work took me out into the country, and I had charge of large sums of money and goods at some times. That is the reason I bought the pistol."

"Where did you keep the pistol?"

"I kept it in my room in my box and it was kept unloaded."

"When did you use it?"

"I only used it when I was out in the country."

"On what occasions?"

"If I had money and goods and I thought I wanted it,

otherwise it remained in my suit case."

"Where was the pistol when you left home?"

"I took it with me."

"Tell me about your father Stanley."

"My father was a quick tempered man, and the way he went on caused a little unpleasantness in the home at times. I thought that he had mended his ways from the time that he met this woman, and after that it made me think that he was not what I thought he was. In my opinion my father had nothing to find fault with in the home."

"No further questions your honour."

"Mr. Kennedy, any questions for the witness?" asked Staines.

Kennedy shook his head.

"The Bench has questions for the witness," said Staines.

"Have you served in the military?"

"Yes, I served in the Infantry arm of the military, undertaken military training."

"How far is it from the Palace Hotel to Carisbrooke boarding house?"

"About four hundred yards."

"Did you take the tram that night?"

"No, I walked that distance."

"How long did that take?"

"That distance would take me five to six minutes."

"How far is it from your residence to the nearest tram lines."

"About three hundred yards."

"Which trams can you get from there?"

"The Ipswich Road, Juliette Street, or Cracknell Road trams."

"How long would it take to walk that distance? To the nearest tram lines?"

"About two minutes."

"How far is your residence from the Five Ways?"

"It would be about five hundred to six hundred yards."

"How long does that take for you to walk there."

"It would take me about five minutes."

"How long would it take if you took a tram from the nearest point to your residence to the Five Ways."

"That would only be one or two minutes."

"How long does it take for the tram to travel from the Palace Hotel to the Five Ways?"

"About fifteen minutes."

"And from the Palace Hotel to the nearest tram stop nearest to where the bodies were found?"

"I cannot say how long it would take."

"How far is it from your home to where the bodies were found?"

"It would be about a mile."

"How long would it take you to walk that distance?"

"It would take me about twenty minutes."

"How would I get from your residence to where the bodies were found?"

"Any outward bound tram could be caught for that purpose going to Ipswich Road, or any outbound car on Ipswich Road."

"Why did you stop at the Palace Hotel before going to see Miss Clutterbuck?"

"I wanted a drink."

"How far would one have to walk if they took a tram from the nearest point of your residence and got off the tram at the nearest point to the scene of the tragedy?"

"I have no idea."

"Thank you Stanley that appears to be all the questions we have for you at the moment, you may step down from the witness box. Sub-Inspector Meldon could you call your next witness please."

"Thank you your honour, we would like to call Mr. James Samuel Walsh to the witness box."

James Walsh repeated what he had told the police as to his whereabouts on the night of the murders. He denied that he had ever ill-treated his wife and maintained that he was on friendly terms with her. The reason for the breakup of the home, he said, was his mother-in-law. He stated that he had no idea she even knew Cumming and had never suspected her of being on intimate terms with any other man.

"Have you ever assaulted your wife?" questioned Meldon.

"Never."

"Are you sure? Did you ever threaten her with a razor?"

"No."

"Absolutely sure?"

"Oh, years ago, before the war, and long before our marriage, she had gone out with another man."

"Did you do anything with the razor?"

"I just told her I'd cut her throat. I never meant it and we made up the row."

Meldon continued his questioning with Walsh responding that he had no idea who committed the murders, and also said that there was no one whom he suspected.

Meldon then requested an adjournment of the inquiry till the next day.

*

The newspapers were distracted from the inquiry by the news that the report by an American Engineer into the feasibility of the application of the open cut system to the Mount Morgan mine was unfavourable. The directors of the company made a statement suggesting that the mine would practically close with operation of a temporary nature confined to the realisation of certain mining assets. The hope had been that the adoption of the open cut system would enable the company to continue operations upon the eight million tons of ore which it estimated the mine still held. However, after returning losses for the past five years, and keenly unsympathetic labour conditions with strikes and sabotage, they felt that nothing was left undone to make possible the continuance of work, and maintenance of Mount Morgan on the map.[lxiv]

*

The next morning Mary Christie, dressed in black, mother of Eileen Walsh, was called to the witness box. Meldon wanted to quickly direct his questioning to Christmas afternoon when Mrs. Cumming visited her but first asked Mary Christie to explain to the court how she believed Eileen had not anticipated meeting Cumming or anyone else on the night of the tragedy. For, dressed in her ordinary house clothes, she went out at about eight o'clock to post a letter. She further stated, to strengthen this view, that she had asked her thirteen year old niece, Ruby Jones, to accompany her to the pillar box, but the child was too tired. She then described how the family searched unsuccessfully for her when her absence became prolonged, and the fact she was missing reported to the police at two thirty the following morning.

"Could you identify this for me please," asked Meldon holding a woman's hat previously submitted as Exhibit 7.

"That is my daughter's hat."

"Could you also have a look at this clothing as well as the shoes."

"Those were hers," said Mary pointing to the shoes.

"And this?" asked Meldon picking up a woman's undergarment.

"That is the princess slip that she had on, and I recognize the bloomers as hers, and also the stockings, the stockings are hers."

"I tender these clothing items and footwear as evidence," said Meldon.

"Ladies attire tendered, admitted, and marked as Exhibit 15," said Staines.

"You told us you had a visitor Christmas afternoon, who was that?" asked Meldon."

"Mrs. Cumming."

"Did she say why she came to your home?"

"At first she said she came to offer her sympathies adding that she didn't know if I would accept it."

"Did you?"

"Yes, I said I did and added, 'I'm awfully sorry for you'."

"Did Mrs. Cumming say anything else?"

"She asked where my daughter's body was and I responded that she was buried the day before."

"How did Mrs. Cumming respond to this news?"

"I thought it an offensive remark when she said 'You got rid of her quick enough didn't you?'."

"Go on," urged Meldon.

"She was curious to know if her husband had ever been at our home drinking and playing cards. I told her, 'No' and she said 'if it wasn't you then it must be someone else'."

"Please," urged Meldon, "tell us everything Mrs. Cumming said that day."

"She said she always warned her husband that this

would be his end, and that he laughed and said it would be a good man that would get him. She then remarked 'evidently the good man got him, but it was from the back'. She said her husband was always fond of beautiful woman and girls, but let him go and 'look at them lying at the morgue twenty-four hours afterwards with their paint and powder off'. I told her my Eileen had no occasion to wear paint or powder. She, Mrs. Cumming, then said how it was 'a strange coincidence' that being 'the only night he went out without his revolver and left it at home on the table'. She then asked me if I thought her husband, meaning Mr. Walsh had done it, or 'had he paid for someone else to do it'. I told her that Walsh had no money to pay anyone to do such a terrible crime."[lxv]

"Mrs. Christie, can you give the court any idea who shot your daughter and the Acting Sergeant?" asked Meldon.

"I don't know who shot either of them."

"Do you suspect any one?"

"I have a suspicion that the person who shot Cumming and my daughter, in my opinion, was someone who knew he was unarmed that night."

"I must object," said Mr. King, "the object of this inquiry is to present facts before the court, not enter hearsay, innuendo, or suspicion! I must protest against this last remark going in as evidence. I ask that instructions be given to the Press that it is not evidence!"

"I cannot issue instructions to the press Mr. King, but I will say to the Press that it was not evidence."

"It is merely an opinion," stated Mr. King, "which might be expressed by any member of the public, but it is not evidence!"[lxvi]

"Your correct," said Staines, "Mr. Meldon could you please ensure that the witnesses are aware that evidence should be provided to support claims of suspicion and please remove that previous comment from the record.

Mrs. Christie do you have any such evidence that supports your suspicion?"

"No your honour," replied Mary Christie, "it was only a suspicion."

"Was your daughter involved with Cumming before the night of the tragedy?" asked Meldon.

"Absolutely not, I never heard of my daughter even speak of him!"

"Are you aware that the letter your daughter posted that night was addressed to Cumming?"

"I have since been told who the letter was written to, that being members of the Police told me."

Meldon produced an addressed and post marked envelope and asked Mrs. Christie if her daughter could have written it.

"That address resembles Eileen's handwriting, but I would not swear that it is hers."

"What do you mean by that?"

"The 'South Brisbane' is more like her writing but the 'Sergeant Cumming' is not."

"What about this postcard, is this your daughter's handwriting?"

"Yes that is her handwriting on the back of this postcard, and the photo is of Eileen."[lxvii]

"I tender this postcard as evidence," said Meldon.

"Postcard tendered, admitted, and marked as Exhibit 16," said Staines.

Meldon indicated he had no further questions neither did Mr. King, Mr. Kennedy however wanted to ask questions on behalf of his client.

"Mrs. Christie," he started, "are you aware that your daughter wrote to her husband recently."

"I believe that my daughter wrote to her husband asking for him to take her back."

"Did you believe this?"

"She said she would go back on condition that he had a proper home for her."

"Have you had contact with Walsh since the tragedy?"

"Yes, he has written to me asking for me to give up the children to him, I will not give them up. He told me that he might make an application to the court to get them."

"Do you know he has made application to the court?"

"I know that Walsh made an application to the court to have the order for maintenance squashed."

"Have you received money from the court since your daughter's death?"

"I most certainly have not!"

"How did you know about the court application?"

"He told me that he went to stop any money being paid to anyone else through that order as soon as he was released from C.I. Branch."

"How long has Walsh known your daughter?"

"Walsh and my daughter kept company together since she was a little girl of fourteen years of age."

"What would you say caused the quarrels between Walsh and your daughter? Jealousy perhaps?" asked Mr. King.

"The quarrels between them were through poverty and drink, but not through jealousy."

"Do you suspect that Walsh may have been near the scene of the tragedy?"

"No, I have not the slightest suspicion that he was anywhere near the scene of the tragedy that night."

"Any further questions of the witness?" asked Staines.

Meldon cleared his throat.

"Mrs. Christie, your daughter's wedding ring, was it

261

loose on her finger?"

"Not that loose that it would slip off, I think a little bit of force would have to be used to get it off."[lxviii]

"Thank you," said Meldon, "that is all your honour."

"The witness may step down."

The next witness called was Eileen's sister Mrs. Madeline Jones. She recounted to the court the same information she had given to Detective Henderson. Her sister had been in good spirits and health when she left the home to post a card and would only be gone for five minutes. She never knew her sister to be on friendly terms with Cumming or that she had met Cumming by appointment or otherwise. Nor was she aware if her sister used to write to him or him to her. After recounting the incident when Walsh had threatened her sister with a razor Mr. Kennedy asked if she had any reason to suspect that her sister's husband had murdered her that night. Madeline replied she did not. Madeline was allowed to step down from the witness box.[lxix]

Meldon then requested that Detective Bonas be resworn on oath as he wished to correct his evidence.

"In my evidence given on the 26th instance it was reported that I said 'at 10 pm on the 22nd December 1926 I was waiting to take charge of the third relief and about to go on duty' should read, 'at 10 pm on the 23rd December 1926'.

"When you discovered the body of Eileen Gladys Walsh did she have a wedding ring on her finger?" asked Meldon.

"No she did not."

"Did she have any mark about the ring finger?" asked Mr. Kennedy.

"I did not notice any mark on her finger to signify that she had a ring on there, recently."[lxx]

"There being no further questions," said Staines checking with the solicitors and Sub-Inspector, "the witness may step down."

Meldon then called Henry Morris who recounted the details given in his statement to police that tallied with Walsh's story that they had been at the Waterloo Bay Hotel till closing time then went to the Liberty Fair before returning home.[lxxi]

Meldon then called Frank Souter, the barman from the Waterloo Bay Hotel to the stand. He identified Walsh as the man he had seen in the bar on the night in question and repeated the statement he gave Detectives regarding the events of that evening.

Mr. Kennedy asked him for an assessment of James Walsh's demeanour that evening.

"As far as I could see Walsh was quite alright that night. We were chatting over old times. He appeared in the ordinary demeanour as when I had met him on previous occasions."

"Did he appear excited?" asked Kennedy.

"He was not excited or morose and appeared to talk to me as if nothing was troubling him."[lxxii]

Charles Clyde was then called to the stand and repeated what he had told detectives, he had seen Henry Morris with another man that he now knew was James Walsh at Liberty Fair. Neither of the solicitors had any further questions and he was allowed to step down.[lxxiii]

Frederick George Chapman was next to be called to the witness stand and he also confirmed that he had seen Henry Morris and James Walsh at the Liberty Fair on the night in question. King and Kennedy had no questions for the witness.[lxxiv]

Meldon then called Constable Francis Eric Baker to the witness stand. Constable Baker repeated the story exactly as he had relayed it to Henderson and Campbell. Meldon however had a few more questions for Baker at the inquiry.

"Was Cumming on good terms with all the Police?"

"To my knowledge, yes."

"Do you know who shot Cumming, or Mrs. Walsh?"

"No."

"Do you suspect any specific person or persons of having shot either or both of them?"

"I have no reason to."

"What type of tram did you see Cumming in that night?"

"It was an open cross bench tram car."

"Can you tell me who this is?" said Meldon handing Baker the postcard with Eileen's photograph.

"I do not recognise the person in that photo."

"Let the record show," said Staines," that the witness is referring to Exhibit 16."

"No further questions," said Meldon, and Baker stood down from the witness box.[lxxv]

Eileen's brother, Frederick Claude Christie, was then called upon to give evidence. He repeated his statement about listening to the wireless at the home of Mr. Slaughter as previously given to detectives. Without further questions being asked he was allowed to step down.[lxxvi]

The next witness to be called was the gunsmith, Joseph Bauman, who stated he was an expert in firearms. Meldon handed him Stanley's pistol and he confirmed it was the pistol he had examined on Christmas Day at the instigation of C.I. Branch. He recalled the experiment he had conducted the next day which had confirmed for him that the shells found at the murder scene were not fired from that weapon.

"How many shots did you fire for your experiment?" asked Staines.

"Six."

"And none of those matched the shells found at the scene entered as Exhibit 2?"

"That is correct, the firing pin hits in a different position to what it did on the six shells I experimented with."

"Could we have those six shells admitted as evidence your Honour?" asked Meldon.

"Six shells discharged from pistol tendered, admitted, and marked as Exhibit 17," said Staines, "Did anyone supervise this experiment?"

"I made the test under the supervision of Sub-Inspector Meldon and other detectives."

"Did the bullets tell you anything?"

"I performed a microscopic examination of the bullets."

"Six bullets discharged experimentally from Exhibit 2 tendered, admitted, and marked as Exhibit 18," said Staines.

"What did you conclude?" asked Staines.

"That the bullet found at the scene," commenced Bauman.

"Exhibit 3," interrupted Staines for the benefit of the court reporter.

"When I compared Exhibit 3 with the six test fired bullets, tendered as Exhibit 18 I observed that Exhibit 3 had passed through a clean barrel, whereas Exhibit 18 showed signs of passing through a barrel which was rusty."

"How long have you been a gunsmith?" asked Mr. King.

"I have been in this work for thirty-three years, and I have frequently been called by the police to give evidence in higher courts."

"Did you experiment with both magazines that

accompanied Stanley Cumming's pistol?"

"I used both magazines in my experiments but they made no difference."[lxxvii]

The court fell silent.

"No further questions?" asked Staines.

"Your Honour," said Meldon, "if it pleases the court could we call for an adjournment till ten o'clock tomorrow morning?"

Staines granted the request.

19 INQUIRY RESUMES JUNE FIRST

On the morning of Wednesday the First of June 1927 the inquiry was reopened by Magistrate Staines. Mr. Kennedy, the solicitor of James Walsh advised the court that periodically he may be called away and asked the court to allow Walsh to represent himself at these times. Staines acknowledged the request to the extent that Walsh would be able to ask questions of the witnesses. The first witness for the day was Mr. Joseph Lionel Herbert the Managing Director of the Trocadero Dansant. He repeated his statement that he had previously given to Henderson and Campbell.

He again stated that when Mrs. Cumming had come to see him after an altercation at the Dance Hall the night before she had asked him what he thought of her husband to which Mr. Herbert stated that he replied 'I don't think I can help you in that'. He then again claimed that Mrs. Cumming said 'Don't you think he ought to be shot?' to which he had replied, 'I am not a judge, but don't you do it'.

"Do you recall when this occurred?" asked Mr. King.

"As far as I remember the argument between Cumming

and his wife at the Trocadero was about the end of 1924 or the beginning of 1925."

"You can't be more precise?"

"It was a special late night, but I cannot trace what date it was on."

"Could it have been New Year's Eve?"

"I cannot remember any special event whether it was New Year's Eve but it was in that vicinity."

"When Mrs. Cumming came to see you the next day, how was her demeanour?"

"She was very much distressed and very worried, she may have been in such a state that she would forget what she said when she spoke to me. On account of her state I did not treat anything that she said as serious."

"So you had a good study of her emotions that day?"

"I sized her up, yes, and her state that day proved to me that her life had not been a happy one."

Mr. Kennedy had no questions.

Meldon asked to approach the witness and handed him a photograph.

"Could you tell the court about this photograph," requested Meldon.

"This is a photograph of Acting Sergeant Cumming in uniform at the 'Phantom of the Opera' dance which was held on the 27th of May 1926."

"Was Cumming on duty that night?"

"I cannot say whether Cumming was on duty that night at the Trocadero or not."

"You stated that after the incident with Mrs. Cumming you requested the Senior Sergeant at South Brisbane not to send you him again for special duty at the Trocadero, yet here is a photograph of him in uniform, in the Trocadero!"

"Cumming used to come to the Trocadero in uniform when he was not on duty there, but on duty in Melbourne

Street."

"Did that happen often?"

"That was a frequent occurrence, not only by him, but by the majority of police there."

"The photo is very bright, what time was it taken?"

"The flashlight photograph would have been taken about nine forty-five pm."[lxxviii]

"I submit to the court the photograph of Cumming in uniform at the Trocadero taken on the 27th May 1926."

"Photograph tendered, admitted, and marked as Exhibit 19," said Staines.

The next witness was William Witt, the sixteen year old who lived with his parents in Annerley Road. He recounted how he knew Acting Sergeant Cumming and Mrs. Walsh and how he had seen Cumming on the night of his death. He stated that he heard two reports like shots on that night at about nine thirty. Neither Mr. King or Mr. Walsh had questions and he was allowed to step down from the witness box.[lxxix]

The next witness to be sworn under oath was James Jamieson of Annerley Road, South Brisbane. He recounted to the court the strange goings on he had witnessed on the night of the murders. He had seen two individuals who he considered to be men loitering outside his home that seemed to remain in the shadows until Cumming and Mrs. Walsh made their way down Annerley Road before turning off towards the laneway that leads to the Gaol.

"They were strangers to me but the way they were dressed they appeared to be men," stated Jamieson.

He then described their clothing and general appearance one taller than the other dressed in dark attire with felt hats. He described how their actions appeared suspicious so he watched them as Cumming, who he had known for over two years, made his way down the street with a woman he described as short, and stout, and appeared to be thick set.

Meldon badgered him with questions.

"Did you hear them speak?"

"I did not hear either of them speak."

"So how did you know they were men?"

"I took them to be two men by the way they dressed."

"At that time did you think they might have been women?"

"There was nothing to indicate to me then that either or both of them were not men."

"Would you recognize them again if you saw them?"

"I think I would recognize the taller of the two again if I saw him, I mean in similar circumstances, or if I saw him."

"Have you seen either of them since?"

"No, I have not."

"Please have a look at this and tell me if you recognize it," said Meldon passing Jamieson a portion of material that had been taken from Exhibit 15, Eileen's dress."

"That is similar to the dress of the woman that I saw with Cumming."

"Have a look at this hat," said Meldon holding Exhibit 7 Eileen's hat, "do you recognize the hat, was the woman you saw wearing this hat?"

"I don't know if she was wearing that hat."

"Would you take a look at James Samuel Walsh," said Meldon pointing at Walsh, "Did you see that man on the night?"

"He was not either of those two men that I saw that night."

"Would you now have a look at Marquis David James Stanley Cumming now in court," said Meldon pointing him out, "did you see him that night?"

"The taller of the men that I saw that night was similar in build to he, but I could not swear that he was one of the men or not."

"Would you also have a look at Mrs. Theresa Jane Cumming now in court," said Meldon, "do you know her?"

"This is the first time I have seen her."

"So you didn't see her that night?"

"I did not see her that night, but I could not say whether she was there that night or not."

"Why is that?"

"If a person like Mrs. Cumming was dressed in men's attire and see her in woman's attire you would hardly recognize her."

"So are you saying that it is possible that they were both there that night?"

"The man I saw that night was of the same build as witness Cumming, but for Mrs. Cumming I can't say anything respecting her regarding the two men that I had seen outside my place on the night of the 23rd December 1926."

"No further questions," said Meldon.

"May I?" asked Mr. King.

"Yes, your witness Mr. King," said Staines.

"When did you first see these two men?"

"It would be nine twenty-six or nine twenty seven when I first noticed them."

"Would you agree that young Cumming's build is a common build?"

"Yes, I would agree with that."

"Do you have any reason to doubt that young Cumming was then at that time in the Empire Theatre?"

"No."

"How precise do you think your estimation is of the height of these men you claim to have seen?"

"The height might be an inch one way or the other."

"Did you hear these men speak?"

"No, I did not hear them talking."

"What impression did you form on that evening of the gender of these two?"

"When I went into my house that night I formed the impression that they were men, they walked like men."

"And you say that you would recognize the taller of these two if you saw him again?"

"Yes I would know the taller man if I saw him again, that being the man about five foot nine inches."

"So you stated earlier that you could not swear that young Cumming was not one of the men you saw that night but you would know the taller man if you saw him again. So what is it? Did you see young Cumming on that night?"

"I meant that the taller I saw of the two that night corresponded to young Cumming, but it was not young Cumming."

"At that time you thought the shorter person was a man?"

"When I went to bed that night my firm impression was that the shorter of the two persons was a man, that being after the two beings had passed within two feet of me."

"Why did you stay in your garden watching them?"

"Their actions were suspicious and it attracted my attention."

"Do you know where the scene of the tragedy occurred?"

"Yes."

"And you believe it is possible that these two shot Acting Sergeant Cumming and Mrs. Walsh?"

"Yes, that is allowing for Mrs. Walsh and Cumming to

reach the spot and allowing time for the two persons to have reached the spot too."

"What would you say of the clothing of these two persons, were they of neat and tidy appearance?"

"They were well dressed."

"And their clothing fitted them?"

"Their clothes appeared to be fitting as far as I could tell."

"How close did Cumming and the woman come near you on the night?"

"The nearest they came to me was about fifteen yards away."

"Could you tell me please how you could see them? I mean, I am told that the sunset on that day at around quarter to seven, and the moon did not rise until ten o'clock that evening. If the moon had been out I could understand given it was only four days after a full moon, but it hadn't risen at the time you said you could see them, I don't think I could recognise someone from fifteen yards in the dark."

"They were walking under the electric light and I could see them."

"And the other two, how could you see them?"

"They were under an electric light."

"And how far is that electric light from your home?"

"About one hundred yards."

"Your honour," interrupted Meldon, "could we call for a recess please."

"Granted," said Staines, "Mr. King, would you like to continue speaking to this witness after the recess?"

"Yes your honour."

"We will take a recess of half an hour and thereafter the witness will be resworn under oath. Court dismissed."[lxxx]

*

After the recess James Jamieson was again sworn in so that Mr. King could continue his line of questions.

"Mr. Jamieson could you tell the court please how long you observed these two persons you saw on the night of the tragedy and why."

"I had the persons in my vision for fully ten minutes till they disappeared from my sight, I was interested in them for about ten minutes as I suspected something."

"And you had a good view of them?"

"I had a good view of the nearest one when he was standing within about two yards of me."

"Do you know Wilton Street at Woolloongabba?"

"No, not by that name."

"The lower end of Peterson Street, towards Ipswich Road?"

"If that is Wilton Street, then yes I know it."

"Which tram was it you caught home again that night?"

"The Dutton Park tram car."

"Did you go past the Gaol?"

"I passed the top end of the Gaol as I was walking down."

"And you noticed the two figures after you saw Cumming and a woman?"

"I noticed the two figures before I saw Cumming and the woman. Cumming and the woman passed the two figures, and they would then be about twelve yards from them when they passed."

"Where were the two figures again?"

"They were on the triangle, near the footpaths of two roads, and Cumming and the woman would have noticed the two figures under the electric light."

"So they would have seen them?"

"No they could not have seen them as they shifted out of the light when they saw Cumming and the woman coming."

"Please, I'm confused," said King, "who was under the light when?"

"I saw the figures shift from under the light before I saw Cumming and the woman come up the street, and I saw Cumming and the woman come up the street about three minutes afterwards."

"Did you hear them speak?"

"I did not hear anything said by the two figures that night."

"What time was this again?"

"After the two men had left and Cumming and the woman passed I went in and had a look at the time and it was then nine-forty."

"Was the time correct?"

"The clock was correct with my watch and about ten minutes afterwards I heard the shots fired, that being nine-fifty that I heard the shots."

"No further questions your honour," said Mr. King.

"Mr. Walsh I see Mr. Kennedy is absent again," said Staines, "do you have any questions for the witness?"

Walsh shook his head.

"Your honour," said Meldon, "if I may."

"Your witness Sub-Inspector."

"When did you consider that one of the two figures may have been a woman?"

"After the night of the 23rd when thinking things over I thought that it was possible that one of the two men that I had seen on the night of the 23rd December 1926 may have been a woman dressed as a man."

"When did you think this?"

"That occurred to me the next day that being after I

had heard of the tragedy."

"Why?" asked Meldon, "Why would you think that?"

"That only occurred to me by the walk of the shorter person of the two."

"Thank you Mr. Jamieson," said Meldon, "No further questions your honour."

"I have a question," responded Staines, "exactly how did you come to the conclusion that the shorter of the two may have been a woman?"

"It came into my mind the next day in the afternoon. I was walking along with my wife and she was taking short steps and I was in a hurry and she was lagging behind so I said to her 'You are lagging behind like the two last night' and then it came into my mind that the shorter one on the previous night might have been a woman."

"So it wasn't because someone suggested it to you?" queried Staines.

-o-

I assumed Staines was looking at Meldon when he asked this question. It appears that up to this point Jamieson had not mentioned that the second person he saw may have been a woman. Then Meldon calls for a recess and on resumption he quizzes Jamieson on this point. It struck me as odd that although Meldon had stated at the outset of the Inquiry that no one giving evidence was under suspicion, he appears to want to continue mounting suspicion on Mrs. Cumming.

*

"That was not a result of anyone suggesting it to me, it was just the manner of the walk of the shorter of the two on the previous night," continued Jamieson.

"When did you comment to your wife of this?" asked Mr. King.

"It was about three or four o'clock the next day, after I had heard of the shooting."

"Might it had been suggested to you when discussing the press reports?"

"I had heard about the tragedy at work but what suggested it to me was that the taller of the two was in front all the time. The matter of the shooting was not discussed at my work at our lunch hour that day. So far as I know it was not published in the paper, as I had not seen it in the paper at that time."[lxxxi]

Staines looked to the others to see if there were further questions. There being none he dismissed the witness and Meldon called Stanley Crane, the Master Painter from The Valley, to give evidence.

Stanley Crane repeated the evidence he had given the detectives. He was driving his motor vehicle down Annerley Road when a man ran across the road looking over his shoulder, with a shorter man watching the first from the right hand side near the railway bridge. He described the first man as about six foot tall with a slight build, sallow complexion, with three or four days growth on his face and about thirty five years old. The second man he described as five foot three inches, very clean shaven, and very slightly built so that his clothes looked to be much too large for him about thirty years old. He estimated the time to be about ten past nine. Mr. King then began to question him.

"Could this have been at about ten o'clock and not nine o'clock?"

"That is impossible!" said Crane.

"Would you appreciate the difference between five foot nine inches and six foot?"

"My business teaches me to be accurate with height and I am a good judge of height. I would not class a man of five foot nine as six feet, nor a man of five feet ten as six feet, but a man of five feet eleven I would say is about six feet."

"Would you mistake a man of five foot three as five six?"

"No I would not make that mistake."

Meldon walked over to the witness box and pointed at James Walsh.

"Is that the man you saw?"

"No," replied Crane.

"What about that man?" said Meldon, pointing to Stanley Cumming, "Is that the man?"

"No, that is not the man," replied Crane.

"Do you have any reason to doubt that the smaller man was a man?"

"No reason whatsoever."

"So nothing unusual came to mind with respect to the ill-fitting clothes of the second man," asked Staines.

"No, nothing unusual came to mind."[lxxxii]

Stanley Crane was then allowed to leave the witness box.

The next witness called was Leonard Jones the railway signalman. He stated that he was in the signal box at Park Road on the night of the tragedy some three hundred and fifty yards from where the bodies were found. He recounted how he had heard two sharp reports and then a duller one sometime between nine fifteen and ten o'clock. The first two shots were in quick succession with about a dozen seconds between the second and third shots.[lxxxiii]

There were no further questions and the police called for an adjournment to the next day.

*

The following morning Maud Crowley was called to the witness box and gave evidence that Stanley Cumming had purchased a cigar from her store on the night in question and was positive that the time was seven forty-five.

"Can you identify that young man in the court today?" asked Meldon.

She pointed at Stanley Cumming saying, "That is the young man that came into the shop, and broke the piece of string."

"When did you share this information?"

"A few days later I told Detective Henderson what I have told the Court this morning."[lxxxiv]

In view of the importance of the evidence given by Mrs. Christie, Mrs. Cumming was again called to the witness stand. She told the court that on Christmas afternoon she had gone to the funeral parlour to view the body of her husband, but when she got there she was told that the corpse of her husband had 'gone through a process' and she was advised not to see it. She then stated that she decided to call on Mrs. Christie to offer her sympathy on the death of her daughter. Meldon quizzed Mrs. Cumming on the evidence that Mary Christie had given attributing some unpleasant and suggestive remarks to her. Mrs. Cumming denied point blank the assertions.

"Then, according to you," said Meldon, "although you were the person that called on Mrs. Christie, you did none of the talking?"

"The conversation was not long," said Mrs. Cumming beginning to weep, "I'm not going to be condemned! They say if it was not through him she would never have been there, and I say if it was not through her, he would not have been there. I would like to say more, but I won't, I do not want to hurt anybody's feelings."

"Say all you want to say now," said Staines, "and never mind about hurting anybody's feelings. We don't want you to go away from the inquiry and tell people that you left anything unsaid through not having had a chance to say it."

"I say the ones who did it were callous to do what they did," said Mrs. Cumming still weeping, "I will say I do not believe that my husband was killed in the position he was found. I do not believe it. The bodies were put that way and the clothes were disarranged by the murderer. People who would shoot two people like that are inhuman."[lxxxv]

"Mr. Herbert states under oath that you said your husband ought to be shot," said Meldon.

"I've denied saying that before, and I deny it again!"

"Did you ever follow your husband?" continued Meldon.

"Yes, I did. I went to a house in Annerley Road after him, and I also went to the Trocadero."

"Do you actually want us to find your husband's killer?" asked Meldon.

"I hope you will discover the murderer and that they are brought to justice. It will be satisfactory to everybody."

"Mrs. Cumming," "said Staines, "could you remove your hat please."

Mrs. Cumming complied and revealed her hair was cut short.

"How long has your hair been cut short?"

"I had it done about a year ago."

"What colour is that?"

"My hair is brown, slightly tinged with grey."

Staines then directed the clerk of the court to measure Mrs. Cumming's height, this was done and the disposition recorded her height as five foot seven and a half inches. Her weight was given as eleven stone three pounds.

"Mrs. Cumming," said Meldon, "could you have a look at this photograph for me. Let the record show your honour that I have handed Mrs. Cumming Exhibit 19.

What do you think your husband is doing at the time the photograph was taken?"

"From my husband's position in that photo I would say that he is trying to keep the crowd back, and he told me that. I have a photo at home similar to that one, but this is not the identical photo as I have mine at home."[lxxxvi]

"No further questions your honour," said Meldon.

"We will adjourn this inquiry for one week from today and reconvene here on the Ninth of June, 1927. Court dismissed."

20 INQUIRY RESUMES JUNE NINTH

A week later, on the morning of Thursday the Ninth of June 1927, the inquiry was reopened by Magistrate Staines. The first witness called for the day was Mrs. Fanny Louisa Howden, widow, and mother of Mrs. Cumming. She was enfeebled by her advanced age and had much difficulty in standing up while taking the oath but she read the formula deliberately and painstakingly.

Under questioning by Meldon she revealed she lived in Jane Street, Fortitude Valley, but at the time of the tragedy she resided at Mrs. Gregory's place in Constance Street of the same suburb. Her daughter was married to Acting-Sergeant Cumming.

"Do you remember the night of December twenty-third?" asked Meldon.

"Yes, my daughter came to see me that night and arrived between seven and eight o'clock."

"Can you fix the time definitely?"

"To the best of my belief that is the time she came."

"May it have been seven-thirty?"

"No, no, not as late as that, only a few minutes after seven. Mrs. Gregory's clock was striking the hour and my daughter arrived a few minutes after that."

Mrs. Howden continued stating that Mrs. Cumming stayed with her for a couple of hours discussing Christmas festivities and presents she had bought that day and how the children would be sent to see her the next day to take her to the stores in the Valley. It was getting on to ten o'clock when her daughter left.

"Are you guessing the time?" asked Meldon.

"Oh no Dear, we had a clock in the house."

"Can you say what time then?"

"My memory is getting faulty, I am seventy-six years old Dear."

"She is eighty-six your Worship!" called out Mrs. Cumming.

"Just a moment," said Mr. Staines.

"Tell them when you came to Queensland Mother," said Mrs. Cumming.

"We came to Queensland in 1861 and I was 20 years old."

"That would make you eighty-six then Mrs. Howden," said Staines.

"Gracious!" said Mrs. Howden.

"If I may continue your Honour," said Meldon, not waiting for a response before continuing his questioning of Mrs. Howden, "Can you say exactly what time Mrs. Cumming left?"

"I could not, because I didn't look at the clock. That is my judgement, that it was approaching ten o'clock."

"Do you remember Detective Henderson?" asked Meldon motioning for Henderson to stand.

"I remember him coming to see me a few days after December Twenty-Third. He had a conversation with me about my daughter being at my place."

"Do you recall telling Detective Henderson that your

daughter left your place about nine or a little after nine?"

"I have no recollection of saying that it was about nine o'clock. What brings it to mind so clearly is that I told her to get away before Beirne's lights go out and that goes out at ten."

"You may have told him that it was nine o'clock?"

"I do not think that I told Detective Henderson it was nine o'clock as Beirne's lights is what I was going on."[lxxxvii]

"Did your daughter at any time tell you that she was unhappy with her husband or that she had any trouble with him?"

"She never told me about her troubles. When I visited them he treated me respectfully. I have nothing to say against the man at all."

"Was your daughter unhappy?"

"I could not tell you, they didn't tell me about it if they had a tiff. I never knew if they had any."

"Was Mrs. Cumming alone when she came to see you?"

"Yes."

"Was there anyone else in the house?"

"I could not say whether there was or not."

"No further questions," said Meldon.

Mrs. Howden stepped down from the witness box, faced the Bench, and curtseyed, and said, "Good Morning Gentleman."

Mrs. Cumming had been gazing moodily at the floor during the majority of her mother's testimony and now assisted the elderly woman to leave the court room. Mrs. Cumming would not return that day.[lxxxviii]

Next to be called to the stand was Francis Waygood the motor-man of the Tramways Service from Tottenham Street that fixed the time of the shootings as nine-fifteen on the night of the twenty-third. He again stated that he heard three automatic pistol shots, two fired rapidly, and one after an interval of less than a minute.

Next was Senior Sergeant Caulfield of South Brisbane Police Station to recount the movements of the Acting-Sergeant earlier on during his shift that evening. He was followed by Walter Hawgood the pawnbroker that retold his story of having sold an automatic pistol on the afternoon of the shootings. Meldon questioned the young man about the appearance of the 'bushy type' that had made the purchase.

"Describe his clothes," ordered Meldon.

"He was wearing a serge suit," said Hawgood.

"What colour," urged Meldon.

"Oh, a dirty black one," said Hawgood, "just like yours!"

"Very complimentary," murmured the Sub-Inspector.[lxxxix]

Hawgood's evidence was followed by that of Frederick Slaughter to verify the whereabouts of Eileen's brother Frederick Christie on the night in question and he told the bench he was quite certain of the date that Frederick Christie was at his home to listen to the wireless.[xc]

Miss Josephine Clutterbuck was then called to the stand. She relayed to the Court how she had accompanied Stanley Cumming to the 'Empire Theatre' that evening. When she told the court how she had kept the ticket butts and handed them to Detective Campbell, Meldon asked her to have a look at two ticket butts.

"I can't be sure of the colour of those tickets," she said.

"Take a closer look," asked Meldon.

"They are dress circle tickets, for Row A, seats fifty-eight and fifty-nine. I notice the date printed on them is the 23rd December."

"But they're not the right colour?" quizzed Meldon.

"I don't recollect the colour."

"Can you identify those as the tickets that you handed to Detective Campbell?"

"No I can't."

"So these are not the tickets that you handed to Detective Campbell, that you claim places you and Stanley at the 'Empire Theatre' on that evening."

"I have no reason to doubt those are the tickets, I just don't recollect the colour."

"I submit to the court tickets to the 'Empire Theatre' dated 23rd December 1926," said Meldon, slapping them on the bench out of frustration.

"Ticket Butts tendered, admitted, and marked as Exhibit 20," said Staines.[xci]

Miss Clutterbuck continued to tell the court that after the theatre, Stanley and herself, had made their way back to Melican's Boarding House and parted ways shortly before eleven forty-five as that was the time on the clock in her room when she got inside. The girl chanced a quick glance and smile at Stanley across the court room. She went on to tell the court that she next met Stanley outside the C.I.B. office on the following Sunday night at about ten o'clock, when she went there in company with Stanley's uncle.

"Did Stanley tell you anything in connection with the tragedy?" asked Meldon.

"No, nothing at all."

"But he must have told you something!"

"He just said 'We have lost the whole support of our family. It is a terrible blow to mother and the family' that was all."

"Are you absolutely sure," said Meldon, "that Stanley Cumming was not out of your company from seven forty-five until eleven forty-five on the night of the 23rd of December."

"Quite certain."

"For a period whatever?" "No."

"They were both lucky they kept the tickets!" said Mr. King.[xcii]

Meldon called his next witness, Detective Acting-Sergeant Henderson.

Under oath Henderson stated that he knew Marquis Cumming but not Eileen Gladys Walsh. On the morning of Friday, 24th December 1926 he arrived at C.I. Branch about 9 a.m. and was informed that deceased Cumming and a woman had been found in a Railway reserve between Park Road and Dutton Park Railway Stations, shot dead. He then proceeded to the scene of the murder in company with Sub-Inspector Meldon where he saw the bodies of the deceased persons exactly as described by Acting Sergeant Bonas in his evidence. He made an examination of the bodies and also the spot where they were lying and the surrounding ground. There were a number of other detectives and the black tracker, George Munro, and a search, under supervision, was made for tracks. There were no tracks discernible as the ground is very hard, stony, bare and dry. No tracks were found that would indicate how the deceased had entered the reserve, nor who would have had any connection with the dead bodies. There was no sign of a struggle. A search was also made for the belt, handcuffs and keys over a large area surrounding the scene of the murder. For several weeks the search continued but up to date no trace of either of the articles missing had been found.

Detective Henderson also described in detail how he had been involved in digging up the ground underneath the head of the body to trace the bullet that passed through Walsh's head. He described how he had visited the house of the deceased Walsh after viewing the bodies and made a search of that location before informing the family of the death of Eileen Walsh. Based on certain information that he had been furnished with by the family, inquiries were made to locate her husband, James Samuel Walsh. About mid-day that day he was found at the Labour Bureau and taken to C.I. Branch where he was closely interrogated by him up till about midnight on that date.

"I heard his evidence given in this court and that was substantially what he told me on the night."

He was positively identified that night by witnesses that placed him at Wynnum the previous evening. He recounted what Walsh had said at the Morgue on the viewing of his wife. He stated he saw witnesses Stanley Cumming and his mother Mrs. Cumming at C.I. Branch that afternoon but had no conversation with them as they were being interrogated by Detective Campbell.[xciii]

He stated that on the next day he and Detective Campbell set out to locate the woman which had been mentioned as accompanying Marquis Cumming to the Picture Show. They managed to achieve this and interrogated her and took a statement from her that on numerous times she had had sexual intercourse with Cumming at an allotment about a hundred yards from the scene of the tragedy. The last occasion had been the night of the 21st December, two nights before the murders. Henderson then described the ritual as relayed to him that Cumming and the woman employed for their trysts. Cumming would remove his belt with the handcuffs and keys on it and place them aside.

He told the court how this woman had told him that on the occasion that Stanley Cumming followed her that he had said, 'My father is no damn good. He has been causing a lot of trouble at home. A man ought to bloody well do time for it!' He described how they had made inquiries of her husband and found that he had been out of Queensland on that date and had not been back since.

He told the court that a woman at Mount Morgan, also the recipient of attention from detectives, had admitted to being the writer of a letter found by Mrs. Cumming and as being the mother of Cumming's illegitimate child.

"You mean this letter," said Meldon.

"Yes she admitted to writing the original of that letter."

"Let the record show that Detective Henderson is referring to Exhibit 8," said Staines.

"She was thoroughly interrogated," said Henderson, "and admitted having written the letter found by Cumming's wife. She said she had been interviewed by Cumming's son and that she had made a statement to him."

-o-

It appeared as though my earlier assumption that Mrs. Cumming may have falsified this letter was incorrect. My concerns about the tone of the letter when compared with the others still held.

*

"And these letters," said Meldon, "previously admitted as Exhibits 9, 10, and 11."

"She handed those letters to the investigating detective having received them from the deceased Cumming. In that statement she also stated that she received a letter that stated not to be surprised if something happens to him and if it did it would be his wife or his son that would do it."

"Do you have that letter?" asked Staines.

"No your honour she didn't have that letter she had destroyed it."

Henderson went on to state that inquiries were made

about the whereabouts of her husband and it was found to be impossible for him to be in Brisbane and as far as could be ascertained she had no other male relatives that would be interested in anything going on between Cumming and her. And that she had no grown up sons and no other admirers were known of.[xciv]

Staines called for adjournment till ten o'clock the next morning.

*

The next morning Henderson returned to the stand and recommenced presenting the details taken from the woman in Mount Morgan.

"In her statement she detailed a number of instances in which she had met Cumming away from her own house and she described what took place on one occasion that deceased Cumming turned her clothes up over her waist, pulled her bloomers right off, undid the front of his trousers and underpants and pulled them below his knees.

From that I would take it that he would be then in the same condition or somewhat similar condition with regard his clothing as the condition in which the clothing of the two deceased when they were found. She also stated in her statement that on one occasion when she was out with deceased Cumming he said to her 'It is always better for a man and a woman when they are having connection to get out in an open paddock so that they could see anybody that would be likely to come on them with surprise and a man could then put up a fight'. I would consider that would account for the two deceased being found on a vacant piece of ground. It was shown that that would be his procedure it being an open space. To my mind it would dispel the idea of the bodies being placed there as suggested by Mrs. Cumming in her evidence and also about her evidence in which she said she believed that the clothes were placed in that condition by someone after the tragedy and before the bodies were found. The evidence of Dr. Dodd, Government Medical Officer, also goes to show that the bodies had not been removed after the tragedy. This also confirms me in my opinion."[xcv]

"This woman also stated in her statement that she received several letters from deceased Cumming in which he complained bitterly about the treatment he was receiving at home from his wife and his son Stanley and that they had frequently threatened to shoot him and that when he was on his holidays, which included June 1925, he told this woman not to be surprised if he was shot, it would be in the dark and it would be one of them, by which she said he was meaning either his wife or his son."[xcvi]

"In her statement she also stated that deceased Cumming told her that they were giving him hell at home over this woman, meaning herself, that his son, the witness Stanley Cumming, had picked the lock of his box and found one of the letters which she had written to him. He told her that he always carried his keys with him and since they had picked the lock he had shifted all her letters to the South Brisbane Police Station and put them in his locker there. The letters from the woman were found in his locker at the South Brisbane Police Station. None of her letters were found in the tin trunk belonging to the deceased Cumming which he kept locked at home. Other letters from various other woman were also found in his locker at South Brisbane Police Station. The letters were taken possession of from the locker by Detective Campbell and I saw them the same day Detective Campbell took them from the locker. This woman also stated that deceased Cumming had told her that his wife and son had two revolvers and she disclosed that she had a passionate love for him and went so far as to say she would have left her husband and gone with him only for the position that he was in."[xcvii]

Henderson then relayed the interrogation of Miss Josephine Clutterbuck and confirmed that her testimony at the inquiry was substantially as she had stated to him at the time. That he had been in the boarding house when she and Detective Campbell had called out to him that she had found the ticket butts in her handbag.

"I have not ascertained anything she has told me to be incorrect. Several of the material things she told me have been corroborated by other people and by other circumstances."

He then recounted how he and Detective Campbell had visited the Cumming home to ask for them to come to C.I. Branch to assist in inquiries and told the court of the hostile attitude they appeared to have taken on the basis of advice given to them by their solicitor at the time, McGrath Junior. Eventually, acting on the advice of another solicitor, Mrs. Cumming did present herself and a very lengthy statement was obtained over four days of interrogation.

"It was also ascertained that he was in intimate relationships with quite a number of other woman in Mount Morgan and South Brisbane. A number of these women were married. Some were single. Inquiries have been made regarding those people, their whereabouts on the night of the murder and their movements have been verified, also the movements of the interested parties."[xcviii]

"A Christmas Card was received by post at South Brisbane Station on the 24th December 1926, having a postmark 'Brisbane, 23rd December 1926' and on it was printed a small verse and underneath the printed word 'from', there was written the word 'Eileen'. That writing was identified as that of the deceased Walsh by her husband and also her mother. That was the only thing denoting any affection between the two deceased prior to the tragedy that was found. No other letters were found either from or to either of the deceased, from either of them. As far as could be ascertained by inquiries of recent years nothing could be found of any immoral relationship between deceased Walsh and anybody else."[xcix]

-o-

The detectives refer to the Christmas card as implying a relationship between Eileen and Cumming. Mrs. Christie though, under oath stated that there were some similarities in the hand writing but also stated that there were some differences. The Christmas Card was not entered into evidence.

*

"We have heard evidence about the time of the shooting that is contradictory," said Mr. King, "what have you surmised from that evidence?"

"From my inquiries I would say that the tragedy occurred sometime between nine fifteen and nine forty on the evening of the 23rd December 1926. I pay serious attention to Jamieson's evidence. I think he is a sound man as an accurate witness."

There being no further questions, Staines allowed the witness to leave the stand.

The next witness was Robert Adamson and he confirmed that on the night in question he met Miss Clutterbuck by chance and as he spoke to her a young man came up to them from the direction of Costa's Cigar Store and was lighting a cigar.

"Is that man in the court today?" asked Meldon.

"Yes," said Adamson pointing at Stanley Cumming, "That is the man I saw. That is the young man that joined Miss Clutterbuck."[c]

The next witness called to the stand was Robert Carius the Yellow Cab Company taxi driver that picked up a fare on the running board as he took a ship's officer, dressed in uniform, to Musgrave Wharf.

"Was that the man you saw?" said Meldon, pointing to Stanley Cumming.

"He was about his build, but it was in the dark, I cannot say."

"Was it him or not!" demanded Meldon.

"I couldn't identify this man."

"Are you positive!"

"I don't know this man."[ci]

Detective Kenneth Campbell was then called to the witness box to give evidence. He commenced by describing the scene of the tragedy and his role in searching in the vicinity of the crime scene for the missing items and a possible murder weapon without success. He then commenced to recount the episode that occurred at the Morgue.

"At about three p.m. on the same date I saw the witness Theresa Jane Cumming and also witness Marquis David James Stanley Cumming. I took them to the morgue. I showed Mrs. Cumming the bodies of the two deceased. On the way to the morgue Mrs. Cumming said 'It is terrible. I have often warned him that he would meet with a sudden end but he would take no notice of me'. On arrival at the morgue when Mrs. Cumming saw the body of her deceased husband she said 'Oh daddy, oh daddy I knew it would come to this. I have warned you that you would meet a terrible end'. She kissed him on the forehead several times and said 'Daddy God forgive you'. She then asked

'Where is the woman!' I uncovered deceased Walsh's face. Mrs. Cumming looked at her and she said to her son who was standing on the opposite side of the morgue table 'That is not the woman he was with at the pictures, she is too stout' and Stanley said 'The other woman was thinner'. She then turned to her husband's body and she said 'Where was he shot?' and I said 'In the back of the head' and pointed to the wound at the back of deceased Cumming's head. Mrs. Cumming did not look at the wound. She said 'It is the woman's fault. I hate all woman'. She then again kissed her husband on the forehead and said 'Daddy God forgive you'. Turning to the deceased Walsh's body she said 'As for you, I will say nothing'."[cii]

"Constable Cook and myself then returned to C.I. Branch with Mrs. Cumming and Stanley. She said 'There has been a lot of trouble between my husband and I, he would never take me out. He always used to go out on his own. I caught him coming out of a picture show in Queen Street with a woman named Mrs. Page'."

Campbell then related the story that Mrs. Cumming had told him in regards to the confrontation with Mrs. Page.

"I then interrogated Stanley and he told me substantially his movements on that night as what he gave here in evidence. I then asked him if there were any firearms at home and he replied 'Yes. My father had a revolver and I have an automatic'. I then accompanied them in a motor car to their home where I took possession of a revolver and automatic pistol, submitted here already as Exhibits 12 and 13. I also took possession of a tin trunk from the room occupied by deceased Cumming. I took the trunk to C.I. Branch. It was locked. There was no key. I forced the lock. The trunk contained wearing apparel and private papers and bank slips for fixed deposits. There were no compromising letters in the trunk. I also examined Cumming's locker at South Brisbane Police Station. That was also locked. I sprung the lock. In there I found a quantity of letters and Christmas Cards, and a pair of woman's bloomers. I later showed those bloomers to Mrs. Cumming and she said they didn't belong to her. I never found out who they belonged to."

Campbell then recalled the hostile position that Mrs. Cumming and Stanley had taken in relation to the police request that they provide a statement.

"Mrs. Cumming said that she thought 'someone in the underworld was responsible for the murder of her husband, that all policeman have enemies, that her husband never stayed out late at night and he always gave her all his money'. Further she stated that 'it is no good the police coming here', 'I am sick of the police coming here', 'It was not done by anyone in this house; it was from the other side', 'he has got his just desserts and I will say no more'."

Mr. Delaney, of Delaney and King Solicitors, was there that day acting on behalf of Mrs. Cumming and Stanley. He had been awaiting the opportunity to question Campbell.

"Up until the 28th December 1926 had Mrs. Cumming given every assistance to the Police?"

"Yes."

"There was no, hostility, as you call it, shown up to that time?"

"Correct."

"When was she first taken to C.I. Branch?"

"She attended on the 24th December."

"Was that the only occasion she was asked to attend, before the 28th?"

"Correct, that was the only day she was asked to attend."

"How long did you keep her there, on the 24th?"

"For about half an hour, but she was under interrogation only for about ten to fifteen minutes."

"Why was that?"

"We could not interrogate her properly on that date because she was weeping at intervals."

"Did you tell anyone else about the conversation you alleged passed between you at the morgue?"

"I told the Sub-Inspector the whole of the conversation that passed between us."

"How would you describe her emotions during the period at the morgue."

"She was in great distress."

"And the information she provided you on the 24th what have you made of those?"

"The statements she made at the C.I. Branch on the 24th have been inquired into and as far as can be ascertained it has been found to be correct."

"Prior to Mrs. Cumming's visit to the morgue had she been told of the circumstances under which the bodies were found?"

"I do not know."

"Up to that time had she been informed that two bodies had been found?"

"I cannot say."

"Do you know what, if anything, the police that visited her prior to her going to the morgue had said?"

"I don't know what she was told."

"And Stanley's statement of the 24th December what did they tell you?"

"Those statements were also tested so far as we considered necessary and as far as we could ascertain the statements that he made were correct."

"Thank you Detective Campbell," said Delaney, "no further questions your honour."

"May I," requested Meldon, before preceding impatiently with his question.

"Did you hear Mrs. Cumming in this Inquiry Court say that she couldn't remember whether she had made certain statements to Detective Henderson or not?"

"Yes."

"Were you also present when evidence was given that she said she was told by Detective Corbett that her husband was found shot with a woman at the back of Boggo Road Gaol."

"So according to that she would know prior to my interview with her that her husband was found shot with a woman. Furthermore on the way to the Morgue Mrs. Cumming told me, without my asking her at all, that she had warned him that he would come to a sudden end."[ciii]

"And you hadn't told her of the circumstances under which her husband was found at that time?"

"That is correct."

Staines looked around the court for a few seconds waiting for further questions. When none were forth coming he adjourned the inquiry till Tuesday the 14th June, 1927.

21 INQUIRY RESUMES JUNE FOURTEENTH

On the morning of Tuesday 14th June 1927 the inquiry was reopened by Magistrate Staines. The first witness called for the day was Gerald McGrath, Articled Law Clerk to James McGrath, Solicitor of Adelaide Street. He was an oval faced young man of slight build, sporting a bowtie and pencil moustache.

As soon as the Law Clerk's name was called out as appearing before the court that day he said he was not compelled to go into the witness-box, and therefore would not do so.

"I do not understand you," said Mr. Staines.

"I have received a subpoena, but I refuse to go into the box!"

"I think you will agree with me that a witness can be called upon to give evidence in any court," responded Staines.

"I plead the privilege between a solicitor and his client!"

"You are not in the nature of a person who may be suspected of a crime, and so far may refuse to go into the box. You only take the question of privilege when you get there and questions are asked."

"I have not been called upon yet?"

"I will call upon you," said Meldon, "I cannot understand why Mr. McGrath has taken up this attitude."

"Mr. McGrath is entitled to plead privilege," said Staines, "if it applies to the questions put by the Sub-Inspector."

"I call on him at this stage," said Meldon very annoyed, "I have no desire to prolong this expensive inquiry. The questions I want to put to him are very simple."

"Quite right," agreed Staines.

"I call on him in the interest of justice," said Meldon.

Gerald McGrath was sworn in and entered the witness box then gave his full name, occupation and address. Meldon then pointed at Mrs. Cumming and asked, "Do you know that woman?"

"I know her professionally. I also know her son Marquis David James Stanley Cumming professionally."

"Did the witness Theresa Jane Cumming call on you professionally after the 23rd December 1926?"

"I refuse to answer that question on the ground that it is privilege as between Solicitor and Client not to disclose any communications or matters that take place between Solicitor and Client and that I am only an Article Clerk to my principal."

"Was the witness, Theresa Jane Cumming a client of your firm at any period since the 23rd December 1926?"

"I refuse to answer the question on the same grounds. I cannot divulge office secrets or anything that took place between solicitor and client."

"Is any interview, apart from what took place, privileged?" asked Staines.

"Between office and client, yes," replied McGrath.

"But an interview is not privileged!"

"I am an articled clerk bound to my principal and I bind myself not to discuss any office business. All article clerks are bound in the same way."

"In office secrets but not office business?" asked Staines.

"Yes I submit it is your Worship."

"Apart from what takes place?"

"Yes."

"If W.J. McGrath Senior came here would he be privileged to refuse to answer?

"Yes, I certainly think that he would."

"You are no more privileged than W.J. McGrath!"

"I think so. I have spoken to Mr. McGrath and he has informed me that it is office business."

"The mere fact of them coming to the office apart from an interview?"

"Yes."

"I am unable to agree with you," said Staines, "although I do think that certain parts of the interview would come under the heading of privilege."

"I ask the bench to consider the matter in light of my being purely an articled clerk working for a principal, Mr. McGrath said I could not disclose the fact that anyone came to his office at all."

"I would like to ask this question," said Meldon, "and get his answer, and I want to follow with another question, I do not care what his answer, but I want to get it done!"

"Did Mrs. Cumming call on you professionally after the 23rd of December?"

"You mean did she call at the office?"

"I don't care whether it was at the office!"

"I refuse to answer that question on the ground that it is privilege as between Solicitor and Client not to disclose any communications or matters that take place between Solicitor and Client and that I am only an Article Clerk to my principal."

"Was Mrs. Cumming a client of your firm at any period since December 23rd?"

"I refuse to answer, on the same grounds."

"Did you advise Mrs. Cumming since that date," started Meldon.

"I refuse to answer that question …"

"I have not finished yet," interrupted Meldon, "did you advise the witness Mrs. Cumming since 23rd December 1926 not to answer any questions put to her by the Police in connection with the murders of Marquis Cumming and Eileen Gladys Walsh?

"I refuse to answer that question on the same grounds."

"Did you advise the witness Marquis David James Stanley Cumming since 23rd December 1926 not to answer any questions put to him by the Police respecting the murders of Marquis Cumming and Eileen Gladys Walsh?"

"I refuse to answer that question on the same grounds."

"Did you tell Detective Henderson at the C.I. Branch since 23rd December 1926 that you did not advise Mrs. Cumming to refuse to answer questions in connection with the investigation of the murders of Marquis Cumming and Eileen Gladys Walsh?"

"No, as I was not asked that question?"

"Did you call at C.I. Branch after 23rd December 1926 for the purpose of getting possession of certain documents, the property of deceased Cumming?"

"I called at the C.I. Branch for the purpose of getting particulars of certain documents or any documents belonging to the deceased Marquis Cumming."

"Was that regarding documents taken possession of by the Police?"

"Yes."

"Did Detective Henderson ask you any questions regarding Mrs. Cumming having told him that she would not answer any questions because you advised her not to do so?"

"To my knowledge, on the day I saw Mr. Henderson he did not ask me any questions concerning Mrs. Cumming. The questions Mr. Henderson asked me were concerning witness Marquis David James Stanley Cumming."

"What were the questions that he asked you concerning witness Marquis David James Stanley Cumming?"

"Whether I had advised Stanley Cumming not to make a statement to the Police."

"What did you tell Detective Henderson?"

"I refuse to answer that question, wait, no, I can answer that question. I did tell Mr. Henderson that I did not advise Stanley Cumming to that effect."

"Was that correct?"

"Yes."

"Did you see witness Stanley Cumming and his mother Mrs. Cumming since 23rd December 1926?

"I have seen them several times together in the street and about the Supreme Court."

"Alright Mr. McGrath!" said the Sub-Inspector, "Did you see them professionally together!"

"I refuse to answer."

"Do you refuse to answer whether Mrs. Cumming and her son Stanley called on you professionally after 23rd December 1926."

"I haven't been asked that question yet."

"I am asking that question now. You are intent on

wasting a lot of time!"

"I am not."

"He is entitled," said Staines, "to refuse to answer on the grounds of privilege if his contention is bona-fide."

"Yes, IF it is," said Meldon sarcastically, "I have put the question and you are not going to tell me how to put it. You are here to abide by what his Worship directs!"

"Answer 'Yes' or 'No'," said Staines, "You have been asked. Do you refuse?"

"I am not trying to waste the time of the court."

"If there is privilege you are entitled to bring it forward, no matter what anybody says," said Staines.

"I refuse to answer the question as it had not yet been put to me."

"And I have ruled that it has been put in the form asked by Sub-Inspector Meldon."

"Then I refuse to answer it."

"That is not the answer!" bellowed Meldon, "There is no answer to my question. Witness has not said 'Yes' or 'No'."

"He takes up the ground of privilege," said Staines, "I will have to decide whether he will have to answer it or not, in other words, whether he carries his professional capacity wherever he goes. Is that the substance of your answer Mr, McGrath?"

"It is not!" interceded Meldon.

"You say that I go professionally anywhere. That is not correct."

"I thought that was the attitude you took up," said Staines, "You may refuse to be interviewed outside your office."

"I insist on an answer to the question, 'Yes' or 'No'," requested Meldon.

"I am afraid I cannot at this stage," said Staines.

"What?" said Meldon, "as to whether to refuse to answer a question! He is not committing a breach of etiquette at all. I am not asking anything between solicitor and client. I am asking whether he refuses to say whether they called on him in a professional capacity."

"That is the question of privilege," replied Staines.

"Then I call for a ruling on that question here and now!" said Meldon.

"A decision cannot be given at this juncture," responded Staines.

"If it is a question of privilege not to answer," said Mr. King, "then the magistrate needs to decide. McGrath could go on refusing to answer questions."

"Did you tell Detective Henderson at the C.I.B. since the date of the murder that you did not advise Mrs. Cumming to refuse to answer questions?"

"I was never asked that question."

"Yes or NO," bellowed Meldon losing his patience.

"I was never asked that question."

"Did Detective Henderson ask you any questions regarding Mrs. Cumming having told him that she would not answer any inquiries because you had advised her not to do so?"

"To my knowledge," said McGrath hesitantly, "on the day I saw Mr. Henderson he did not ask me any questions about Mrs. Cumming. I can easily clear this matter up," he said addressing Staines, "The question asked of me had been about the son Stanley Cumming."

"I wish he would give his answer to the questions," said Meldon.

"I wanted to save time," replied McGrath.

"You are not saving time!" snapped Meldon.

"The question he asked me was about her son Stanley."

"Is that your answer?"

"Yes."

"You told us now that you did not advise the witness Stanley Cumming to the effect, 'That I did not advise Stanley Cumming not to make a statement to the Police'."

"No I told Detective Henderson 'To the best of my knowledge' I did not tell Detective Henderson that I advised Stanley Cumming not to make a statement to the Police."

"To the best of your knowledge!" stated Staines, "You won't go further than that?"

"I can't, your Worship."

"Is that a qualification?" quizzed Meldon, "It makes it just the opposite now! I understood from you that you told Detective Henderson that you did not advise Stanley not to make a statement!"

"Not that way," said McGrath, "I didn't tell…"

"Not to make a statement?" quizzed Staines.

"Is that correct?" said Meldon, "That contradicts. What did you tell Detective Henderson!"

"I told him that I did not advise Stanley Cumming not to make a statement to the Police."

"Did you tell him that in response to a question put by him?"

"Yes."

"Did Detective Henderson ask you if you had advised the witness Mrs. Cumming not to answer questions or make a statement to the Police respecting the murders of deceased Cumming and Walsh?"

"Detective Henderson never asked me that question."

"Did you call at C.I. Branch on or about the 29th December 1926 and ask for Detective Henderson at the counter?"

"To the best of my knowledge I asked for Detective Meldon on the day I called, and on that day I saw you."

"Did you see Detective Henderson before you saw me?"

"I did."

"Did you say to Detective Henderson I am acting for Mrs. Cumming and her son. I want to see some documents taken possession of by your men from her house on the 24th of this month?"

"I think I did."

"Did Detective Henderson say 'She told me you are acting for her and that you had advised her and her son not to answer any questions to any of the Police'. Did you do that?"

"I am compelled to answer Yes and No."

"Well, answer it fully!"

"Detective Henderson did tell me that Mrs. Cumming had told him that I was acting for her. He then asked me if I had advised Stanley Cumming not to make a statement to the Police."

"What did you say?"

"I have already answered that question. I told him that I did not advise Stanley Cumming not to make a statement to the Police."

"Did the Detective say to you, 'She, (Mrs. Cumming) told me you were acting for her and that you had advised her not to answer and questions put to her by the police'?"

"He did not ask me that question."

"Did you reply, 'Certainly not, I wouldn't do that!'"

"I did not."

"Did Detective Henderson say to you, 'You will have to see Sub-Inspector Meldon about the documents'? And did he take you into my office, show you I mean, not take?"

"Yes."

"You saw me there?"

"That is so."

"Did I ask you if you had advised Mrs. Cumming and her son not to answer any questions put to her by the detectives or make a statement?"

"No."

"And did you tell me you did not?"

"As to going to your office with Henderson, he went into the room, and approximately five seconds later he beckoned to me from your office to come in. I was standing in an adjoining room and could see Mr. Henderson from where I was standing."

"What about it?"

"You asked me did Henderson take me in!"

"It was quite clear, and you are very, very technical Mr. McGrath!"

"Pardon me, Mr. Meldon."

"Please answer the question!"

"No."

"So you will not answer the question?"

"No, my answer is no."

"In your interview with me there was only the two of us there?"

"I think so. I think Mr. Henderson went out just after I came in."

"Do you deny I asked you anything about you having advised Mrs. Cumming and her son not to make a statement to the Detectives or answer any questions regarding the murders?"

"Yes."

"And if I go into that witness box and swear that I did I am lying?" said Meldon slightly exasperated.

"Either that or your memory is tricking you."

"And the same applies to Detective Henderson that if he swears in the box that you told him that you did not advise Mrs. Cumming not to make a statement or answer any questions respecting the murders?"[civ]

"The same would apply to that question but he did ask me concerning the son, so, yes, either he is lying or his memory is tricking him."

"He is lying or his memory is tricking him!" Meldon shook his head then continued with his questions, "Did you know that prior to this interview with the detectives at C.I.B. office that he and Detective Campbell made inquiries at your father's office concerning Mrs. Cumming and her son having been there?"

"Yes."

"Do you know that your father told them that there was no record in the books of the Cummings as clients?"

"No, I didn't know."

"Had you heard it?"

"No."

"Would you be surprised to know that your father had told the detectives that?"

"Very much so."

"Would you be surprised to know that when Mrs. Cumming refused on December 28th to make a statement or answer questions, that she had her solicitor's advice, that I instructed two detectives to interview the solicitors, whose name was given as McGrath?"

McGrath was silent for a period of time before he responded.

"I don't know what it has got to do with it. I have nothing to do with those instructions."

"I know that. Have you any reason to doubt that I gave those instructions?"

"Oh, no, not at all!"

"I don't suppose, Mr. McGrath, you know of any reason why I insist, and am prepared to substantiate under oath, that you did tell me that you did not advise Mrs. Cumming and her son not to answer questions or make a statement to the Detectives? If you didn't tell me."

"I don't know of any personal reason. I don't know of any reason other than your memory may have tricked you."

"Have you any reason to believe that I have got a defective memory?"

"No, I suppose our memories are equal."

"Why?"

"We are both people with full capacities of memory I suppose except that mine may be better, I am younger."

"How much younger," snapped Meldon, "do you know?"

"Er, no-o-o."

"Well, what are you basing your opinion on!"

"Well perhaps I am younger."

"Do you know whether you are or not, younger than me?"

"I do."

"Do you know anything about whether my memory is trained or not?"

"I don't, any more than the average person."

"Do you know anything about my memory or not?"

"I don't see what that has to do with it."

"You will before we finish! What about Detective Henderson? Is there any reason why he would say and has substantiated it under oath, that you did tell him that you did not advise Mrs. Cumming not to make a statement or answer questions?"

"None that I know of."

"You have known Detective Henderson in his official capacity for a number of years I understand?"

"Known him as a member of the Criminal Investigation Department, yes."

"And as far as you know is he dependable?"

"So far as I know he is a dependable officer."

"And as far as you know am I a dependable officer?"

"So far as I know."

Meldon paused.

"Are you suggesting I am not?" asked McGrath.

"Where did you get that inspiration from? There is nothing that I have said. Did you go to Finney Isles and see witness Stanley Cumming to collect a professional fee for advise that you had given him?"

"I refuse to answer that question as to whether I went to see Stanley Cumming at Finney's professionally on the grounds already stated."

"Do you think those grounds are good under these circumstances as disclosed at this Inquiry?"

"In the first place I do not know what grounds have been disclosed at this inquiry and secondly what business I do in W.J. McGrath's office is the business of W.J. McGrath Senior and I do consider those grounds as good."

"Even though your client, or ex-client to be precise, has given her reasons that she acted on the advice of the solicitor in not answering and that you were the solicitor?"

"I refuse to answer that question on the grounds already stated."

"I think I've heard enough," said Mr. Staines, "The court will take a short recess while I consider the question of privilege."

*

After the recess Gerald McGrath was sworn in again and before a question could be asked he began to address the court.

"As to the question of privilege as disclosing

information or communication between solicitor and client…"

"I will stop you there Mr. McGrath," said Staines, "the Bench holds that the question of privilege operates as to all matters between solicitor and client as well as client and solicitor and his clerks in so far as they are acting as agent or intermediaries between him and his client. That does not apply to the matter of the bare fact of an interview as against what takes place at the interview."

"Thank you your Worship," said Meldon "Mr. McGrath did you have an interview with the witness Mrs. Cumming at any time since the 23rd December 1926?"

"Yes, the first interview I had with Mrs. Cumming was on the evening of the 27th December 1926 in a professional capacity. I did not have a professional interview on that date with Stanley Cumming, he was not present."

"Where was that?"

"At the office of W.J. McGrath solicitor of Adelaide Street."

"And the next?"

"To the best of my knowledge witness Stanley Cumming interviewed me at my residence at Cameron Street South Brisbane. The next interview was with the witness Mrs. Cumming and her son Stanley two days later at the office of W.J. McGrath about the 31st December 1926 and two or three days subsequent at the office of W.J. McGrath Senior on three or four occasions I interviewed in a professional capacity the witness Mrs. Cumming and her son Stanley. About two days later I interviewed Mrs. Cumming at the office of Mr. Meldon, Criminal Investigation Department. That I think is all the interviews I had with either Mrs. Cumming or her son Stanley."

"Would you say approximately there were three interviews with Stanley Cumming and approximately six or seven with Mrs. Cumming and Stanley conjointly?"

"Yes, some of those interviews were concerning the administration of the estate of the late Marquis Cumming."

"You won't give evidence as to the nature of the other portion of the interviews?"

"It isn't that I won't. It is that I am not allowed."

"Even though your ex-client Mrs. Cumming gives her consent?"

"Even though she does I would still refuse."

"I suppose you understand that it is important to Mrs. Cumming to establish that she was legally advised to take up a certain course?"

"I won't answer that question."

"She states that she acted on that advice and this was her reason for refusing to answer questions in interrogation?"

"I refuse to answer that. I refuse to answer any questions concerning what took place between myself and Mrs. Cumming in a professional capacity other than the fact of interviews or attendance. I was acting for my father, W.J. McGrath senior in respect of all interviews and attendance between myself and Mrs. Cumming and Stanley Cumming or any dealings in this matter."

"Don't you think it peculiar that Detective Henderson only asked you about the advice tendered to Stanley Cumming and not Mrs. Cumming?"

"He is the best judge of that."

"Even though they had both refused at the same time to answer questions? Giving their reasons that they were acting on legal advice."

"I won't express an opinion on that."

"Don't you think it peculiar for the detectives to go to W.J. McGrath concerning Mrs. Cumming and her son having been there if they did not go there for the purpose of verifying the statements made by Mrs. Cumming and her son?"

"I won't express an opinion."

"Why have you told us that you didn't advise Stanley Cumming not to give a statement?"

"Who do you mean by us?"

"The Court?"

"I didn't tell that to the Court!"

"What did you tell the Court?"

"I did not tell the Court that I had advised Stanley Cumming not to give a statement but I told Detective Henderson that I did not tell Stanley Cumming not to give a statement at the time of my interview with Detective Henderson of the Criminal Investigation Department."

"It is a wonder you told Detective Henderson so much!"

"What I did tell him had nothing to do with any interview between myself and Stanley Cumming."

"When Stanley Cumming swears that you did advise him not to give a statement or answer questions he is not telling the truth?"

"I refuse to answer on the same grounds as previously stated."

"You refuse to answer that question although you told Detective Henderson that you did not give him that advice?"

"Yes, I refuse to answer on the grounds already stated."

"No more questions your Worship," said Meldon shaking his head.

"Even though Mrs. Cumming gives her consent," stated McGrath, "to communications between solicitor and client being stated I would still refuse to answer any of those questions as I am not entitled to; the principle, W.J. McGrath Solicitor is the person to decide and give authority as to whether I should or not."ᶜᵛ

"Thank you Mr. McGrath," said Staines, "I think we are all aware of your position. Now if you wouldn't mind would you please vacate the witness box!"

*

Detective Henderson went into the box again, and swore that he had had an interview with McGrath at the C.I.B. office, at which that solicitor had informed him that he had not given Mrs. Cumming or Stanley advice not to make statements or answer questions.

He proceeded to tell the court that on December 30, the detectives had called again, but McGrath was out, so they spoke to W. J. McGrath, who informed them that there was no record of the Cumming wife and son in his clients' book. He explained how he thought that they had gone to the wrong office.

Sub-inspector Meldon then asked Henderson about his enquiries into the Cumming-Walsh murder, concerning firearms and vendors of those weapons, but the Court was informed that the investigations had been negative, and that nobody thought to have had a possible connection with the crime had bought an automatic of the kind which had perpetrated the shooting.

Mr. King asked Detective Henderson about the men seen by witness Crane. Henderson stated that the men seen by the witness Crane might have had something to do with the slaying of the police officer and his consort of that night, although Henderson did not think it very probable.

Of course, they could have walked to the scene of the murder in 10 minutes from where they had been seen. Henderson stated that in his opinion, Cumming had met Mrs. Walsh at or near the terminus of Annerley and

Stephens roads. That would have been about half-past eight.

Mr. King suggested, and the detective agreed, that the motive for the murder might have been the outraged feelings of a husband with whose wife Cumming had had immoral relations. The detective also admitted that not all the women with whom Cumming had misconducted himself had been traced, and that only those definitely known to have been his mistresses had been examined, and their movements and those of their husbands had been traced on the night of the murder. It was stated by him in addition that the main reason for the names of those women not being made public was that tragedy might eventuate in their families if the fact that they had been loose in their conduct with Cumming was known.[cvi]

After Henderson finished giving his evidence the court was adjourned by Staines until ten a.m. on Friday the 17th June 1927.[cvii]

22 INQUIRY END

On the morning of Friday 17th June 1927 the inquiry was reopened by Magistrate Staines. The first witness called for the day was Mrs. Cumming who confirmed to the court that Gerald McGrath was known to her, that she had called upon him for advice and that the advice she had received from him was not to answer any questions or make any statement to the Police. She also stated she was quite willing for Mr. McGrath to divulge anything that he told her at her interviews with him, noting that her meeting had been very brief.[cviii]

Sub-Inspector Martin John Meldon then called himself as a witness and swore on oath with the object of refuting the evidence given by McGrath on Tuesday. The officer said that he was in charge of the C.I.B., Brisbane. About the end of December, he continued, Detective Henderson told him that McGrath wished to see him. McGrath came into his office and said that he was acting for Mrs. Cumming and her son, and that he desired to inspect certain documents of the murdered man.

"During the course of that interview," added the Sub-inspector, "I told Mr. McGrath that Mrs. Cumming and her son had informed the detectives that they would not come to the C.I.B. office or answer any further questions or make a statement respecting the murder of Acting-sergeant Cumming and the woman Walsh. I told him that Mrs. Cumming had stated that he (McGrath) had advised her not to do so, and I asked him if this was correct. Mr. McGrath replied, 'No, I never gave her that advice!'"

"The suggestion by McGrath that my memory would be tricking me, or that I was speaking untruthfully was not correct with regard to the interview between myself and the solicitor at the C.I. Branch."

"I would like to submit to the inquiry this clipping from the 'Patriot' newspaper dated 12th June 1927 respecting this inquiry and the suggestion therein of the employment by police of third degree methods towards witness Marquis Cumming. I categorically deny this and state that the article is not correct. As far as I know at this inquiry that paper never had a representative here."[cix]

"Newspaper clipping tendered, admitted, and marked as Exhibit 21," said Staines.

Detective Henderson was recalled, and in answer to Mr. King, said that he was quite satisfied that Mrs. Cumming had told him that her solicitor, McGrath, had advised her not to make a statement.

Regarding the evidence of Mrs. Howden, mother of Mrs. Cumming, the detective said he had no reasonable ground to disbelieve her. He told Sub-inspector Meldon, in answer to further questions, that he had interviewed Mrs. Melican, proprietor of a boarding-house where Josephine Clutterbuck worked in consequence of an anonymous letter received by Meldon, intimating that she had some information. When the detective saw her and her son and made inquiries from them he had obtained no information which would assist his investigations. He also spoke to other residents of the house. He found nothing in his investigations which would contradict anything that Josephine Clutterbuck had told him. He had gone to the house where the girl worked with a view to testing the credibility of the story told him by the girl.

All rumours received by the C.I.B. concerning the circumstances surrounding the deaths of Acting-sergeant Cumming and Mrs. Walsh had been run down, he told the inquiry.

"Can you say what parts of the Cumming house were searched?" asked Staines.

"It was all searched."

"Inside?"

"Yes, as well as the ground outside and underneath the house."

He added that all receptacles inside the house had been carefully looked into and an extensive search made. He and Detective Campbell had undertaken that examination on the day after the tragedy.

"What were you searching for?" asked Meldon.

"We searched with a view to finding the handcuffs, keys, and belt missing from the person of Cumming after he had been found dead. We also looked for any weapons apart from those which had been handed to the C.I.B."

"Searches were also made at places other than the Cumming house for those things?" asked Mr. King.

"Oh, yes," responded Campbell.[cx]

From the evidence of another woman, he said, Cumming was in the habit of taking his belt off, and it would probably be lying on the ground some little distance away from them. No doubt the belt, handcuffs, and keys had been destroyed or hidden in a place where they would never be found.

"Do you have a theory on why the belt, handcuffs and

keys would be missing?" asked Meldon.

"In the dark it might be reasonable to assume that there was a weapon with that belt. It would be possible that they might mistake the handcuffs for a weapon, any person approaching the deceased at the time for the purpose of doing them an injury would probably take the precaution of taking those things, thereby thinking he would be disarmed."

"Mrs. Cumming says that he wore his handcuffs loose, and never on the belt," stated Mr. King.

"If Mrs. Cumming says that he never wore his handcuffs on his belt I could not deny it. She would be in the best position to know."

"Mrs. Cumming says he always carried his revolver in the hip pocket, would you be surprised to know that?"

"No. that would not surprise me."

"And the fact that he is said to carry his handcuffs on his belt?"

"As a general rule the Police carry their handcuffs on their belt."

"Do you believe the evidence of witness Jamieson?"

"Yes, I do."

"And do you believe witness Crane saw the two men he said he did?"

"Yes."

"Do you doubt the times he gave in evidence?"

"I have no reason to doubt his times."

"How do you reconcile these two views then?"

"I do not attach any connection between the two men that Crane saw and the two men seen by Jamieson. I think they are two different sets of persons."

"Do you believe the evidence of Josephine Clutterbuck?" asked Mr. King.

"I could not disprove the statement that Stanley had

been with her, and I think that his movements on the night of the murder had been accounted for from about 7:30 p.m. until sometime after 11 o'clock the same night."

"Do you believe that they had anything to do with the murder."

Detective Campbell took a long pause before answering.

"That is a hard question. They may have."

"Have you any doubt that Mrs. Cumming went to the home of her mother at the Valley on the night of the killing?"

"I have not been able to prove otherwise."

"You have no doubt?"

"I have not been able to disprove it."

"And that she stayed there until sometime about 9 o'clock or a little later, and passed the South Brisbane Town Hall on her way home about 9:45 o'clock?"

"I have not been able to disprove it."[cxi]

The court was silent for a few moments and Campbell was allowed to step down. He returned to the gallery and sat with Henderson.

"Do you have further witnesses Sub-Inspector?" asked Staines.

"Not at this time your worship."

"But you think there may be further witnesses at some stage?"

"Absolutely!"

"Might I suggest," said Staines, "that you call for an adjournment sine die[13]?"

"Before the court adjourns your Worship, could I address the court?" asked Mr. King.

---

[13] Adjournment without assigning a day for a further meeting or hearing

"Permission granted," responded Staines.

"For the record I would like to state my opinion, that the system under which this inquiry was held is antiquated and obsolete. I wish to stress the point that on the night of the murder there were surely other persons in the lonely reserve whose evidence, if they came forward, would materially assist the police to sheet the crime home. Those persons who were there no doubt have reasons for not coming forward, and doubtless they did not wish to disclose the fact that they had been in the reserve at night. Certain things have been said against Mrs. Cumming and Stanley which could not have been said in a police court."

"I will point out," interjected Staines, "that it was necessary for the inquiry court to have wide latitude."

"It means you give people a weapon to attack persons who cannot reply, with detriment to the reputations of those attacked! It is possible for the public to be unconsciously biased by what was said at the inquiry, the system is wrong!"

"Thank you Mr. King," said Staines, "for now the inquiry is closed with the proviso that it might be reopened if necessary."[cxii]

The exhibits were gathered up, the photographs and letters were filed with the signed statements of evidence, while the clothing, firearms and shells were placed in boxes to be stored in the C.I. Branch property room.

*

Magisterial Inquiries Officer, Arthur Staines Esquire J.P. spent the next few weeks producing a Certificate of Particulars regarding the Inquiry into the deaths of Marquis Cumming and Eileen Gladys Walsh for attachment to the evidence taken during the Inquiry. In reviewing all the statements that had been taken in evidence he came to the conclusion that there did not appear to be enough indication to definitely connect any particular person with the crime. In his certificate however, he took the opportunity to submit matters that he considered pertinent to the case and warranted noting, numbering each matter in turn.

(1) Cumming used to generally carry a revolver (one of the factors in such evidently being for use if he were caught by interested parties in his illicit sexual connection with other married women) but Staines found it strange that he evidently did not have it on him that particular night, which he considered made it appear that the murderer or murderers knew of the omission. Further he reported that although Mrs. Cumming said she did not know of his not having his revolver that night, Mrs. Christie said that on coming to see her on the 25th December 1926 that Mrs. Cumming had said among other things that the deceased had said, when spoken to by her about his illicit connections, 'It will be a good man that will get me' and added that she also said 'evidently the good man has got him, but he got him from the back'. Mrs. Christie had also contributed comments to Mrs. Cumming such as 'He was always fond of beautiful girls but let him look at them laying at the morgue 24 hours afterward with their paint and powder off' and that 'it was a strange coincidence that was the only night that he went out without his revolver'.

(2) Cumming and his wife were evidently most unhappy in their domestic and marital relations.

(3) Mrs. Cumming states that she left her home between 7:15 and 8 p.m. on 23/12/26 and took a tram to the Valley to see her mother, Mrs. Howden, who lives in Constance Street, where she says she arrived about 8 p.m. going alone. She says she left about 9:15 p.m. noticing the

time by the South Brisbane Town Hall clock as 9:45 p.m. reaching home about 10:05 p.m. She did not cite anyone she saw, nor any incident on the way. Mrs. Howden who is 85 years of age and who evidently and naturally suffers from defect of memory stated that Mrs. Cumming called at her place on the night stated and left about 9 p.m. or a little after.

(4) Deceased Cumming's son Marquis David James Stanley Cumming (usually called Stanley Cumming) had an automatic pistol, but it seems the shots were not fired from that pistol, although of the same calibre as the cartridges which with deceased were murdered.

(5) It seems indisputable that James Samuel Walsh, husband of female deceased, had nothing to do with the crime.

(6) Deceased Cumming and his son Stanley were evidently at enmity which was accentuated by the fact that Stanley interviewed a married woman and obtained a signed statement from her that she bore an illegitimate child to deceased, and that deceased had, on many occasions, had sexual intercourse with her, and of which Stanley Cumming had acquainted his father.

(7) Stanley Cumming attended the Empire Theatre (Albert Street) on the night in question with Miss Clutterbuck arriving there about 8:05 p.m. and leaving at the end of the programme about 10:30 p.m. He seems undoubtedly to have attended and his time of arrival and departure seem to be totally established, but so far as the time between he does not in evidence state anything about the programme or anything else. Miss Clutterbuck has done so, but she states they were sitting together during the whole period. However Detective Campbell says that Stanley Cumming told him, on his interviewing him, about an old man sitting next to him and deeply interested in

Mary Laurence (one of the performers) from the singing point of view, and he considered him a bit of a nuisance.

(8) Joseph Lionel Herbert, Managing Director of the Trocadero Dansant, says that on account of an altercation Cumming and Mrs. Cumming had there one night while a dance was on, Mrs. Cumming came to him next morning, and told him of their domestic unhappiness, and amongst other things said to him 'What do you think of him, don't you think he ought to be shot?'. Mrs. Cumming denies making that statement.

(9) Detective Acting Sergeant Henderson states that on interviewing another married woman whom deceased had on at least three occasions sexual intercourse with, she stated that on one occasion Stanley Cumming had followed her and amongst other things he said to her 'My father is no damn good, he has been causing a lot of trouble at home, the man ought to bloody well do time for it'. Stanley Cumming admitted following and talking to the woman, but denies making that statement.

(10) Mrs. Cumming states in evidence 'I have warned my husband of the dangers he was running by carrying on with other woman in the position he held, and he has said to me it would take a smart man to catch him'.

(11) Mrs. Cumming states she went to the scene of the tragedy a day or two after the bodies were discovered, to view the surroundings to see whether anyone could see what was going on, and also on account of being told that people in the locality did not hear the shots that were fired, and that she had never been there before, nor since, and did not know that her husband frequented that locality at night.

(12) Mrs. Cumming said it was between 2 and 3 a.m. on 24/12/26 that she first exhibited anxiety about her husband.

(13) Letters Exhibits 9, 10, and 11, tendered, but Mrs. Cumming and Stanley Cumming deny practically all statements made by the deceased in those letters as to his home life.

(14) Detective Constable Campbell and Detective Acting Sergeant Henderson state that on 28th December 1926 Mrs. Cumming told them 'he has got his desserts and I will say no more' and Detective Acting Sergeant Henderson states that at an interview Stanley Cumming said 'while you are questioning us here, he or she who did the murder are going free' and Mrs. Cumming said 'By the way you men keep coming here it looks as if you are trying to make us out guilty'. Mrs. Cumming and Stanley say they do not remember that being said, but the latter said he could not deny its being said, but he didn't recollect its being said.

(15) Detective Constable Campbell states that Mrs. Cumming on the way to the Morgue told him without his asking her at all, that she had warned her husband that he would come to a sudden end, and that he (Campbell) had not up to that time told her the circumstances under which her husband had been found. Mrs. Cumming says she does not remember saying so, and Stanley Cumming says he does not remember anything his mother said then, but he said he was not denying it.

(16) Leaving Mrs. Cumming and her son Stanley Cumming out of the question in reference to this paragraph (16) no one has been brought under suspicion by the evidence elicited at the Inquiry save for the persons stated by Jamieson as having followed the two deceased.[cxiii]

*

The Court Clerk also prepared a written summary for

the Crown Solicitor as a result of Inquest 626/27 - M. Cumming & E.G. Walsh.

The Crown Solicitor,

The two deceased were shot dead by some person or persons on the night of 23rd December last sometime between the hours of 9 &10 p.m. – the precise time not being definitely ascertained, but probably being about 9:45 though one witness places it as early as 9:15.

Deceased Cumming was seen on an out bound tram proceeding along Stanley St in the direction of Woolloongabba at a little after 8 p.m. and later alone in Annerley Rd going in the direction of Boggo Rd Gaol.

Deceased Walsh left her home in Stephens St at between 7:45 and 8 p.m. saying she was going to the pillar box to post a letter and would not be long away; she could have gone to either one of two, equidistant, one in Annerley Rd, one at Gloucester St station.

Evidently she went to the one at Annerley Rd for some time later a witness saw Cumming and a woman corresponding to the description of Mrs. Walsh walking down Annerley Rd & turn up the gaol lane. This meeting seems not to have been prearranged for when leaving home deceased Walsh had informed her relatives that she would not be away long and her mother says she did not, at 6:50 that night, intend going out at all that night.

Shortly after the above mentioned witness saw the two deceased turn down the lane towards the gaol he heard shots from the direction of the gaol giving the time as about 9:45. He says there were two shots and it seems clear they were the shots which caused the deaths of the two deceased.

So far as the evidence discloses any particulars of the

actual shooting it establishes that it must have been done at very close range for in both cases the bodies were powder marked & that Cumming was shot in the back & Walsh in the face.

The dispositions do not definitely establish that this is a case of double murder. In the case of Cumming the G.M.O. says that his wound would not have been self-inflicted but that that of deceased Walsh could have been. It seems more probable however that it is a case of double murder than one of murder and suicide because the Doctor says that the same size bullet caused the injuries to both deceased making it almost certain that the same revolver fired both shots & if deceased Walsh had shot herself the revolver would most likely have been found nearby and it has not been found.

Suspicion has been directed to several persons, (1) Mrs. Cumming, widow of deceased Cumming (2) M.D.J.S. Cumming, son of deceased (3) James Samuel Walsh, husband of deceased Walsh (4) Two unknown persons seen to follow the two deceased on the night of the tragedy (5) Two men seen coming from direction of gaol about the time of the tragedy (6) Other persons with whom the deceased Cumming is known to have been entangled and persons possibly interested on their behalf (7) A woman in Mount Morgan and persons possibly interested on her behalf (8) A brother of deceased Walsh (9) A number of persons seen waiting round the South Brisbane Police Station on the night of the tragedy.

As to the persons seen waiting around the Police Station and also other persons with whom deceased Cumming is known to have been entangled the Police Witnesses have testified that their movements have been fully investigated & satisfactorily accounted for but they point out it is possible he was entangled with other persons whom they do not know of. The woman from Mount Morgan is definitely established not to have been near the scene at the time.

F.C. Christie (brother of deceased Walsh) was, on his own evidence, out on the night in question. He left home at 6:50 p.m. & went to the house of people named Slaughter at Highgate Hill, leaving there to return home at 9:30. Slaughter was called & said Christie was at his place from 7 to 9:40 p.m. It is possible that he may have seen the two deceased and followed them but there is nothing to establish that he did so that no charge could be made against him.

At about 9:30 p.m. on the night in question one of the witnesses says he saw two figures in male attire standing in Annerley Rd watching in the direction of Gladstone Rd. He stood inside his own gate and watched and shortly saw deceased (both) coming down the road and turning into the gaol lane whereupon the other two followed them.

He was asked as to the descriptions of these two figures, he said that James Samuel Walsh was not either of those figures but that M.J.D.S. Cumming was similar in build to the taller figure though he could not definitely swear that he was one of them & then says definitely Cumming Junior was not the taller figure. He also says that either of the two figures might have been a woman. The identity of these two figures is not established.

Another witness gave evidence that he was proceeding along Annerley Rd about 9:10 p.m. on this night when he saw two men one of whom ran across the road from the direction of the gaol and the other seemed to be covering him. He says however that his watch from which he took his time might have been minutes slow or minutes fast.

A third witness (a pawnbroker) says that on the afternoon of the day of the tragedy a man came to the shop and purchased an automatic revolver of similar pattern to that belonging to M.J.D.S. Cumming but smaller.

These three witnesses have each given descriptions of the men seen. There is a marked resemblance between that given by the pawnbroker and that given by the second witness of one of two men seen by him. Both agree that the height was 6ft, that the man was sallow, that he needed a shave & that he was dressed in a dark suit. This man is the one the second witness saw running from the direction of the tragedy & another witness, who had considerable experience during the war, heard the shots & swore definitely that he could tell from the sound that they were fired from an automatic. That witness fixes the time at about 9:10 p.m. which is near the time fixed by the second witness. This seems to lead to the conclusion that probably the man at the pawnbrokers had some connection with the matter though there is no more than a probability. The description given by the first witness does not agree with that by the other two. But there is this feature about it – He gave the height of one of the men at 5 feet 9 inches but his estimate might have been an inch out either way. If this be so the height might have been 5ft 8 inches, Mrs. Cumming's height is 5 feet 7½ inches. In addition he estimated that man's weight at about 11 stone 8 lbs and Mrs. Cumming's weight is about 11 stone 3 lbs. This is all the connection that can be established between Mrs. Cumming & these two men and is not very strong whilst the only thing to connect Stanley is that a dark suit was worn by him and these men.

Mrs. Cumming & Stanley have each given evidence of the domestic circumstances prevailing in their home over some years immediately preceding this occurrence and have also given some account of their doings on this particular night.

It is clear from the evidence of both that circumstances in this household were unhappy and in the main they give the same account. There are however cases in which they do not agree e.g. (a) Mrs. Cumming says certain letters were found in June 1924 & that her son first wrote to the writer & later went to Mount Morgan & interviewed that writer, & got a statement from her which statement she (Mrs. C.) later destroyed; on the other hand Stanley admits being shown the letters and having an interview at Mount Morgan but says nothing of writing to Mount Morgan first and he puts the date as sometime later than June 1925; (b) Mrs. Cumming says her son left home on one occasion on account of domestic rows but he emphatically denies that as a reason. There is, apart from these two instances, no substantial difference between what each says & these do not appear of any evidential value beyond suggesting the possibility that they have agreed amongst themselves as to the evidence they should give.

Stanley Cumming has given an account of his movements on the night in question & had it for the greater part corroborated by another witness or witnesses. After careful comparison of his account from 7 p.m. to 10:30 p.m. with that of the person whose company he is supposed then to have been there does not appear any discrepancy between them; after that time there is two differences; he says they reached a certain place at 11:10 p.m. & parted 11:30 p.m. which the other witness says they reached there at 11 p.m. and parted at 11:45 p.m.

After leaving this witness he says he hailed a motor taxi-cab to overtake a tram. He gives certain particulars in connection with that cab & these particulars are substantiated by a driver of a cab but that driver being asked to identify his fare said he was of Stanley Cumming's build but he could not identify him.

In Mrs. Cumming's case she is not so clearly supported. She says she left home between 7:15 and 8 p.m. and went to her mother's place in the Valley arriving there somewhere about 8 p.m. and remaining there till 9:15 p.m. and went along Stanley St in a tram at 9:45 p.m. Her mother however swears that Mrs. Cumming reached her place not as late as 7:30 & only a few minutes after 7 p.m. & left two hours later but later said she remained on till getting on to 10 p.m. It is therefore not at all clear as to when she actually left the Valley.

From careful perusal of the evidence of all witnesses it appears impossible to definitely associate any person with the murders. Though it seems possible as Mr. Staines points out that persons seen do in description somewhat tally with the widow and her son.

G. Bond

21.7.27

23 COVER THE TRACKS

Weeks passed and Henderson had been assigned to investigate a rash of robberies that had occurred. Campbell had been assigned to work automotive theft.

*

By mid-August 1927 Meldon was on an inspection tour in the north of the state. Detectives Burns and Mullaly were on the graveyard shift at CI Branch.

The residents of Brisbane were woken from their dozy state by what sounded like a very large explosion from the vicinity of George Street. Within a hundred yards of C.I. Branch, situated at the corner of George and Elizabeth Streets the streets were filled with iron and timber rafters. Most windows had been shattered and glass lay everywhere. A full view of C.I. Branch or more precisely what remained of the building indicated that the roof had been blown off and part of the stone wall facing George Street had been shattered. Rescuers stumbled through the debris and found Mullaly holding up Burns. Mullaly had stepped out for supper and Burns had fallen asleep when the explosion occurred. Mullaly had rushed back to find Burns who had been thrown to the floor from his bed. Burns was obviously suffering from shock and would need medical attention. Rescuers went to enter the building but Mullaly cautioned them as he feared there may be further bombs in the building. Fires had started to burn and the bells of the Fire Brigade could be heard approaching. A detective entered a nearby store and notified Roma Street to send a squad from Police Headquarters.

The greatest destruction caused appeared to be in the middle part of the building. The whole section of the roof had been lifted and a shower of woodwork and masonry had been hurled skyward to fall into the streets. Around the building could be seen the debris had also been hurled into the State Government Insurance Building opposite and the Treasury building on the other side with the parapets and ledges lodged with scraps of iron, wood, and stone. In the centre of the building for a depth of some 60 feet was an indescribable jumble of splintered and smashed timbers, broken partitions and office furniture. The masonry of the wall just above the George Street entrance was blown out and the wall was leaning forward at such a dangerous angle that it appeared likely to fall at any moment. Another of the doors leading to George Street was blown out and the partition between the property room and the Commissioner of Police's office torn down. The Senior Sergeant's Room and the fingerprint room escaped damage although it appeared that the 'dust of ages' had been showered upon them. The bricks in the top of the wall separating the property room from the office of Sub-Inspector Meldon were blown out and the wall slightly stove in. The partitions of the wall in the clerk's room were thrown about the floor along with furniture, typewriters and documents.

A large gaping hole in the roof allowed a clear view of the evening sky that caught the white sheets of paper that appeared to be flying about in all directions. The middle part of the building had comprised the property room in front while immediately behind was the clerks room and the office of the 'Police Gazette'. Detectives were convinced by the debris pattern that the explosion had occurred in the property room. The window of the property room had been left open. 'Someone must have thrown a bomb through the security grill into the property room'.[cxiv]

Anything that had survived the blast was damaged when the Fire Brigade began to spray water on the spot fires burning amongst the debris.[14]

*

The next day Mr. John Henderson, Government Analyst for Queensland, made an examination of the site of Criminal Investigation Branch and concluded that the damage had been caused by a high explosive. Gelignite he concluded was the most likely explosive used. With probably a weight of no less than five pounds having been used. He knew that gelignite would need to be detonated to explode and that would require a fuse or electricity. He reported to the police that the explosion of 5 lbs of gelignite thrown through the George Street window by someone outside could have caused the damage done.[cxv]

The police had established two definite facts in respect to the wrecking of the police headquarters. That there were no explosives in the building prior to the explosion

---

[14] Figure 10 – Photograph of CIB headquarters after bombing

suggesting that the damage was caused by high explosives, a bomb or other explosive missile thrown or dropped through the window of the stolen property room as concluded by the Government Analyst. They developed the theory that the bomb was attached to a fuse, thus giving the perpetrator an opportunity to get away from the building before the crash. This was borne out when pieces of fuse were found within the building.[cxvi]

The authorities were satisfied with the assumption that a deliberate attempt was made to wreck the room in which stolen property was stored as the motive. It appeared that the destruction of evidence was the motive as some of the property would certainly have furnished a conviction. Working on these lines the police were confident that the author of the damage would be promptly brought to justice.

A man named John Joseph Cahill called at the C.I. Branch and spoke to Henderson. He told Henderson he had seen two men standing near the Office of the Commissioner of Police at about eleven-forty the previous evening and he had also seen these two in the same vicinity and time the previous Wednesday night. The description given matched one of the men Henderson had been investigating for robbery and he proceeded, in company with other detectives, to the premises of Joseph Rappaport, pawnbroker and second-hand dealer, where he found his suspect.[cxvii]

That afternoon Albert Orchard was identified by Cahill in a line up and taken into custody.

Orchard was on bail awaiting trial for the burglary of the Premier Shirt and Pyjama factory. He had been caught red-handed by Detective McCulloch on the night of July 26th. McCulloch dressed in plain clothes had been standing at the corner of Grey and Russell streets on that night and saw a motor car pull up at the kerb outside Tritton's furniture factory. He walked down Russell Street towards Stanley Street and when he was about four yards from the car he saw the passenger get out of the car and walk up Russell Street in the direction of Grey Street. He recognized the car as belonging to Rappaport, a second hand dealer, whose property's back fence adjoined the Laidlaw Buildings. The building where the Premier Shirt and Pyjama Manufacturing Company had their factory.

When he reached the front of the car he saw Albert Orchard sitting at the wheel of the car. He heard Orchard call out to the other man, 'Tell those other fellows to hurry up. I can't stay here all night'.

McCulloch walked up the opposite side of the street and saw Orchard get out of the car and walk down Grey Street for about 50 yards where he met the first man. This man had come from the direction of the building where it is now known that a robbery had taken place. They stood there talking for a few moments before both returned to the car and got in the front seat.

Detective McCulloch was now standing near the abutment of the railway bridge on the opposite side of the road. He then saw Sergeant Heggarty walking towards him and they met on the other side of the street where the car was standing and they walked to the car together.

When they reached the car Orchard looked at McCulloch and said 'Good night Mac'. The other man alighted from the vehicle and walked to the front of the car he also greeted McCulloch similarly. McCulloch addressed Orchard and asked 'What have you got in the back of this car?' to which Orchard replied 'I don't know what's in there'. McCulloch opened the side rear door and as he examined the contents the first man made a dash up the street.

Concealed beneath two rugs McCulloch found forty-seven rolls of 'Tobralco' and six pieces of 'Zephyr', along with a false number plate, 4/- worth of sandwiches, two bottles of beer and a tin of oil.

"Well," said McCulloch, "apparently you are ready for a very long trip!"

The rolls of shirting material had been taken from the Premier Shirt and Pyjama factory and after the robbery an attempt had been made to burn the factory down. When detectives visited the scene of the crime, after the flames had been put out, they noticed a strong smell of petrol. It had apparently been sprinkled about the floor and walls. On examining the building they found that a window near the rear door had been forced open.[cxviii]

Orchard was committed for trial again and released on bail. This was not opposed by the police as they wanted to put a tail on him to surface the man who had been in the car with him on the night McCulloch found the stolen fabric. They now believed that man was James Fitzgerald.

*

On the 23rd August 1927, David Cumming, father of the deceased Acting-Sergeant, passed away after a long illness.

*

On the night of September 29th, at about seven-fifteen, Detective McCulloch in company with Detective Rochford stood on the footpath at North Quay when they observed Albert Orchard and a woman talking to Fitzgerald on the other side of the street. The three stood there talking before crossing the street to sit on a rockery about forty yards from the Detectives. Detective Rochford went for assistance as McCulloch kept the group under observation.

About fifteen minutes later a posse of Detectives arrived and they went to the position where Orchard and Fitzgerald were sitting.

"Hullo Fitz," said McCulloch, "stand up!"

The man spoken to had his hat pulled down over his eyes and rose to his feet.

"My name's Clark," he said, "I'm waiting for my wife."

Suddenly his hand went for his trouser pocket. Rochford moved just as quickly and caught hold of his arm.

"What have you got here?" asked Rochford.

"A gun," was the reply.

Rochford searched the man's pocket and found he had an automatic pistol fully loaded, with one cartridge in the breech and six others in the magazine. Rochford took possession of the weapon.

"There is a warrant out for your arrest," said McCulloch, "for the robbery and wilful destruction at the Premier Shirt and Pyjama factory. I see you have your mate Orchard with you."

"I don't know him, I've only just met him," responded Fitzgerald.

"I saw you talking to Orchard across the street not half an hour ago!"

"The game is up, I'll go quietly with you," said Fitzgerald.

"Cuff him boys."[cxix]

Back at the station Fitzgerald's pockets were thoroughly searched and an additional fourteen revolver cartridges were found in his pockets.

"What's the idea of carrying a pistol?" asked McCulloch.

"I always carry one," replied Fitzgerald, "you never know when some of these burglars might have a crack at you!"

Later James Fitzgerald was charged with having broken into and entering the premises of Premier Shirt and Pyjama factory on the night of the 26th July and with having stolen material valued at £180. The evidence however, was also lost in the bomb explosion.

*

While at the watch house Fitzgerald was visited by Detective Henderson.

"While we have you here," said Henderson, "I intend bringing along two men who had seen Albert Orchard and another man on the night of the explosion at the C.I. Branch."

"I knew you were putting this on me."

"Did Orchard tell you?"

"I have nothing to say as to who told me."

"They have positively identified Orchard and I have every reason to believe that you were the other man. You will be in a line-up for these two men to identify as the man seen with Orchard."

"I know these two fellows will pick me. I'll bet you a 'fiver' they pick me!"

"You seem pretty certain about being picked," said Henderson, "you must be the right man. You know Orchard do you not?"

"I don't know him."

"Did you not live with him for a while at Rappaport's? You have been seen in his company."

"I have never lived at Rappaport's" responded Fitzgerald, "The only time I have been with Orchard was the other night, when you chaps picked me up on North Quay. I met him by accident, he asked me if I had seen a man in a fawn overcoat waiting about."

"Well where have you been living then?"

"I've been in Brisbane about four and a half months and been living at a house in Warry Street in the Valley," replied Fitzgerald, "I have been keeping in 'smoke' all the time on account of that New South Wales matter."

"So what were your movements on that night, the night of the 13th August."

"On that night I was at the Empire Theatre and returned to my room about eleven thirty. I can call my Landlady to give evidence. I was with a mate."

"What's your mates name?"

"No, I refuse to tell you that."

Fitzgerald had sent for clean clothing and this had been brought to him in a portmanteau. As he began to unpack some clothes Henderson noticed a writing pad.

"It that yours?" he asked, "Mind if I take a look."

Fitzgerald grunted.

Henderson examined the blotter that was attached to the writing pad. He took a pencil and using the side of the pencil he highlighted the indentation left on the paper in the pad, that sat beneath a page that had been torn out.

"Mrs. A. Orchard, 8 Dick Street, Marrickville, Sydney," read Henderson, "I thought you said you did not know Orchard, that is his wife's address in Sydney."

"I don't know anything about it."

"The line-up is ready, let's see how you get on then."

John Joseph Cahill was the first to view the line-up and Fitzgerald was picked out from six other men as the individual he had seen with Orchard near the C.I. Branch about eleven-forty on Saturday 13th August and about the same time on the previous Wednesday night. Next to view the line-up was Edward Henry Randall and he pointed at Fitzgerald and said 'That is the man, the man I saw with Orchard at the mouth of York Lane and Elizabeth Street about two minutes after the explosion at the C.I. Branch took place'. Both witnesses remarked how Fitzgerald must have grown a moustache since they saw him with Orchard.[cxx]

"James Fitzgerald," said Henderson, "I hereby charge you that, conjointly with Albert Orchard and with intent to destroy a quantity of shirting material, the property of Buss and Turner, and Bayard's Ltd., you put gelignite in the offices of the Commissioner of Police, George Street, City."

"That's the charge is it? I am not worrying about it."[cxxi]

24 THE MISS X ENQUIRIES

Two weeks after Orchard and Fitzgerald were committed to stand trial on the robbery and bombing, the 'Truth' newspaper made sensational claims of a new clue coming to light in the Cumming-Walsh murder case. They claimed that out of the depths of tortured conscience a young woman had made a most startling statement to them. They claimed that it had, or appeared to have, a very important bearing on the murder which hitherto had been classed as one of the most mysterious and dastardly crimes known to Queensland.

The 'Truth' impressed upon their readers that the girl who makes the statement alleges that she has been shockingly treated by a man, a member of the police force of Queensland, therefore her statement was to be viewed carefully. Nonetheless, the editors felt that there was sufficient in her story to warrant the reopening of the magisterial inquiry.

The claims had been sensationalised no doubt to boost public sales. With snippets such as, 'His letters to one woman – mother of an illegitimate child of his – showed an almost poetic passion'. 'He rounded off his phrases with expressions which, in parts, actually ranked beside classics of lovemaking', must have had the detectives shaking their heads.

They claimed that 'whoever was responsible for the slaying had gone to work with a greater deal of caution than is usual in the class of person who commits murder. It all pointed to skill, self-confidence, forethought', 'it was a cold blooded murder'. They conveyed my thoughts exactly. That this was not a crime of passion, for those are usually bloody affairs that lack any premeditation.

At least the reporter had recognised the efforts of the police department when he wrote 'The dead man's character was searched out with a searing light. Unerringly the police traced his movements for many a long past day, and subjected his unofficial seraglio to a very thorough investigation'. 'But from all the welter of statements came forth not one jot or tittle of evidence which would focus a clear light on the crime, its perpetration, or its motive'.

For me the reporter captured the crime succinctly. Cumming had been murdered, with a woman, the time had been checked off, a figure or figures were seen running away from the scene of the murder within a few minutes of its doing, taking his belt, handcuffs and keys, and that the weapon that dealt death was a thirty-two calibre automatic pistol.

I imagined how the veins at Meldon's temple would be throbbing when he read that 'the magisterial inquiry dragged its weary length for about four weeks – at spasmodic intervals – and ended as helplessly as it had begun'. 'And the position is that the police do not know who murdered Cumming and Mrs. Walsh. Every line of inquiry led to nothing, and apparently, the police had nothing new to go on'.

I thought that this was not entirely true. They might have got somewhere with the evidence, if it hadn't been blown up!

I wanted to skim read the article to get to the section that covered the 'new clue' but each paragraph seemed to contain some hook that had me reading the whole thing. Then I got to the crux of the article, a young woman had approached the newspaper with a strange story to tell.

She was a daughter of the Australian bush – but now broken into the ways of the city. She did not pose as a broken lily, nor did she desire to portray herself as a virtuous girl who had been melodramatically wronged. She told her tale without frills and with a full sense of the terrible import of the things which she had to say. Yet she believed she had been done a great injustice by a certain man and her statement was to be judged accordingly. She swore it was true and made a statutory declaration to that effect before a Justice of the Peace.

To maintain her anonymity they called her Miss X. They described Miss X as a tall, slim young woman with a pair of pretty eyes, although they are for the time dimmed and circled with black due to the shedding of many tears. Her hair was described as golden and her carriage graceful. She appeared to be well enough educated although she lapsed into the vernacular when talking excitedly, slightly slangy, but attractive.

She captivated the heart of a police officer of the Queensland force and admitted that she subsequently became his mistress. She insisted though that he promised to marry her – someday. That day was long in coming and had not arrived up to that point in time. But she trusted....and waited....and suffered.

She was now 22 years of age having been born in New South Wales before she came to Queensland were her father took to farming not far from Brisbane. When she was 18 ½ years of age she left school and life seemingly opened up for her. She entered the employ of a business house until the October of 1924, then giving it up in favour of domestic employment.

At a beachside resort she met the police officer, who was destined afterwards to throw such a shadow over her youth. They became friends, just casual acquaintances. She stated that they walked together as young people do, and chatted amicably together, it was a pleasant friendship for both of them. She transferred to Brisbane securing employment in a hostelry and continued her outings with her friend. She knew Cumming for she had been introduced to him by his cousin.

Then, according to her story, her friend the policeman became pressing in his advances and very soon their platonic relationship ripened into passionate love-making, leading to the inevitable, but Miss X evaded motherhood.

Soon they rowed over a girl who plays a very important part in the supposed connection between the policeman and the death of Acting-Sergeant Cumming. Over this girl Miss X and her friend quarrelled he had been taking her out although the policeman had not admitted it, but he said a great deal more, things that burnt and seared into her mind at the knowledge that her lover was faithless and untrue.

But they came together again in the following April, and once more she was called upon to pay the price, and, once more she evaded it. But later she was unable to evade the scourge that had ruined many a life. He, she says, admitted that he was responsible.

She was now convinced of his faithlessness. It disgusted her. The green-eyed monster soon perched on her shoulder, making leering glances at her, and she was furious, jealous, outraged, mad with him, but she still loved him. A few nights later she would see him standing at the corner of the street near the Exhibition in Gregory Terrace, she observed him unnoticed. When, from the other side of the street, it was apparently an appointment, but Miss X intervened and after solidly rowing at her lover she took him away with her, leaving the other girl standing. A patched up peace followed.

Four nights later she noticed the girl in Queen Street as if waiting for a tram. Miss X jealous and suspecting another appointment, did some private detective work. She caught the same tram. The girl alighted at the Five Ways and walked up the left hand side of the street going back towards town. And she saw this girl meet Acting-Sergeant Cumming at South Brisbane. She told the reporter that she 'knew Cumming, as I had been introduced by his cousin. I saw Cumming and the girl talking. Then he put his hand in his pocket and took something out, which he gave to the girl. I could not see what it was'. He left her standing there and went back to Five Ways. She went as far as a nearby shop and stood there. After about fifteen minutes Cumming returned and again chatted to her before they both took a tram going towards the city.

She then told the reporter that she 'followed her and Cumming. He got off the tram at Stanley Street and she continued into town'. She followed the girl into town, but once there did not follow her anymore.

On the night of the 23rd December she had an appointment to meet her policeman lover at 7 p.m. There was to be a special celebration that night, it was his birthday. 'He said he was 30 years of age, though I believe he is four years older than that'. She had made a cake for him so they retired to her room, not far from Gregory Terrace in Berry Street. They ate cake and talked. But then, according to Miss X, at around nine o'clock although she could not be certain of the time, her police officer sweetheart said that he had to leave. It was unexpected. But she declares that he told her to swear that he did not leave her until quarter to twelve, as he had to return to the barracks in Roma Street by midnight. She was to wait for him in case he came back and that they were to meet the following night at half past seven if he did not.[cxxii]

He appeared to be very worried about something, and in spite of her solicitations and protestations, he left. He did not come back although she waited up into the early hours of the morning. The following night they met again as arranged in George Street where he burst out 'I suppose you know Cumming had been murdered! And a woman with him!' She had not read the papers and responded 'I wonder who did it?' to which he replied 'Oh, that's best kept to myself!'.

From that time on, she said, he was a changed man, He appeared at times to be practically demented. Any reference to the Cumming-Walsh murder affected him. Later that same night, in her room, seeing that he was very altered of personality and apparently bearing a mental burden of secrecy, she asked him what was the matter. 'I have a lot of worry on my mind' he allegedly responded. She pressed him again to tell her what it was, 'Oh, if only I told you, you would never speak to me again. I am a murderer!'

He appeared to be in a highly excitable and nervous state. Frequently in the following days she asked him to confide but the only response he would ever give was 'I am very worried!'.

As fate would have it his troubles were driven out of her mind when the burden of women was again upon her and again she spoke to her lover of it. There was another scene. 'I feel a coward and a dog' she alleges he said, 'I have brought disgrace on you. If you don't leave Queensland I will scatter your brains like I did Cumming's!' He then pulled out a pistol saying 'You had better say your prayers for the last time'.

With the barrel pointed at her she had said 'Yes, let's die together. If you are going to kill yourself, kill me first. I don't want to be left alone'. But the thought of it made him recoil and he put the gun away.

'I am a coward' she recalled he said, 'Forgive me, I lost control of myself'. Again she pressed him to tell her what his worry was but still he refused to say.

Then he began to drink.

She said this was unusual for him and she took it that he had some sorrow to drown. Eventually she listened to his pleas and left Queensland sometime during March not returning until June. She had carried her burden with her, but in Sydney, she was freed from it.

Since her return she stated that she had not renewed her association with her erstwhile lover. But it had played on her mind, she was worried and didn't know what to do. Then she had approached the newspaper.

'I think he knows something about the Cumming tragedy' she told the reporter, 'ever since that night he had not been himself. He has been acting strangely, as if he has a great secret on his mind. He and Cumming were friendly with the same girl. I know my lover was intimate with her and I know that Cumming met her'.

She also added to the fact of knowing Cumming, that he often besought her to go out with him some night, but she refused.

The newspaper reported that her statement was worthy of investigation. It had been sworn to. And although by her own admission she had broken the moral laws of society she is a jealous woman cast aside by the man she once gave of herself, if the statement had been made from spite then it was only fair to the man that her tongue be silenced. The need for further investigation was imperative. It merits inquiry, they argued, and as the magisterial inquiry conducted by Staines was not closed, merely adjourned, then surely there was sufficient in her tale to cause the authorities to put her on the witness stand and examine her.

They offered to provide the statement, along with her name and address to the proper authorities for it was up to them to demand that she repeat her story in the proper place.[cxxiii]

*

I imagine that Meldon exploded with a tirade of expletives from his temporary office at Roma Street. The unfortunate victim of his abuse was probably Detective Campbell, whose only mistake would have been to ask the Sub-Inspector if he had enjoyed his Sunday off. Henderson stayed out of Meldon's way until Campbell retreated from the office.

"Come with me," he said on spying Henderson.

He took up his coat and hat from his desk.

"Where are we going?" asked Henderson.

"The bloody 'Truth' where else!"

"Hang on," said Henderson, "I'm on robbery now and you're on auto-theft, why do we need to go to the 'Truth'?"

"Do you want me to tell you on the way, or would you prefer Meldon tells you?"

"Walking then are we?" asked Henderson as he checked behind him to ensure Meldon wasn't about to pounce upon him as well.

As they made their way to the office of the newspaper they discussed the article and if there may be some truth in it.

"It's ludicrous!" said Campbell, "the suggestion that a copper would shoot another."

Henderson didn't respond. He was deep in thought. He recalled the temper of his early days in the force. Ten years previous he had been on duty at Albion Police Station when he had an altercation with Constable Joseph Griffin. Griffin had charged Henderson with assaulting him. Constable Griffin swore that he had gone to bed at the station when Henderson, who was still on duty, entered the office and turned on the light. After five minutes Henderson walked out the office onto the back verandah. Griffin, who was trying to get to sleep, then entered the office and turned out the light. He then claims that Henderson re-entered the office and said, 'What the bloody hell did you want to put the light out for, does you think you can do as you like here'. Griffin claimed that Henderson then struck him several times with clenched fists about the head and shoulders saying, 'I will kill you, you bastard!'.

"A penny for them," said Campbell.

"Oh, nothing," said Henderson on being brought back to the present.

"At least we know it wouldn't be either of us," said Campbell.

"What do you mean?"

"Neither of us will be the Constable that Miss X claims killed Cumming."

"Neither of us named you mean?"

"Well you're safe," said Campbell sarcastically, "who would believe the word of some wee young lassie over a Royal Victorian Medal recipient? How is His Royal Highness these days? Keeps in touch does he?"

Campbell was referring to Henderson being awarded the medal by the Duke of York during the recent royal visit when Henderson had been assigned to escort duty. The Duke had been so impressed by Henderson's conduct that he bestowed the award on him at Government House earlier in the year.

"What about you Campbell," retorted Henderson, "still frequenting the track are you?"

Detective Campbell was known to spend a large portion of his free time at the race course. His fellow officers knew of this, but were not aware of the full extent of his gambling habit.

"Shut your cake hole!" replied Campbell.

＊

Although the paper didn't publish the name of her policeman lover there was enough identifying information. Miss X had met the Constable in the April of 1924 while working as a waitress at Sandgate.[cxxiv] The gossip would have been quick to travel outside of the sea-side village of Sandgate and soon everyone was talking. Was it the Constable that had been promoted so quickly to Detective, Martin Elford?

-o-

Constable Elford was stationed at Sandgate during 1924. He had been transferred there from Mount Morgan where he was under the supervision of Acting-Sergeant Cumming. According to Sergeant O'Grady, Cumming had been the source of discontent among the officers stationed there. Elford had been sent to Mount Morgan to gather the correspondence between Cumming and F.A.D.

I also contemplated if Elford had been sent to Mount Morgan so that detectives could interview his wife. Had she been named in the letters from the locker?

＊

Henderson and Campbell spent the week after Meldon's outburst intensely investigating the claims of Miss X. She had been questioned and cross questioned both at her home and within the confines of the Criminal Investigation Department. Nothing that they uncovered could be used as a sound argument against re-opening the magisterial inquiry.

Yet, that had not happened. The 'Truth' found that it was its duty to publish the full sworn particulars which they did with 'certain obviously necessary reservations'.[cxxv]

Thus, with the elimination of names and particulars which might irreparably damage persons who can only defend themselves in the Court, the newspaper published the girl's sworn statement. Along with photographs of Henderson and Campbell as the officers engaged in the investigation of the Cumming-Walsh murders.

The police force closed ranks, so much so that all the paper could report was that an air of mystery hung over C.I.B. as no one was anxious to discuss the matter with the press. That the detectives were puzzled about the girl's statement was no secret however.

Time after time portions of the girl's story were doubted, only to be proven correct. Her policeman lover was asked to give account of his movements on the night of the tragedy. This was accepted.

As long and loud as the 'Truth' called for the inquiry to reopen, the Police would not be goaded. Meldon had been made to look foolish by Gerald McGrath so I doubt if he wished to see the inquiry reopened. The words of Mr. King Would have stuck with them when he charged that with a magisterial inquiry, 'you give people a weapon to attack persons who cannot reply, with detriment to the reputations of those attacked'.

*

Three days after the newspaper article, on a Wednesday, Miss Elizabeth Josephine Clutterbuck married Mr. Archibald McKissock.

*

At the end of November police in New South Wales made an arrest in connection with the sale of bogus art union tickets. The tickets were replicas of the Queensland Golden Casket Tickets and the result slips were also similar to the Casket Results, save for the fact that the numbers coinciding with the tickets sold had been eliminated. By the time the police became aware of the fraud the tickets had been sold in their thousands.[cxxvi]

*

December 16th brought the end to the trial in the Supreme Court of Fitzgerald and Orchard. Although charged with breaking and entering the jury found them guilty of receiving stolen goods. Mr. Justice Woolcock in handing down sentence said he was convinced that Fitzgerald was a dangerous and desperate criminal and sentenced him to eight years imprisonment. In sentencing Orchard to seven years hard labour he said that he was taking into account the fact that it was Orchard's first offence and he was working at the time.[cxxvii]

*

Exactly twelve months to the day after the Cumming-Walsh murder Mr. Justice Woolcock sat in criminal jurisdiction in the Supreme Court. An application had been made by the Crown Prosecutor, Mr. Sheehy, for a 'nolle prosequi'[15]. This was granted. Albert Orchard and James Fitzgerald would not stand trial with having attempted to destroy the C.I.B. office by means of explosives.[cxxviii]

No one was ever brought to trial for the destruction of the physical evidence in the Cumming Walsh murders.

*

In the April of 1928 the Home Secretary (Mr. James Stopford) announced the promotion of Sub-Inspector Meldon to Inspector First-Class as from the 1st May.[cxxix]

At forty-one years of age, Meldon was the youngest Inspector ever appointed in the Queensland Police Force. In announcing the promotion Stopford said of Meldon that he was 'a man of exceptional ability as a police officer. He has the power to control his subordinates in such a way that he obtains the best results without impairing the efficiency, and commands respect. He has been commended by Bench and Bar for his splendid work on innumerable occasions'.[cxxx]

*

In the beginning of 1929 the company known as the Trocadero Dansant Limited was placed into voluntary liquidation and a new company was registered as Trocadero Dansant Entertainment Limited. Mr. J.L. Herbert transferred his interest in his contract for the purchase of the Trocadero land to the new company.[cxxxi]

---

[15] do not prosecute

25 PERFECT SYSTEM

The 'Truth' newspaper stopped pressing for the inquiry to reopen and no progress was made at all over the next twelve months in trying to solve the murders. In the May of 1929 the Labour Government lost power and although James Stopford was returned to serve Mount Morgan he no longer held the position of Home Secretary. He was replaced by Mr. Jens Christian Peterson in May. At first Petersen had represented the Labor Party, winning the Queensland seat of Normanby at the state election of 1915. He resigned from the Labor Party while still an elected member for the seat of Normanby and joined the Country Party because he was disillusioned with Labor's socialist policies. In his resignation speech he blamed the government for maladministration, the crippling of industry, the restriction of development and the creation of financial stringency and unemployment because of legislative measures.

When questioned in December of 1929 concerning allegations the Golden Casket Tickets purchased by some people outside of Brisbane had not been sent to them, Petersen stated that he was not yet prepared to comment.

But stated that the matter was still in the hands of the police, who had been instructed to probe the matter to the fullest extent.

Early in the new year the Minister for Labour and Industry, Mr. H.E. Sizer M.L.A., was invited to the Golden Casket to undertake a tour of inspection of the administration of the office. A number of newspaper representatives were also invited. The manager, Mr. W.S. Noble, explained that the mail received at the Casket Office now averaged five thousand letters a day. On arrival from the post office the mail was opened by a staff of about twenty cashiers and the application form was checked against the amount of money enclosed. Noble continued to explain the processes in place to ensure that applications, money, ticket issues, and result slips passed through different areas to enable cross checking to be conducted. The inspection had impressed the Minister so much he was reported to say that he thought 'the system is as near perfect as is humanly possible to make it'.[cxxxii]

There was one person who must have thought differently. He wasn't sure how he should proceed but knew he couldn't go to the police directly. Stanley Cumming took his story to the independent tabloid newspaper, published weekly in Sydney but read all over Australia, 'Smith's Weekly'.

*

Mr. Noble sat at his desk at the Golden Casket Office with three tickets and envelopes in front of him. The reporter from 'Smith's Weekly' had been to see him after running an article discrediting the claims of the Minister and left the tickets with him. Noble had been compelled to call the police. He waited now for Detective Sergeant

O'Driscoll and Detective Troy to be escorted to his office.

When the Detectives arrived he handed the three Golden Casket tickets, in draw No. 236 Art Union, numbered 8268, 8287, and 12779 to O'Driscoll along with the envelopes.

"Do you know whose hand writing this is?" quizzed Troy.

"Yes," replied Noble, "I've just sent for Miss Hunter to join us."

Miss Margaret Ann Hunter joined them in Noble's office and he explained what was going on.

"Inquiries are being made about an article that appeared in 'Smith's Weekly' today, and I have seen the tickets, which the Detectives now have in their possession and I have informed them the hand writing is yours."

O'Driscoll told her that the three tickets had been handed to Mr. Noble by a representative from the newspaper.

"Do you know anything about it?" he asked.

Miss Hunter appeared reluctant to speak at first then said, "I found the envelopes with the tickets in them among the result slip envelopes on the day after the draw and I took them home to my flat as I was afraid that Mr. Noble would be annoyed with me because they were not sent to the persons to whom they were addressed."

"This is a very serious matter," said O'Driscoll, "you had no right to take the tickets out of the office."

"But I didn't intend to use the tickets to try to win any prize!" pleaded Miss Hunter.

"So how did the newspaper end up with them?"

"I was keeping company with a boy named Stanley Cumming, in June last year, and when I found out who he was, I decided to part with him. We had a dispute and one night he found the tickets and envelopes in a drawer in the duchess in my flat. He took them away with him, as well as letters of mine, and a photo."

"Why would he take them?" asked detective Troy.

"He did this for spite as I refused to have anything further to do with him."

"How do you know it was spite?" asked O'Driscoll.

"He came to the flat about a week later and he threatened to take the tickets to Mr. Noble and get me sacked unless I made it up with him. I refused to do so and he held that threat over my head for months."

"But why did he go to the newspaper now, he's had these for six months?"

"About a fortnight ago he came here to the Casket Office and he showed me the three tickets and he said 'How would they look in Smith's Weekly'. I got annoyed with him and told him to take them down to Smith's if he liked'.

"Why did you have the tickets in your flat?"

"I did not want Mr. Noble to know that they had not been posted."

"The newspaper representative has suggested to me that you took away a number of other tickets and that Cumming states that he has seen you tearing tickets up. Is that correct?"

"I don't recollect anything like that occurring," said Miss Hunter.

"What would you say if I suggested that you, Cumming and a man named Collingwood, set out to swindle the casket in such a way as to draw prizes?"

"That's absurd, it would be impossible for us to swindle the Casket!"

"Could you show me the room where you work," requested O'Driscoll.

Mr. Noble escorted the Detectives and Miss Hunter to

the room. There he explained the method employed in dealing with tickets and result slips. Noble then pointed out the three envelopes to Miss Hunter.

"These are white envelopes, and if you found them as you say you did, amongst the result envelopes, you would not get into any trouble by handing them to me. You would not be held responsible for that at all. That is not your funeral. It is the sorter who would be held responsible for a mistake like that."

Miss Hunter did not respond as she turned her gaze to the floor.

O'Driscoll took Miss Hunter into custody on a charge of having stolen three Golden Casket tickets valued at 15 shillings and nine pence, the property of the committee of Queensland Golden Casket Art Union.

*

O'Driscoll managed to track down Stanley Cumming just after midday on Friday the 13th of December 1929 and asked him to escort him to C.I. Branch. Stanley was led to a room and asked to take a seat while O'Driscoll excused himself.

On his return he had Miss Hunter in his company.

When she saw Stanley she exclaimed,

"This is the man that stole my photograph and my underclothing, and he is the man that took three tickets out of my duchess and threatened to hand them to Mr. Noble to get me the sack!"[cxxxiii]

*

On the 24th of February the case against Miss Hunter was heard in the Police Court to determine if there was sufficient evidence of stealing for the accused to be committed to trial at the criminal sittings of the Supreme

Court. Sub-Inspector Lipp would prosecute with Mr. McLaughlin appearing on behalf of Miss Hunter. They would present their case before Magistrate Hishon.

Mr. Noble was called as a witness and was asked of Miss Hunter's employment by the Casket Office. He responded that she had been with the office since 1920 and in 1926 she was appointed supervisor of ticket writers, with five girls under her, that attracted a weekly wage of £4. The case proceeded as follows,

"Have you thoroughly investigated the matter since Miss Hunter was suspended, Mr. Noble?" asked McLaughlin.

"Yes, I have."

"In other Casket drawings has it been found that a similar mistake had been made?"

"Yes, it has happened twice since Margaret Hunter was suspended."

"In your opinion, knowing the story the girl told, is she dishonest?"

"I object!" roared Lipp.

"I will not require the witness to answer," said the Magistrate.

"I would say that Miss Hunter was a capable clerk," said Noble.

"As the person who laid the complaint and as the manager of the Golden Casket, do you believe that Margaret Hunter was guilty of any dishonesty in what she did?"

"According to the circumstances as I know them she was not dishonest. It was irregular for her to take those tickets. I have checked her work for six months back and I have found it exact and good. There is no sign of dishonesty."

"Having heard the girl's story, do you believe it true?"

"I object," said Sub-Inspector Lipp wearily.

Again the Magistrate stated that he did not require the witness to answer the question.

"I would say her explanation is reasonable," said Noble.

"Now, could it be that Margaret Hunter, fearing dismissal, took those tickets away without any idea of wrongfully using them?"

"The system is as near perfect as possible. It is not quite accurate to say that a mistake made by an employee would bring instant dismissal. That is a matter for the Casket Committee to deal with."

Miss Claire Foreman was the next witness called to the witness box and as the flapper entered the Court Room she smiled at the Court and nodded cheerfully to Miss Hunter in the dock. She proceeded with the utmost candour to tell the court that she had discovered an envelope with a ticket in it appertaining to Casket 236. This envelope having been misplaced among those in which the result slips had to be sent.

"What did you do when you discovered the envelope?"

"I drew Maggie's attention to it, sorry Margaret Hunter's attention to it, and I looked at the ticket and saw that it was in the name of the 'Missing Link' and I said to Maggie, 'It will be a missing link'."

"What did Miss Hunter do?"

"Maggie showed me two other similar envelopes she had found and she took them all away with her."

"How often does it happen at the Casket Office that tickets are found not posted after a Casket had been drawn?"

"Often enough."

"Were the tickets ever mentioned again?"

"Shortly after Maggie took the ticket to her flat she

approached me and said 'the two tickets I found and the ticket you found have been taken from my duchess where I put them by Stan Cumming after I had a row with him, I asked him to give them back, but he would not do so. He kept them for a while and then he threatened to give them to Mr. Noble if I did not make it up to him again'. I used to be in the office when Cumming called to see Maggie and he would threaten her that he would give the tickets to a newspaper."

"You heard him say that?"

"No, I did not hear him say that," said Miss Foreman, "but Maggie told me this after Cumming went away."

"Did you tell Mr. Noble that Miss Hunter took the tickets to her flat?"

"No I did not," she replied, "If I told tales like that about Maggie I would have tales to tell about the other girls. I hope I am not a tale-teller."

"Was this something new, finding tickets amongst the envelopes for the result slips posted them to the subscriber after the Casket is drawn?"

"It was nothing new, no."

"What do the girls do with the tickets they find? Do they take them home or tear them?"

"It is not for me to say. Sometimes Mr. Noble hears of it and sometimes…" she said, smiling broadly and shrugging her shoulders.

Miss Foreman was allowed to step down from the witness box while Thomas O'Hagan was called as the next witness. O'Hagan stated that he was a journalist and that Stanley Cumming came to him on the 4th December the previous year and handed him three tickets in Golden Casket Art Union No. 236. These he locked in a safe then later he took them to Noble, the Casket manager.

The next witness called was Stanley Cumming. Who

was described by the press as a well-groomed young man, with restless eyes that darted hither and thither from beneath bushy eyebrows. When asked for his name and occupation, Stanley stated his name and that he was a waterside worker.

"Do you know the defendant Hunter?" asked Sub-Inspector Lipp.

"Your worship," answered Stanley, "I decline to answer the question."

"What rot!" commented the Magistrate, "answer the question."

"I have known her since June 1928, and kept company with her till June 1929, often visiting her flat at Kia Ora in Wickham Terrace."

"Do you also know Miss Claire Foreman?"

"Yes, I do know her."

"Do you know Thomas O'Hagan?"

"I refuse to answer that on the grounds it may incriminate me," responded Stanley.

"Do you know that man?" pursued Lipp, pointing at O'Hagan.

"I refuse to answer."

"Did you call on Margaret Hunter at the Casket Office?"

"I refuse to answer on the same grounds as the other refusals."

"Did you see those tickets before today?"

"I also refuse to answer that."

"Your Worship," said Lipp somewhat exacerbated, "Could you please direct the witness to answer the questions."

"I'm sorry Sub-Inspector," responded Hishon, "but I hold that he has a perfect right not to say anything if it might incriminate him, and, I think he is entitled to some latitude."

"Look here Cumming," said Lipp, "when did you see those three tickets last!"

"I've already said I refuse to answer, on legal advice, on the grounds that the question may incriminate me."

"Did you see them in Hunter's flat?"

"I refuse to answer."

"Were you shown those tickets at the C.I.B. on January 22nd."

"Yes, I saw them there."

"When did you see those tickets prior to the time you saw them at the C.I.B.?"

"I refuse to answer that as well. I think I made it quite clear that I will not answer anything that might incriminate me."

"But you did write a letter to Margaret Hunter, didn't you?"

"I again refuse to answer."

"Were you associated with Margaret Hunter in the stealing of those tickets?"

"I object," interjected Mr. McLaughlin.

"And I refuse to answer," said Stanley.

"Did you induce Hunter to remove the tickets from the Casket office?"

"I refuse to answer."

"I ask that this witness be treated as hostile!" snapped Lipp at the Magistrate.

"No," replied Hishon considerately, "I won't do that."

"I can't carry it any further," said Lipp pushing himself back into his chair.cxxxiv

"This is ludicrous," roared McLaughlin, "if this is the best the police can come up with then I ask the Court to dismiss the charge against my client!"

Hishon was quiet for a moment before stating that he

was satisfied that an offence had been committed and the case would go to trial on the 7th April. Bail was set at £20.[cxxxv]

*

A week later and the Attorney-General, Neil Francis MacGroarty, filed a nolle prosequi in the case of Margaret Hunter. It would not proceed to trial.[cxxxvi]

*

Mrs. Ellen Stopford, wife of Mr. James Stopford, M.L.A. for Mt. Morgan, died, at a private hospital at Gympie on Thursday morning, 22nd May. She was a Brisbane native, 52 years of age, and had returned only a few days before from a tour through New Zealand with her husband, whose health is not by any means good. Both of them were on their way to Alpha, in Central Queensland, when at Palmwoods railway station she became very ill. At Gympie she was taken from the train to hospital where she died.[cxxxvii]

*

Early in December of the same year, in what was reported as tragically sudden circumstances, Dr. J. Espie Dods passed away at his home in Wickham Terrace aged fifty-six.[cxxxviii]

26 COLD CASE

I assume that case of Margaret Hunter was Stanley's attempt to expose the Golden Casket system, and the link to his father's death, thereby exonerating himself and his mother. His plan had failed. The Cumming-Walsh murders were now officially a cold case with the removal of all detectives from the active pursuit of the guilty person or persons. What remained of the police files were bundled up, secured with 'Restricted Access' tape, and sent for storage. The restricted access meant that the files could not be accessed for sixty-five years without the express permission in writing from the Police Commissioner.

*

In the September of 1931 Mrs. Mary Philomena Smith, daughter of Mr. James Stopford, passed away at a private hospital in Gregory Terrace a week after giving birth to a son.[cxxxix]

*

During 1932 the Labour Party won back control of the Queensland State Parliament. Mr. James Stopford was elected the member for Maryborough contesting that electorate after the seat of Mt. Morgan was abolished under a redistribution adjustment. He was returned as the Home Secretary.

*

On the Sixth day of September 1932 it was charged under the Police Acts and Rules that Detective Campbell, between the 12th day of April 1932 and the 1st day of July 1932, at Brisbane and Cloncurry, that he, then being a member of the Police Force of Queensland, was guilty of misconduct and conduct unbecoming a member of the Force; in that he associated with three men known as Roy Phillips, alias Wilson, alias Howard, alias Dean, alias Curtis; Frank Rance, alias Frank Young, and Douglas Lawrence Phillips, alias Edwards, knowing that these men were implicated in the theft of motor-cars reported to the police as stolen in Brisbane; and that he received various sums of money, amounting to £80 from said Roy Phillips, alias Wilson etc. and Douglas Lawrence Phillips, alias Edwards, to condone the offence of stealing.[cxl]

During the trial Rance gave evidence that he first met Campbell in relation to the theft of a motor-car from Sydney, that he had sold in Brisbane, due to getting into difficulties with a bookmaker. Campbell was the only member of the Police Force to interview Rance and at that time Campbell suggested that he obtain a car on hire purchase for on selling, reporting the car as stolen to the police, as Campbell was in charge of automotive theft at C.I. Branch. When he met Campbell at the races he told him that he had got the car. He gave Campbell a sum of money for the information relating to a Pontiac that had been impounded at C.I. Branch and sold to Rance by Campbell. Rance had been induced to purchase it by Campbell who told Rance there would be more.

Rance then met Campbell at his home and when Campbell asked for £25 it was handed over, as Rance thought he might get into serious trouble for selling the car he brought from Sydney. He alleged that Campbell said 'I did not ask for a receipt for that car, I could make things unpleasant for you'. Rance alleges he said to Campbell 'You ought to have plenty of money, what do you do with your money', to which Campbell had replied, 'Oh, horses. I've been sticking to a couple of fellows here'.'[cxli]

Detective Martin Elford also called upon to give evidence.[cxlii]

Campbell was dismissed from the Force and sentenced to imprisonment with hard labour for eighteen months. A jury found him guilty but also asked for leniency. In his sentencing the Judge said he had taken into account that Campbell had received 17 favourable records and rewards whilst he was at C.I. Department, but he had deliberately embarked in crime and had used his position as a sergeant of police for the purpose of facilitating its commission and to prevent its detection. However he found it difficult to forgive him for calling upon his wife to give evidence. The other troupe of perjurers did not matter so much. His honour then asked Campbell what cases had he provided evidence in, as he felt that no doubt the court would hear from those convicted.[cxliii]

-o-

Campbell was now a discredited officer. He had been the detective that was alone with Josephine Clutterbuck when the theatre tickets were produced in support of

Stanley's alibi. Was Campbell implicit in concealing the identity of the Cumming Walsh murderers?

Detective Elford had also been called to give evidence and appears to be one of the witnesses that Justice Macrossan called a 'troupe of perjurers'.

*

Later that year, Mr. Talty, Secretary of the Police Union, made allegations of corrupt practices against certain parliamentarians and administrative officers of the police force, during a general meeting of the Police Force Union. The executive unanimously agreed that further action by the Union was not warranted. The Police Union Secretary and the Home Secretary were known for the animosity that existed between them with numerous allegations and counter allegations being made in the privilege of parliament and in the Police Union Journal.

*

During May of 1934 an appeal was heard before the Police Appeal Board against the decision by the Commissioner of Police in dismissing Ex-Sergeant Sexton from the force following a charge of conduct unbecoming to a member of the Police Force in that he disrespectfully spoke of a superior officer to a constable.

Evidence was given by a constable that in the early hours of March 28th Sergeant Sexton had a conversation with him in Queen Street, in which it was alleged that Sexton said, among other things, that a licensee of the Arcadia Hotel was very friendly with Jacky Meldon, that he had got Jacky to go to the Marathon Club, and that they would fix Jacky's friends.

The Arcadia Hotel was across the road from the Marathon Club and complaints had been received about rowdy drunkenness about the vicinity of the Marathon Club.

Sexton denied that the conversation had taken place saying that he had not visited the constable at the time it was alleged to have taken place. A visit to a constable at the time, he said, would have been disclosed in his book.

The Board consisted of Mr. Ferguson, Police Magistrate, Inspector Ferguson of Toowoomba representing the Commissioner, and Mr. Talty secretary of the Police Union.

Mr. King appeared for the appellant and Inspector Meldon for the Police.

"Please explain your report Constable Barrett," asked Meldon.

"Around twelve thirty in the morning at the intersection of Queen and Albert Streets, I was standing near the T&G Corner. Sexton approached me and he said 'How are things' and I said 'Good'. Then he said 'that complaint that was read out tonight about the Marathon Club came from Dallon. Dallon is very friendly with Jacky Meldon. Dallon has got Jacky to go to the Marathon Club. I will take you down one night and we will catch Dallon. He is a friend of Jacky's and I am going to get square with him'."

"What did you say to that?" asked Meldon.

"I said, ' It may be hard' and Sergeant Sexton said, 'I will get a friend of mine to go inside and at a given time open the door and we will go down the lane and rush in'. He then said 'Come on down and we will take a look'. We then went down to the Arcadia Hotel and went on the verandah of the hotel and Sergeant Sexton had a look at the door and window, and he said that there was a peephole."

"To whom was he referring when he said Jacky Meldon?"

"Inspector Meldon, yourself, sir."

"Why wasn't this conversation in your first report?" asked Mr. King.

"The first report was not full, I made the second on instructions."

"Why did you not put the visit to the Marathon Club in your first report?"

"The first report was not a full report."

"I put it very emphatically to you," said Mr. King, "that you and Sexton went down and had a look at the Arcadia Hotel and then went back to the corner of Queen and Albert Street. You were not at the club!"

"I was at the club."

"If the Sergeant can bring evidence to the effect that he was talking to an ambulance bearer at the ambulance station at Ann Street at the time you said you had a conversation with him at twelve thirty, what would you say?"

"It is false. We went to the Marathon Club. A man opened the door from the inside and Sergeant Sexton stepped in and asked me to follow him. We went up the stairs to the back portion of the club. The attendant asked Sergeant Sexton if we were looking for someone and he replied we were looking for a chap. We then left the club and returned to the intersection of Queen and Albert Streets. Sergeant Sexton then said 'We will fix Jacky's friends' then he went down Albert Street towards Adelaide Street."

"How do you know he was referring to Inspector Meldon when he was saying Jacky Meldon?" asked Meldon.

"I have heard Mr. Talty mention Jacky Meldon at union

meetings."

"That is the schoolmaster," said Inspector Meldon.

"Did you report this matter on your own instance or at the invitation of anybody?" asked Mr. King.

"On my own instance," said Barrett.[cxliv]

Sergeant Francis Fahey then gave evidence and told the board that Patrick Dallon, licensee of the Arcadia Hotel had made a complaint to him about the conduct of people visiting the Marathon Club in Elizabeth Street and he had furnished a report to the Inspectors at Roma Street.

Peter Sexton was then called to give evidence and stated that he had visited him on the evening of April 27th and reprimanded him for his slovenly bearing, a reprimand which he appeared to resent.

It was reported that a cook at the Marathon Club by the name of Panos remembered the Sergeant and Constable being at the club at twelve thirty.

When cross-examined Sexton said that at various times he had reported illicit drinking at the Marathon Club and Panos was prosecuted by the traffic police for sly grog selling. He knew Panos as a friend of Dallon's. He admitted that he had been reprimanded by Inspector Meldon about gambling adding that each time he reported gambling, Inspector Meldon seemed to resent it.

"Did I not tell you," said Meldon, "you were not to go into betting shops without a warrant!"

"Yes, but I went into Swanson's which is a known betting shop looking for a man wanted by C.I. Branch for assault and robbery," responded Sexton, "I saw betting going on and thought it my duty to take the cards and instruments of gaming that were being used."

Herbert Thomas Cabell, ambulance bearer, stated that Sexton was talking to him at the ambulance centre from twelve twenty to twelve thirty a.m. on March 28th.

The Chairman of the Board then announced that the decision would be communicated to the Commissioner of Police.[cxlv]

-o-

In 1936, James Stopford died of heart disease and cirrhosis of the liver at the Mater Misericordia Hospital, Brisbane. He was fifty-eight years of age. After a state funeral he was buried in Toowong cemetery.[cxlvi] Inspector Meldon was assigned to the Rockhampton District at his own request.[cxlvii]

-o-

Henderson passed away suddenly in 1939 at the age of fifty-one with the reputation of being one of the best men in the force, taking particular care to be fair to both sides.

He had a special aptitude for dealing with embezzlement and fraud cases. He became an acting-Sergeant in 1923, Sergeant in 1929, and Senior-Sergeant in 1932. He accompanied the Duke and Duchess of York throughout their tour of the State and was appointed Sub-Inspector in 1934.[cxlviii]

Was it possible that Henderson was sent on 20 days leave at a crucial point in the murder investigation as it was felt that his aptitude for embezzlement and fraud may have uncovered the truth?

Later that year, December 1939, Stanley Cumming joined the Royal Australian Airforce then being 34 years old commencing duty as a flight mechanic.

-o-

In 1941 Joseph Henry Stopford, the younger brother of the former Home Secretary and Minister for Mines, James Stopford, passed away suddenly at the age of 57 years.

Joseph Stopford had been employed at the Golden Casket Office since 1924 often officiating at the Golden Casket drawings. He became unwell at his desk after having assisted to overhaul the Golden Casket machine at City Hall. Prior to joining the Golden Casket Office he had been employed as a moulder at the Mount Morgan mine.[cxlix]

-o-

In 1942 Mrs. Alice Elizabeth Herbert filed a claim for maintenance in the Brisbane Summons Court on the grounds that she had been left without means of support. Joseph Lionel Herbert, by then a Warrant Officer with the Australian Infantry Forces, frankly admitted that twelve months after he parted from his wife on November 11th 1929, he had become fond of another woman and had since been living with her as husband and wife. His allegations of his wife's adultery with a man, whose name he said he knew but would not divulge to the court, were strenuously denied by his wife.[cl]

Was this the truth? If Alice Herbert had been involved with Marquis Cumming then Herbert may have had another motive. Framing Mrs. Cumming with his evidence would certainly have removed the spotlight from him.

At the end of 1942 Stanley Cumming was discharged from the Royal Australian Air Force.

-o-

During 1943 Inspector M.J. Meldon passed away at the age of fifty-six years in Toowoomba. He had moved from Rockhampton to Toowoomba two years earlier where he retired in August 1942.[cli]

Stanley Cumming married Marmion Barbara Kearns in

St Stephens Cathedral.[clii]

-o-

In 1944 a retired Policeman, Acting Sergeant Robert Stewart Christie, no relation to Eileen Gladys Walsh nee Christie, had the good fortune to win first prize in the Golden Casket on two occasions, six weeks apart. The prizes totalling £7,800. At the time, Casket officials stated that the odds against winning two first prizes in such a short period, with tickets bought from the same agent, were almost incalculable.[cliii]

Robert Christie had been stationed at Roma Street during 1926 and was promoted to Acting Sergeant in 1929. In the same year he commenced a series of transfers to regional centres throughout the State until his retirement in February 1941. Robert had little time to enjoy his incredible stroke of luck as he passed away in March 1945 survived by his wife E.G. Christie.

Mrs. Theresa Jane Cumming also passed away, in 1945, at sixty-nine years of age.[cliv] After his mother's death Stanley's behaviour became erratic presumably from grief.

-o-

In 1946 Stanley pleaded guilty to a complaint of unlawful assault. Stanley was now a residential proprietor, renting out rooms in a boarding house in Little Edward Street, the 'Kenross Private Hotel'. William John Robinson had entered the residential to see his wife, who had a room, and requested that he be allowed to stay in the room for the night. Stanley told him it was against regulations and an altercation ensued that culminated with Stanley striking several blows to the man's head with a lead pipe.^{clv}

-O-

Then in 1947 Stanley was charged with having attempted to kill George Webster. Stanley conducted his own defence. He pleaded not guilty before Chief Justice Macrossan and a jury. It was alleged that on the morning of September 19th Webster saw Stanley and asked for a room. Stanley had asked to see his identification papers. Webster complied and went out. On his return Stanley believed he was under the influence of liquor, although Webster claimed that he had only had a few drinks, Stanley told Webster to get out. Webster got his belongings and stood on the footpath outside the premises. Stanley then appeared with a shotgun, which he discharged at Webster, who was unhurt. Stanley claimed he had fired a blank. It is then stated that Stanley went inside and loaded a live shell into the gun. He reappeared and fired at Webster, hitting him in the leg.

Stanley alleged that he had been resting in his room when he heard stamping and quarrelling in Webster's room. He went out and saw Webster go into the yard where his wife was washing. He heard Webster offer his wife £5 and make an improper suggestion to her. Then he told Webster to get out. He said that he fired the blank shell at the ground and aimed the live shell at the palings of a fence.^{clvi}

Detective Sergeant McNichol said that he arrived at 'Kinross' at three-thirty p.m. were he saw Stanley Cumming in the kitchen with Sub-Inspector Talty. The Detective took possession of a double barrelled 12 gauge hammer type shotgun and two boxes of cartridges. Later he accompanied Stanley to the Brisbane General Hospital and saw Webster who had suffered injuries to both legs. Stanley was then taken to C.I. Branch and arrested.

Two schoolboys from St. Joseph's College Gregory Terrace gave evidence that they heard a man with a shotgun held at his waist say 'I'll give you two seconds to get away' before firing at a man outside the private hotel. Webster, they said, 'grabbed his legs' after being shot and they could see his legs were bleeding.

At the end of November 1947, Chief Justice Macrossan found Stanley Cumming guilty of having unlawfully wounded George Webster on September 19th. He passed a sentence of six months imprisonment stating, 'You are evidently a man of very violent temper. I feel I must impose some sentence. I cannot treat the offence of discharging a loaded firearm at a man as a mere peccadillo.

It is a very serious offence. The fact that a man is married with dependents, cannot be used as a shield to enable him to discharge loaded firearms at people and escape punishment'.

His Honour remanded Stanley, after his conviction, for medical observation. The report of the G.M.O. (Dr. Cameron) was that he showed no signs of mental defects or disorders but that he was of excitable temperament and emotionally unstable.[clvii]

-o-

In February 1951 Stanley Cumming had been motivated to approach Brisbane Detectives by fresh information that had recently come into his possession. The Criminal Investigation Branch reopened the case but refused to discuss the matter with the press beyond confirming that Stanley Cumming had made two statements to the police, and that these were being investigated.

Stanley Cumming was quick to talk to the press and was considered frank in his discussions with them.

'There are some people, I know, who have always held the suspicion that either I or my mother did the shooting', he told the 'Truth' newspaper, 'This is a dreadful lie, a complete mistake, which has followed me for a quarter of a century. Naturally, I should like the mystery solved, to clear my dead mother's name and my own. The police questioned me at the time, once for 12 hours on end, and kept a girlfriend in an adjoining room for six hours, questioning her along the same lines. When they found that our independent stories of my night's movements, we were in a theatre, completely dovetailed, they dropped the matter, realising it was impossible for me to have been responsible for the shooting.'

'The fact that both mother and I knew that dad had had various love affairs with women in Mount Morgan and Brisbane, gave police, and other people, what they thought would be a motive for either of us to shoot him and Mrs. Walsh. Fortunately for us we were both able to establish incontrovertible alibis which showed it was impossible for either of us to have been near the place that night.'

'Naturally, I have seldom had the crime out of my mind. Whatever my father's faults he was still my father, and a good father. I have always hoped that, someday, his murderer would be caught. Recently I happened on some information which, it seemed to me, formed three clues that could very easily be of value in leading the police to a solution of the mystery, and I have passed this on to them, together with the names of persons to be interviewed'.

'I have always leaned to the theory that my father and Mrs. Walsh could have been done to death by a jealousy crazed woman, one of several whom unfortunately, he found it so easy to deceive simultaneously. Did one such follow them to the paddock at Park Road that night, and mad with jealousy at what she saw, shot them both, and then hurry away unseen?'

Stanley told the press that this was the direction that one of the new clues he had given police lead, the other was of a quiet different nature and concerned a man with whom Acting-Sergeant Cumming was on ill-terms.

The following week Stanley approached the newspaper and informed them that he was offering a £1500 reward for information that will lead to the conviction of the murderer, or murderers. Stanley stated that he 'did not know that they had made any progress at all' and he wanted the thing to move so he decided to offer '£1500 hard cash as a reward'.

The detectives reviewed the case documents, added Stanley's information, then placed another sixty-five years access restriction on the file.

-o-

In 1957 Stanley had his name changed by deed poll. He felt burdened with the name Marquis David James Stanley Cumming that he had only used for official documents. Preferring the simpler Stanley James Cumming.

-o-

In October 1963, Stanley wrote to the RAAF to inform them of his name change and to seek a change of his discharge papers to reflect this so that he could access repatriation services. Included with this request is a twenty-three pages long letter, a rambling, at times incoherent, discourse of portions of his life and the Queensland economy. There is a marked difference in the hand writing and tone of this letter to that which he had written to the Department in 1946. He complains of being unwell, with the, at times, indistinguishable contents of his letter attesting to his state of health.

At one stage he recounts his altercation with George Webster. 'Well, I fired a blank 12G pigeon gun blast at the ground and he bent up and died for that one and you could hardly hear it so to get more noise effect I fitted a live bugger in the right choke barrel and let go at the 3 $^5/_8$" hardwood paling fence 3ft from his blasted feet and one, only one, pin head No.7 pigeon shot sphere soft lead hit him on the ankle and only one blasted 70 year old paling fell off the fence and he jumped aside as the old batten hung in the nob nail for a second or two then fell out on the footpath. I then saw the cow pull up his trouser leg and I knew I was done for. I knew I had drawn first blood with a firearm. I planted hid the blank shell safely, too safely, and couldn't find it until 4 moons after the show was all over. 12 of the CIB did not find it either...'[clviii]

What I found curious was that Stanley admitted to concealing evidence. So well concealed that 12 men from CIB couldn't find it. Was it possible that Stanley had concealed the evidence from his father's murder? Did Stanley have something to do with the disappearance of this father's belt, handcuffs and keys? Could Stanley have committed patricide?

-o-

Permission to access restricted material must be obtained from the responsible agency, the Queensland Police Service. The murder files are now held by the Queensland State Archives and are not available for public access. Unless permission is granted prior by the Commissioner of Police.

This restriction applies to the following files:

Item ID 790800 Murder File **CUMMING STANLEY MARQUIS DAVID & WALSH EILEEN GLADYS** – Restricted to 20th February 2024

Item ID 666221 **Murder file: Cumming, Marquis Joseph; and Walsh, Ellen Gladys** – Restricted to 27th April 2034.

Item ID 666212 **Murder file: Walsh, Ellen Gladys; and Cumming, Marquis Joseph** – Restricted to 27th April 2034.

27 SCAFFOLD OF SHAME

At the time of writing, the Cumming-Walsh murder remains a cold case. After spending many hours researching the facts of the case it has been difficult not to develop conspiracy theories. There are even websites now dedicated to cold cases where subscribers attempt to ply their detective skills to solve this very mystery. One such site makes the claim that they, 'just as Meldon, like Mrs. Cumming for it'. Which is completely understandable given her alibi was loose on exact times and supported by a woman, her mother, who had trouble remembering how old she was. But she was the only one to have offered an alternate scenario to the jealous lover theory.

The problem with the jealous lover theory is that the crime scene did not fit the pattern of a crime of passion. The Cumming-Walsh murder was committed by someone who coldly fired one shot to the head of each. If Mrs. Cumming was guilty, it would be of conspiracy to commit murder and not the actual act. A hired hit-man would need proof that he was the one who performed the deed. The missing belt, handcuffs, keys and wedding ring could have provided that proof.

Mrs. Cumming denied having hired an agent to follow her husband, but then, she denied a great many things. But there is no available evidence that she was ever asked directly if she had sought such a deal, a contract for the life of her husband. Had Herbert planted a seed in her mind when he states he told her, 'don't do it yourself'?

However, Mr. Herbert is a conundrum himself. Why did he come forward with the information he did? There was no reason that can be established from the available information as to why the police would have needed to speak to him. He had been convicted for sly-grog selling and his dance hall had been resumed for the widening of the street before the murders. After he gives evidence at the inquiry the council sells the property back to him on generous repayment terms, provides him with the funds to move the building frontage, and establishes a lane way into the rear of the dance hall.

He was under surveillance by the predecessor to A.S.I.O. at the time. He lied about his age on his attestation papers to gain entry to the Australian Military in World War One[clix] and again in World War Two.[clx]

After the insolvency of his company and the transfer of his share of the Trocadero he left Brisbane for Adelaide, leaving his wife to manage the venue. In Adelaide he established 'The Floating Palais', a dance hall on a barge, on Lake Torrens, only to have it sink after a muffled explosion is heard by the caretaker.[clxi] Another bombing, another coincidence.

He returns to Brisbane and takes over management of 'The Jungle Club' in Brunswick Street New Farm. While there he is charged with assault on two separate occasions, one against Wenzel Horachek[clxii], the other against William Joseph Howden[clxiii]. I have been unable to prove a connection between William Joseph Howden and Mrs.

Cumming nee Howden.

Herbert then leaves Brisbane for Sydney, where he tries to find investors for a casino in Noumea.[clxiv] Apparently this was unsuccessful as shortly after he has an appeal against a conviction dismissed by the High Court. He had been found guilty upon four charges of the Bankruptcy Act and sentenced to four months imprisonment.[clxv]

In 1942, while serving as a Warrant-Officer in the Australian Army, his wife files a desertion suit. She alleges that in 1929 he knocked her about and blackened both her eyes due to his being confronted with seeing another woman. He counter-claims that the altercation was as a result of her adultery. He further admitted to at one time having assets of £90,000 but declared that business failures had eaten them up.[clxvi]

Eventually his restaurant in Sydney was also declared bankrupt. At the time that Stanley Cumming comes forward with new information Herbert is living in Western Sydney, working as a restaurant manager. There is no trace of him after this time.

Although circumstantial, it would appear as though Herbert did receive favours immediately following his appearance at the Magistrates Inquiry. If these were favours for services rendered then the obvious question that follows is who were the favours for? Was the favour purely for providing incriminating testimony or for something more sinister?

One thing that can be established beyond doubt is that most witnesses at the Magistrates Inquiry lied about something. The denials of what was said by various people means that either one of the participants in various conversations must have lied. Most however have at their core Mrs. Cumming. But the inquiry was notable by the absence of two key witnesses, Jessie Cumming and Mrs.

Page. Their statements were presented to the court by Detective Campbell, who was later discharged from the service, placing in doubt all testimony he had ever given. If he perjured himself in those cases then why not this one?

But if Campbell and Herbert lied then who were they lying for? If it was someone who could influence the Brisbane City Council to return the Trocadero to Herbert then they must have held some position of power. It may be purely coincidence that the State Member for Mount Morgan was also the Home Secretary. A position with considerable influence over the Police Force. A position with oversight of the lucrative operations of the Golden Casket. A position responsible for the establishment of the Brisbane City Council. A position that continually denied calls for a police station to be opened at Spring Hill. A position were the incumbent found that his future son-in-law had the great fortune to win thirty-thousand acres of land in a government ballot and first prize in the casket. This coincidence must have been the driver for Stanley's later court appearance. But that case never found its way to trial, thanks to the decision by the Attorney-General. Had there been pressure brought to bear there as well?

Did that pressure rise again to ensure that Orchard and Fitzgerald would not stand trial for the bombing of the C.I.B. Office. An act that may have eliminated all physical evidence in the murder case. The word 'may' is used deliberately. Without access to the Case File it can only be assumed. Unfortunately as there is no meta-data for the case file, there is at present no way for anyone outside the Police Force to know exactly what is in the file, if anything. Did someone know that the target of the bombing was not the robbery material that would convict Orchard and Fitzgerald? Would taking them to trial for it lead to scrutiny of the inventory of what else was held in the property room that night?

The physical evidence would reveal far more about the case than the testimonials gathered at the Inquiry. Yet the act of bombing did not remove all that could be learnt from the physical evidence. The photograph of the murder scene, entered as Exhibit 1 at the Inquiry, appears to still offer clues. The dark shadow about the Policeman's neck appears to be more than a shadow. If this was blood, as suggested by the testimony of the Train Driver and his Fireman, then it appears to contradict the evidence of the G.M.O. For that amount of blood to be present about the front of the chest, after being shot in the back of the neck, would have meant that the Acting Sergeant must have been on his front for a period of time before being positioned where he was found. The distance between the bodies also seems to be counter to the G.M.O.'s evidence. The fact that no bullet was found beneath Eileen's head is also counter to this evidence. Might the bombing have been ordered to prevent any re-evaluation occurring?

The bombing may have also destroyed the many letters referred to at the Magisterial Inquiry as pointing to the numerous affairs of Cumming. Letters that were retrieved from the Acting-Sergeant's locker by the disgraced Campbell. These were not entered into evidence at the Inquiry merely referenced by the detectives. The only letters entered into evidence were correspondence that it is said occurred between Cumming and the woman from Mount Morgan retrieved by Detective Elford. A man that appears to be implicated by Miss X and grouped with a 'troupe of perjurers' in Campbell's trial. The letter attributed to the woman from Mount Morgan indicates that she and the Acting Sergeant were not on the best of terms at the time as she takes exception to being 'classed in the low set'. Is it possible that this woman had attempted to blackmail Cumming with the knowledge of an illegitimate child? And yet the Detectives introduce three letters reportedly from this woman and written by Cumming that suggests that they are very much in love. One of the letters raises suspicion as it is incorrectly dated, as Wednesday the 21st December 1926, when the 21st of December 1926 was a Tuesday. Twice in these letters, those dated the 5th and 12th of December 1926, reference is made to Cumming's four children, when in fact he had five children living at the time.

Although both Mrs. Cumming and Stanley Cumming identified the handwriting as that of Marquis Cumming, and although there are similarities, there are also enough differences for a hand-writing expert to place some doubt that the letters were written by him. Which would account for the denials of the content of the letters. But to convince those closest to the writer that the author was the Acting-Sergeant would require considerable skill in counterfeiting. Skill enough to escape undetected with producing bogus Golden Casket Tickets perhaps?

These questions may be answered by reference to the murder file as well as other documents that have been placed under restricted access, including,

Item ID 566416 Police Service File **Cumming Marquis** sealed until the 24th July 2046,

Item ID 559370 Police Service File **Martin John Meldon** sealed until the 24th July 2041,

Item ID 560016 Police Service File **Martin Elford** sealed until the 1st January 2040,

Item ID 559755 Police Service File **Francis Baker** sealed until the 1st January 2049,

Item ID 559390 Police Service File **William Bonas** sealed until the 1st January 2035,

and,

Item ID 559876 Police Service File **Percy Mullally** sealed until the 1st January 2036.

There is a process whereby a request can be made to view restricted access files. A process that I have completed three times for the murder file over the past ten years and on all occasions the request was denied. I am in no way questioning the decision. But I do fail to understand, when a restricted access file is added to, why the sixty-five year restriction period is reset for the entire file?

The dates set for restriction mean that any number of conspiracy theories cannot be disproven until the last date is passed, one hundred and twenty-three years after the murders. No doubt the culprit has by now died of old age as was feared by the newspaper reporters at the time. Of cause this is a cold case, there is no reason for an official active investigation to solve near one hundred year old murders. One can only assume that the information contained in the files does not identify the culprit, otherwise, someone would have been brought to justice. So the usefulness of the files is purely their ability to disprove alternate theories. But they should at least demonstrate that alternatives were considered and the reasons for not pursuing those particular lines of inquiry.

-o-

The following is my honest opinion of the events surrounding the murders of Marquis Cumming and Eileen Gladys Walsh based on the information available.

The murder was premeditated and not a crime of passion. It was a deliberate hit of the policeman. A member of the Cumming household was asked to provide information pertaining to the Acting-Sergeant leaving the house without his revolver. The most likely candidate is

Stanley. Stanley has been described as quick to temper, emotionally unbalanced, and was afraid of his father, having run away from him on two occasions. It may also be assumed that Stanley hid the weapon from his father that night to ensure his father left without it. Cumming would have removed it from his hip pocket, where he is said to have carried it, to sit down for the evening meal. At one stage Mrs. Cumming said the weapon was on the table when her husband left the house, yet detectives found it in his bag the next day. I doubt that Stanley was aware that the use of this information was to allow the murder to be perpetrated.

Stanley was probably able to be induced to provide this information by the offer to provide an alibi. He states that when living at Stephens Road he had no particular girlfriend. However, shortly afterward, Miss Josephine Clutterbuck provides his alibi. The collaborating evidence, the theatre tickets, were produced in the presence of Detective Campbell. Campbell was later convicted of perverting the course of justice, while Miss Clutterbuck married Archibald McKissock within twelve months of the murders. A letter from an anonymous source apparently indicates that Mrs. Melican, Miss Clutterbuck's employer, had evidence that would contradict Stanley's alibi but was said by Campbell to lead to nothing.

Further, I believe that the person Stanley notified, that the Acting-Sergeant had left home without his revolver, was Joseph Lionel Herbert. I don't believe that Mrs. Cumming arranged for the hit on her husband.

Herbert appears to be pivotal to the case. Given his conviction and the resumption of his dance hall before the murders only to see the land and building returned along with funds to undertake substantial improvements after his testimony. Herbert proclaims that he had amassed assets to the value of £90,000. A substantial amount for the time. Managing the Trocadero must have been a very lucrative business. And Cumming was at the Trocadero the night before he was killed.

Had Cumming uncovered a bogus Casket Ticket racket. Had he sent such a ticket to F.A.D. to determine if the bogus ticket could be passed off as legitimate? When he heard that the ticket was accepted had he approached the counterfeiting syndicate for a piece of the action or to expose it? Were Herbert and Jamieson, a printer by trade, part of the syndicate?

I do not believe that Herbert was either the gunman or the financier, but rather an accomplice, a middle man, the 'bag man'. Although I question the veracity of Jamieson's evidence what if there is some truth in it? The shorter of two men sighted in the vicinity of the crime that night he described as between five feet three inches and five feet six inches of moderate build. Herbert was five feet five and a half inches and eleven stone. The shorter of the two was described as having a shorter gait such that it was suggested that the second man was in fact a woman. Might someone who had recovered from having their leg crushed by a boulder also have had a restricted gait?

However this possibility, that the second man was in fact a woman, appears to have been suggested to Jamieson during the magisterial inquiry. Much credence is given to his testimony over the other witnesses that were called. The number of shots fired being a major point. At least three other witnesses confirmed hearing three shots on the night, Johns, Waygood, and the on duty prison guard. This would seem to be for the purpose of supporting the theory presented by the arrangement of the bodies. The other issue I have with his evidence is that he states that he saw Cumming and a woman proceed down Annerley Road then turn into a laneway that leads to Burke Street. There is no line of sight from his garden to this laneway. Jamieson could not have seen this occur as he has described.

The evidence of the actual shooting suggests to me that the Policeman and Eileen where standing facing each other when a shot was fired from behind Cumming. His reaction was to scrunch his shoulders and lower his head. A second shot was fired with the passage of the projectile through his back to the base of his skull consistent with the bullet holes in his tunic and undershirt. He fell face down on the ground and his blood flowed to drench the front of his shirt. The third shot fired struck Eileen in the face and exited from the base of her skull. Witnesses suggest that there was between 15 and 60 seconds between the second and third shots.

I believe that their assailant then set about arranging the bodies and clothing as they were found. The concern I have with the GMO's evidence was only raised when I learnt that he had signed off Cumming as medical fit for duty after Cumming had had an operation, yet stated at the Magisterial Inquiry that he did not know the Acting-Sergeant. The only inference that can be drawn from the presence of spermatozoa is that Eileen was close to ovulating and had sexual relations sometime during the five days leading up to her death.

I believe that sometime after Mrs. Cumming had visited Mrs. Christie, Stanley informed his mother of what he had done. Adding that the people who had approached him warned him about speaking to the police and possibly threatened her children. This would account for the supposed legal stance taken and Mrs. Cumming asserting that 'the bodies were arranged that way to put that as a motive' and for her denials for having made the remarks to Mary Christie and those she made at the morgue, for her comments had the effect of making her appear guilty. Her guilt, I believe, was in her protection of Stanley and possibly her other children.

In all probability it appears unlikely that Eileen Walsh had a prearranged meeting with Marquis Cumming. It would appear that she was lured to the railway reserve, either on the pretence of looking for a stray dog perhaps, or, the prospect of being provided information as to the whereabouts of James Delacour. However she would have been cautious, remembering that Spider Raper was shot just five days earlier and within seven hundred yards of her Stephens Road home. It must have been someone she knew or trusted. A policeman other than Cumming or a former one-time resident of Stephens Road perhaps, Stanley Cumming.

The only evidence that links the two victims was a Christmas card and an entry in the relief book at the South Brisbane Police Station. The Christmas Card supposedly sent from Eileen to Cumming was not submitted as evidence at the inquiry and her mother could not positively identify the handwriting as her daughter's. Eileen's mother and her husband both state she was not in receipt of a pension yet it was stated that there was an entry in the relief book at the station. Given Cumming was known to have taken money from an account while at Mount Morgan it is not inconceivable that he falsified such records for personal gain.

Personally, I don't believe that Cumming was the only one guilty of falsifying records. The marked discrepancy between the tone of the first letter from the woman in Mount Morgan and those supposedly sent subsequently from Cumming suggest forgery. The letters however contain topical information regarding the Acting-Sergeant's life, so if falsified, it must have been by someone with close contact. Reference is made to his father's illness and the shooting of Spider Rapper. The person who collected the letters was Detective Martin Elford who appears to be the policeman implicated by Miss X. If it was Cumming's knowledge of a counterfeiting syndicate that lead to his demise then presumably these letters could have as easily been forgeries.

In 1925 Francis Annie and Robert Doak were living in Gordon's Lane in Mount Morgan were Robert worked as a miner. This would have been a difficult time for the family as the mine was due to close resulting in the displacement of 3,000 workers. No other connection between these individuals and anyone else involved in the case has been established at this juncture. She was not called to testify to that effect at the inquiry. She may have been paid off or had no knowledge that she had been implicated as the source of the letters.

The many letters that were reportedly found in the Acting-Sergeant's locker by Campbell were not admitted as evidence at the inquiry. If such letters did exist they were either destroyed by the bombing or are in the restricted access files held in Queensland State Archives.

There are two possibilities for the letters to have been found in the Acting-Sergeant's locker. Either they were placed there after the murder, using the keys from his belt. In which case there may have been items removed that would have pointed to the true motive. But to gain access to the locker would require the perpetrator to have been a police officer or impersonator to gain entry to the police station. Or alternatively, they were planted there by the person who found them, Detective Campbell. Both scenarios seem plausible in the circumstances.

It is only in recent times that the catch phrase, "follow the money", has been used to suggest a money trail or corruption scheme within political office. In this case "following the money" would seem to lead to Herbert and the Golden Casket. I am of the belief that winning Golden Casket tickets were used as a means of distributing payments for illegal activity and money laundering for it was common practice for purchasers to use nom de plumes to buy tickets ensuring anonymity. This belief is based on the fact that the Casket Office was under the control of the Government, although the Office described the processes as a "perfect system" evidence is found to the contrary. The fact that the brother of the Home Secretary worked for the Casket Office and Stanley's unexplained motive for trying to expose the flaws of the "perfect system" appear too coincidently for it not to be so.

I was nagged by Campbell's question of Mrs. Cumming about her husband being on a pension. I then remembered the evidence given by Jack Herbert 'the Bagman' at the Fitzgerald inquiry held during the late 1980s. Jack Herbert testified that the protection money that allowed illegal gambling and prostitution to flourish in Queensland was part of a racket known as 'the Joke'. Could the payments for illegal activity at the time of the murders been known as 'the Pension'?

The common surname is a coincidence. Jack Herbert was born in 1924 in London, the year after Joseph Lionel Herbert married Alice Conway in Brisbane.

I believe it is possible that E.G. Walsh nee Christie may have been mistaken as E.G. Christie wife of Police Constable Robert Stewart Christie who was lucky enough to win two first prizes in the Colden Casket, the odds of which were considered incalculable at the time. The odds of the coincidence in the names of the murdered woman and the policeman's wife would presumably be similar.

It also seems highly implausible for Herbert and

Campbell to have acted alone. The money trail suggests Herbert was paid off while Campbell due to his poor education, or rather bad education as reported in is personnel service record, appears to be merely a foot soldier. The most likely associates appear to be Meldon and the constable referred to by Miss X suggest that Elford was the 'Hit Man'.

The conjecture against Meldon and Elford is purely circumstantial. Both were promoted rapidly. Meldon held a strong position in determining the course of action regarding gambling, he was favoured by the Home Secretary, and was notably absent when the C.I. Branch was bombed.

On the death of the Home Secretary, Meldon transfers out of Brisbane. It would appear as though his protection had been removed. Elford had been promoted to Detective Sergeant stationed in Toowoomba by that time.

Although this is all purely conjecture it does seem to offer a plausible alternative to the jealousy crazed woman scenario that Stanley Cumming proposed twenty-five years after the murders.

I could have written a work of fiction loosely based on true events, but I actually doubted that an audience would believe some of the coincidences. What you have just read is the accumulation of my research into a true crime murder mystery. Unfortunately it was never solved and is unlikely to ever be.

*

Eileen Gladys Walsh nee Christie, my Great-Grandmother, had a child when she was seventeen years of age. The father's name was not included on the birth certificate. That child, my Grandfather, was adopted when he was six months old, something he did not learn until later in life. His dying wish was for his birth mother to be found. And she was. He never knew the story of her passing, murdered in the company of a policeman, in the process of sexual intercourse.

Eileen Gladys Walsh has been condemned to stand on the scaffold of shame for eternity, along with Marquis Cumming, as justice has not been found.

I could not leave her story there and I made it my mission to research the case as deeply as possible. I have not been able to delve as deeply as I would have liked, due to the restricted access of some records, but, from the information readily available to the public I soon found myself agreeing with the newspaper reports of the time, 'that the whole business is fishy, and very fishy indeed'.

-o-

On the Christmas Eve of 2006 I stood in the South Brisbane Cemetery before grave number 2H-338, the final resting place of Eileen. An unmarked paupers grave. When I say grave, I mean a bare patch of sloping earth at one side of the cemetery beneath a fifty year old iron-bark tree. I don't know what I was expecting but it wasn't that. I was suddenly filled with the same emotions of two small boys who would have stood at that very spot eighty years before me. And, yes, I cried.

Antony W Rogers

Figure 1 - The Murder Scene clxvii

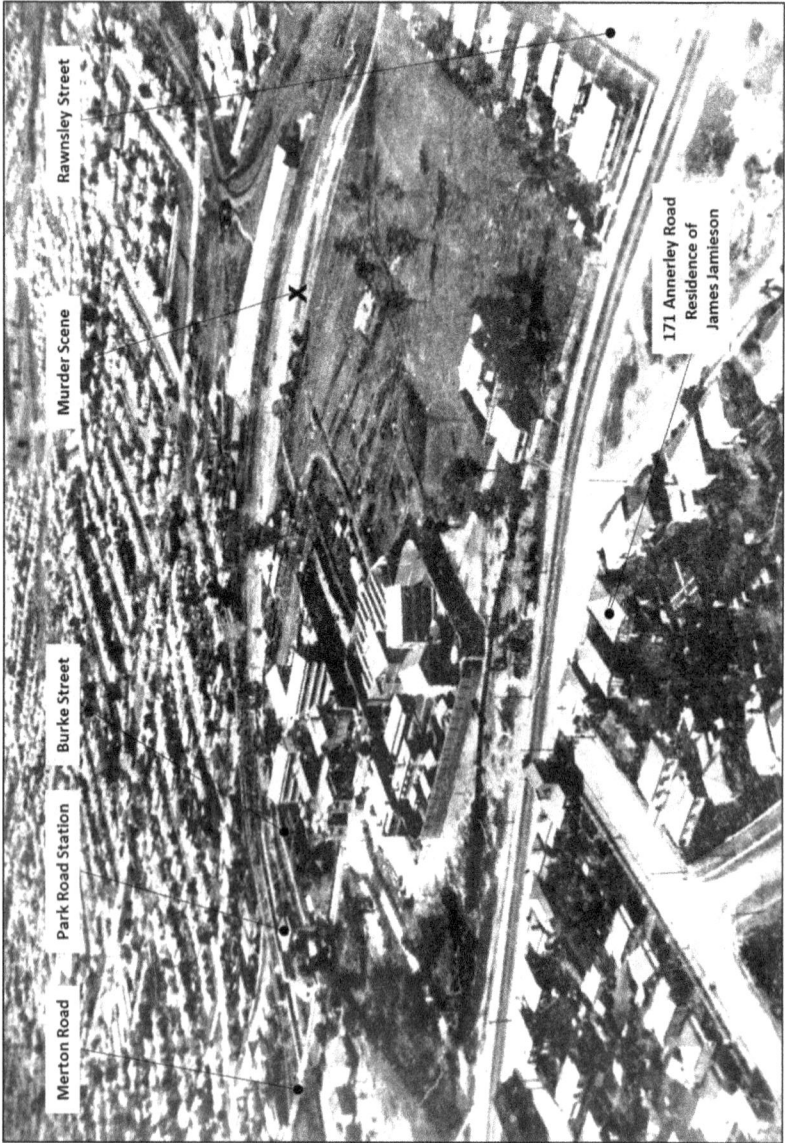

Figure 2 - Aerial view of Boggo Road Gaol, Brisbane, 1929[clxviii]

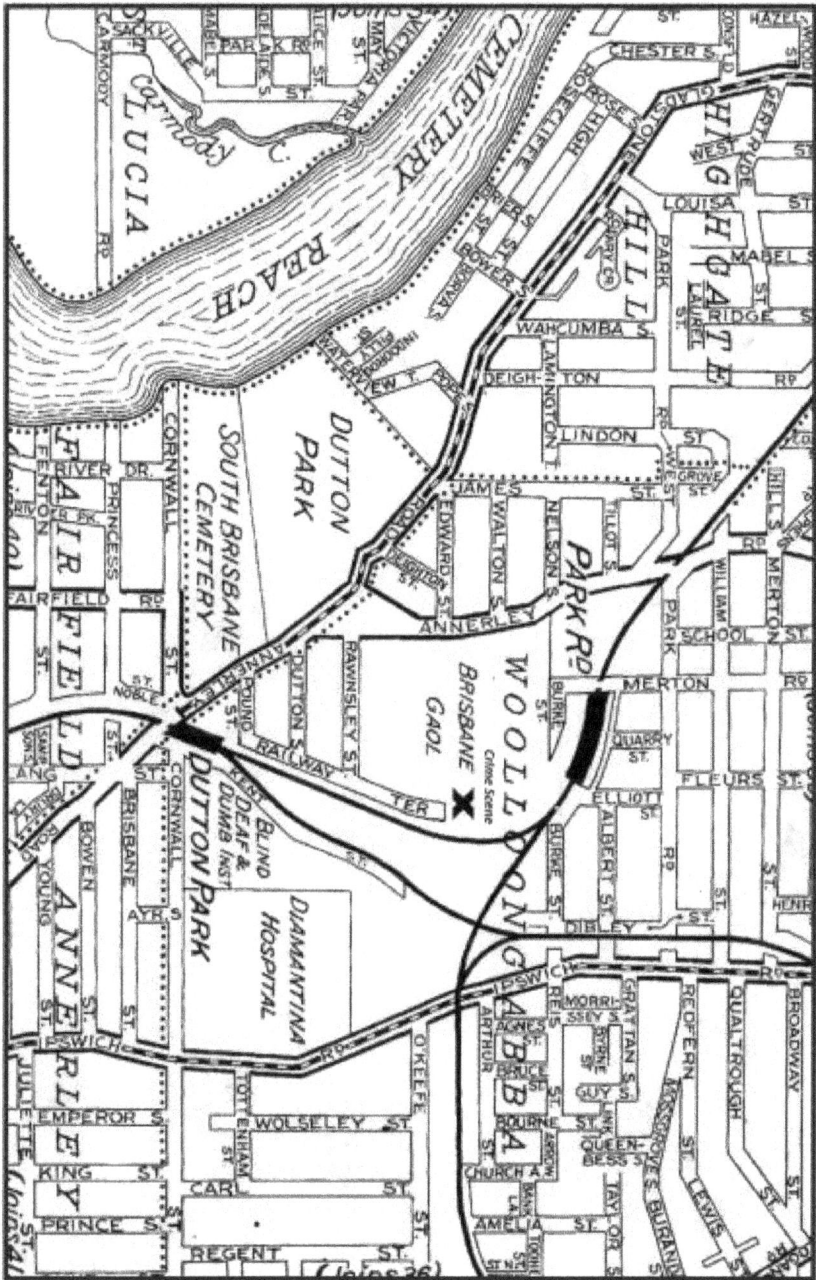

Figure 3 - Refidex Directory 1926 Map 35 Page 73. Crime Scene indicated by X

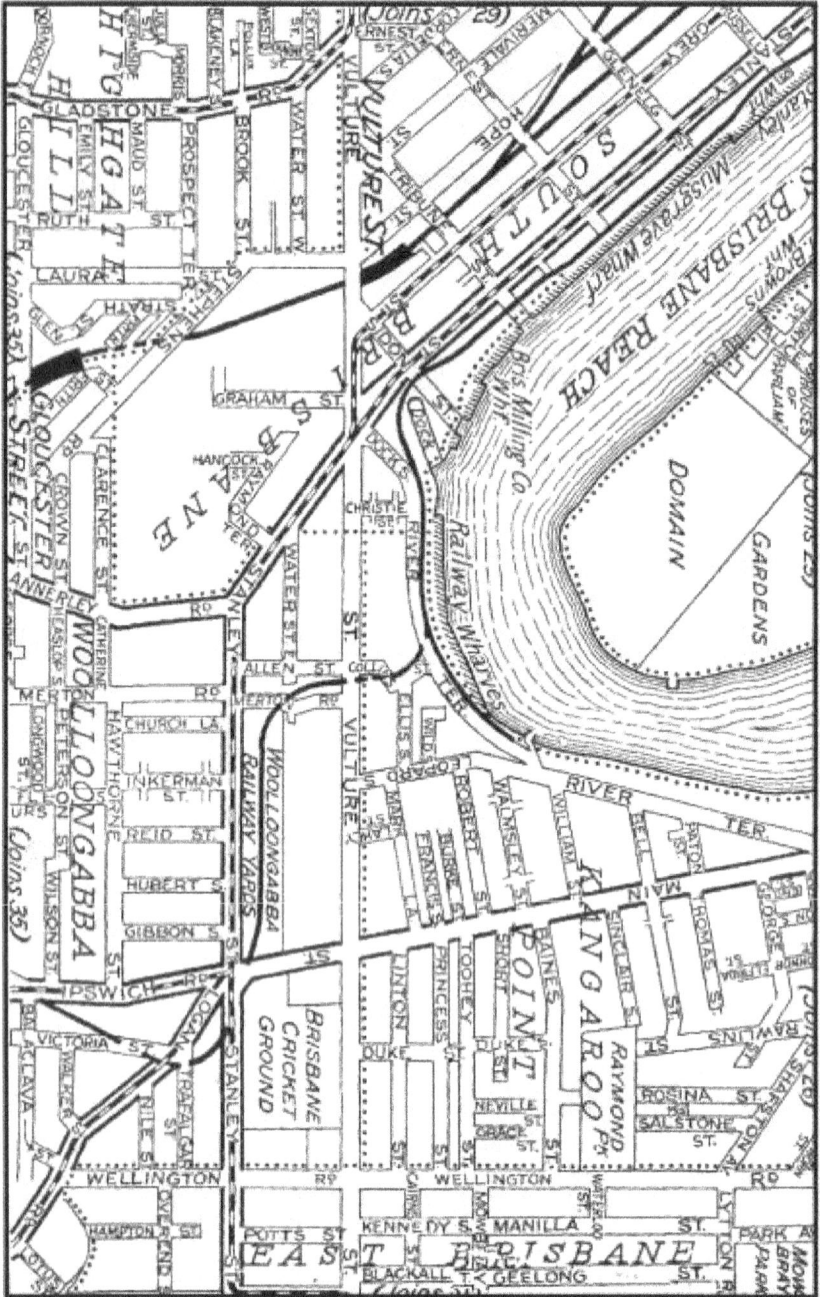

Figure 4 - Refidex Directory 1926 Map 30 Page 63

Note: Wilton Street is incorrectly labelled Wilson Street

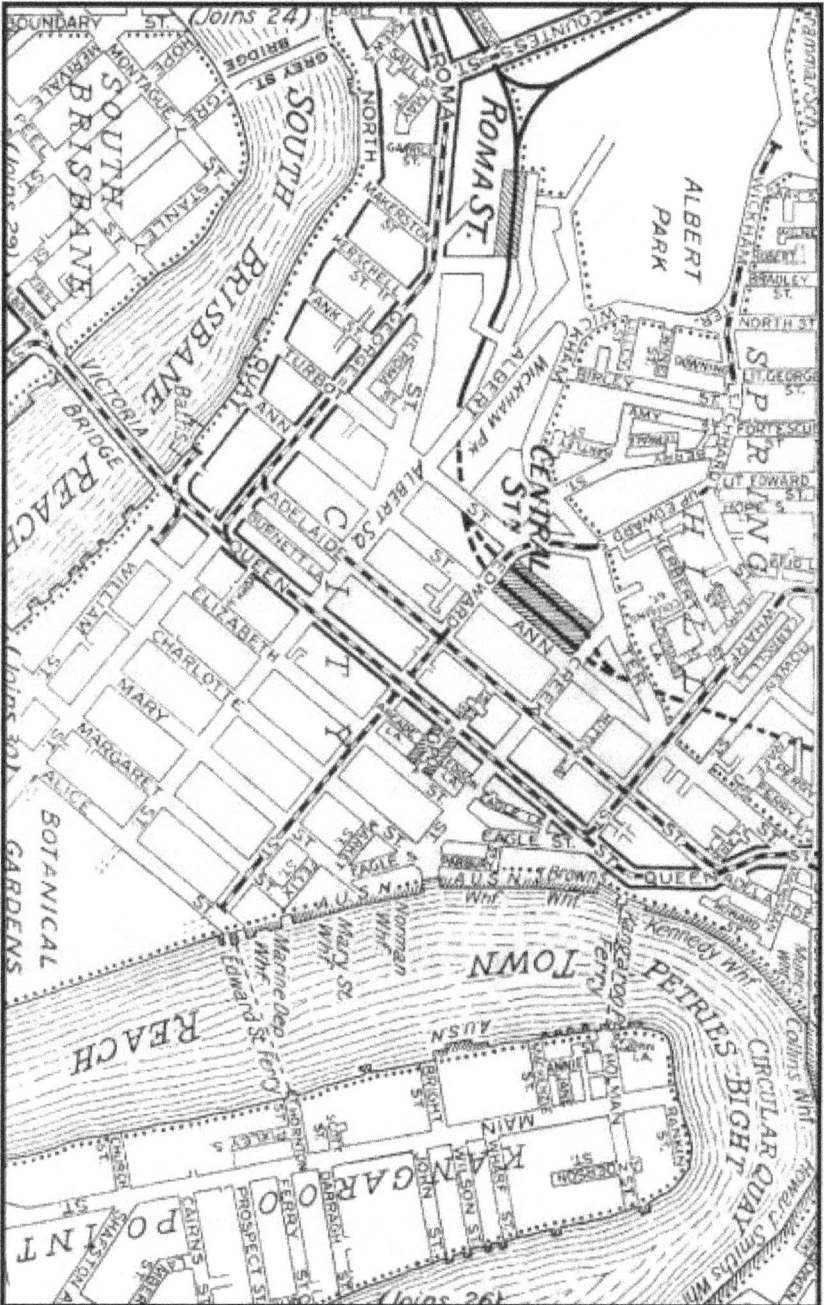

Figure 5 - Refidex Directory 1926 Map 25 Page 53

Figure 6 - Acting Sergeant Cumming at the Trocadero Dansant 1924[clxix]

Figure 7- Mrs. Eileen Gladys Walsh (nee Christie) Circa 1916[clxx]

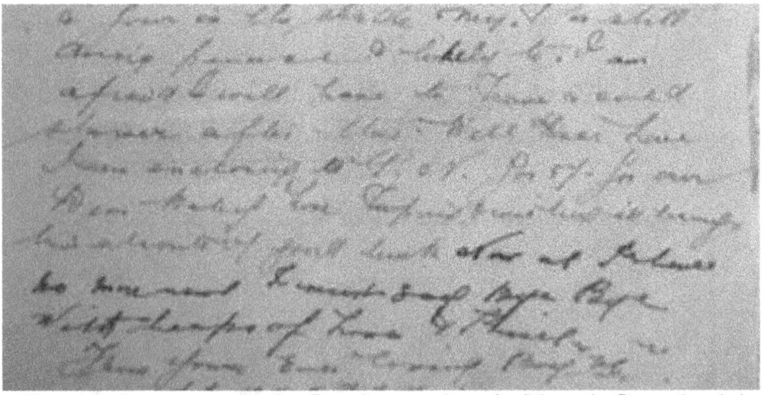

Figure 8 - Letter presented to Inquiry as written by Marquis Cumming[clxxi]

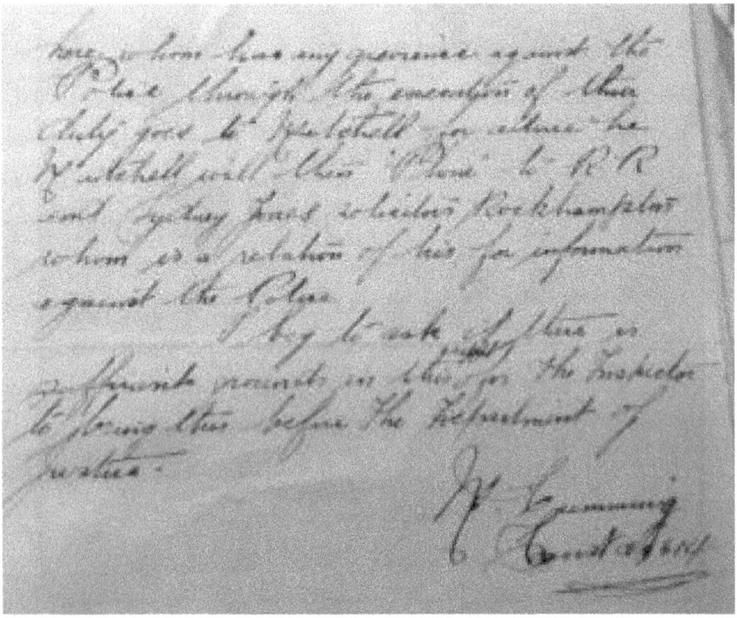

Figure 9 - Letter written by Marquis Cumming held on his Police Service File[clxxii]

Figure 10 - Aftermath of CIB Bombing 17 August 1927[clxxiii]

ABOUT THE AUTHOR

Antony W. Rogers and his family have a long association with Brisbane. His paternal Great-Grandfather immigrated from Cornwall in 1858 and settled at what is now known as Nundah. He is also a descendant of Job Stone, whose son James became known as the founder of Stones Corner when, in 1875, he purchased land on the corner of the present day Logan and Old Cleveland Roads. In the 1930s his maternal grandfather served as an altar boy at the Church of the Ascension at Morningside. His grandfather also attended Cannon Hill State School leaving to take up an apprenticeship at the blacksmith's works in Wynnum Road before his marriage. Antony was also baptized and confirmed at the same Church and his marriage was solemnized there, as well as being the location for the renewal of his wedding vows under the same Minister twenty-five years later. Antony completed tertiary studies in Mechanical Engineering and Business Management that supplied the foundations for his career in information technology project management. His interests include fly-fishing, travel and genealogy. The latter sparking him to produce the family history book 'Australian Rosemorder Diaspora' as well as the narrative non-fiction title 'The Ascension'.

[i] 1926 'DOUBLE-MURDER AT SOUTH BRISBANE', The Telegraph (Brisbane, Qld. : 1872 - 1947), 24 December, p. 9., http://nla.gov.au/nla.news-article179228594

[ii] 1928, The True facts of Australia's greatest double murder mystery : who murdered Act. Sgt. Cumming and Mrs Eileen Walsh at Brisbane, 23rd December, 1926? Nielsen & Simmons, http://nla.gov.au/nla.obj-603489374

[iii] 1926 'DOUBLE MURDER.', The Northern Herald (Cairns, Qld. : 1913 - 1939), 29 December, p. 47., http://nla.gov.au/nla.news-article149383621

[iv] 1926 'DEATH STRIKES GUILTY PAIR IN LAST EMBRACE', Truth (Brisbane, Qld. : 1900 - 1954), 26 December, p. 1., http://nla.gov.au/nla.news-article199286675

[v] Di Maio, Vincent J. Gunshot Wounds: Practical Aspects of Firearms, Ballistics, and Forensic Techniques, Second Edition, CRC Press, New York, 1999.

[vi] Queensland State Archives Item ID349443, Inquest file, Page -B-

[vii] 1928, The True facts of Australia's greatest double murder mystery : who murdered Act. Sgt. Cumming and Mrs Eileen Walsh at Brisbane, 23rd December, 1926, Nielsen & Simmons, Brisbane, P. 15 http://nla.gov.au/nla.obj-603497476

[viii] 1927 'VITAL CLUE IN CUMMING—WALSH MURDER MYSTERY HAT WITH A HISTORY', Truth (Brisbane, Qld. : 1900 - 1954), 6 February, p.1., http://nla.gov.au/nla.newsarticle199290432

[ix] 1927 'VITAL CLUE IN CUMMING—WALSH MURDER MYSTERY HAT WITH A HISTORY', Truth (Brisbane, Qld. : 1900 - 1954), 6 February, p. 14., http://nla.gov.au/nla.newsarticle199290432

[x] 1927 'SOUTH BRISBANE DOUBLE MURDER', Smith's Weekly (Sydney, NSW : 1919 - 1950), Queensland Edition, 12 February, p. 3.

[xi] 1926 'DUTTON PARK MURDER.', The Evening News (Rockhampton, Qld. : 1924 - 1941), 31 December, p. 5., http://nla.gov.au/nla.news-article202408459

[xii] 1924 'GOLDEN CASKET', Northern Star (Lismore, NSW : 1876 - 1954), 3 October, p. 5., http://nla.gov.au/nla.news-article93459318

[xiii] 1924 'Golden Casket Allegations.', Truth (Brisbane, Qld. : 1900 - 1954), 7 September, p.6., http://nla.gov.au/nla.news-article198671125

xiv 1924 'GOLDEN CASKET DRAWINGS.', The Longreach Leader (Qld. : 1923 - 1954), 5 September, p. 20., http://nla.gov.au/nla.news-article39333791

xv Queensland State Archives Item ID349443, Inquest file, Page J

xvi 1928. The True facts of Australia's greatest double murder mystery : who murdered Act. Sgt. Cumming and Mrs Eileen Walsh at Brisbane, 23rd December, 1926?, Commonwealth (ill.) 2nd ed, Nielsen & Simmons, Brisbane, Page 35

xvii Queensland State Archives Item ID349443, Inquest file, Page u

xviii Queensland State Archives Item ID349443, Inquest file, Page A

xix Queensland State Archives Item ID349443, Inquest file, Page I

xx 1927, Smith's Weekly (Sydney, NSW : 1919 - 1950), 5 February, p. 9. , http://nla.gov.au/nla.news-page25332257

xxi Queensland State Archives Item ID349443, Inquest file, Page c

xxii Queensland State Archives Item ID349443, Inquest file, Page e

xxiii Queensland State Archives Item ID349443, Inquest file, Page -F-

xxiv Queensland State Archives Item ID349443, Inquest file, Page -o-

xxv 1925 'CONVICTED OF ASSAULT.', The Daily Mail (Brisbane, Qld. : 1903 - 1926), 17 March, p. 8., http://nla.gov.au/nla.news-article219084204

xxvi 1926 'SECRET WHICH LIES BEHIND THE HIGHGATE HILL SLAYING', Truth (Brisbane, Qld.: 1900 - 1954), 26 December, p. 9., http://nla.gov.au/nla.news-article199286711

xxvii 1927 'MURDER CHARGE', Queensland Times (Ipswich) (Qld. : 1909 - 1954), 7 January, p. 6. (DAILY.), http://nla.gov.au/nla.news-article116911499

xxviii Queensland State Archives Item ID349443, Inquest file, Page -U-

xxix 1923 'FIRE AT ZILLMERE.', Daily Standard (Brisbane, Qld. : 1912 - 1936), 18 April, p. 2. (SECOND EDITION), http://nla.gov.au/nla.news-article183907667

xxx Queensland State Archives Item ID349443, Inquest file, Page -z-

xxxi Queensland State Archives Item ID349443, Inquest file, Page -y-

xxxii Queensland State Archives Item ID349443, Inquest file, Page -E-xxxiii 1926 'SECRET WHICH LIES BEHIND THE HIGHGATE HILL SLAYING', Truth (Brisbane, Qld. : 1900 - 1954), 26 December, p. 9., http://nla.gov.au/nla.news-article199286711

xxxiv 1922 'SPRING HILL GANGS.', The Daily Mail (Brisbane, Qld. : 1903 - 1926), 21 January, p. 6., http://nla.gov.au/nla.news-article220524244

xxxv 1934 'Theorist Sleuths Baffled By Trunk Murders', Truth (Brisbane, Qld. : 1900 - 1954), 22 July, p. 18., http://nla.gov.au/nla.news-article198229506

xxxvi Queensland State Archives Item ID349443, Inquest file, Exhibit 9

xxxvii Queensland State Archives Item ID349443, Inquest file, Exhibit 10

xxxviii Queensland State Archives Item ID349443, Inquest file, Exhibit 11

xxxix 1926 'DEATH OF MRS. A. MEE.', The Evening News (Rockhampton, Qld. : 1924 - 1941), 17 December, p. 4. , http://nla.gov.au/nla.news-article202418301

xl Queensland State Archives Item ID349443, Inquest file, Page -Q-

xli Queensland State Archives Item ID349443, Inquest file, Page -W-

xlii Queensland State Archives Item ID349443, Inquest file, Page m

xliii 1915 'Jamieson's Jokes', Truth (Brisbane, Qld. : 1900 - 1954), 28 February, p. 10., http://nla.gov.au/nla.news-article203047612

xliv 1927 'DOUBLE MURDER MYSTERY', Truth (Brisbane, Qld. : 1900 - 1954), 23 January, p. 14., http://nla.gov.au/nla.news-article199288767

xlv 1927 'VITAL CLUE IN CUMMING—WALSH MURDER MYSTERY HAT WITH A HISTORY', Truth (Brisbane, Qld. : 1900 - 1954), 6 February, p. 14., http://nla.gov.au/nla.newsarticle199290432

xlvi NAA:B2455, HERBERT J.L. 1413

xlvii NAA: A402, W290, HERBERT, Joseph Louis (or Leonard), AIF, Sub-manager, Trocadero Dancing Palais, South Brisbane. Communist sympathiser and subscriber to funds.

xlviii Queensland State Archives Item ID 2828915, Ecclesiastical (will) file

xlix Queensland State Archives Item ID566416, Police service file

l Queensland State Archives Item ID566416, Police service file

Antony W Rogers

───

li 1938 'Obtained Divorce After 35 Years Of Married Life', The Telegraph (Brisbane, Qld. : 1872 - 1947), 8 April, p. 9. (SECOND EDITION), http://nla.gov.au/nla.newsarticle183477583

lii 1927 'GOLDEN CASKET.', Morning Bulletin (Rockhampton, Qld. : 1878 - 1954), 1 February, p. 9., http://nla.gov.au/nla.news-article55265987

liii 1926 'Family Notices', The Telegraph (Brisbane, Qld. : 1872 - 1947), 27 December, p. 6., http://nla.gov.au/nla.news-article179229160

liv 1931 'AFTER SHORT ILLNESS.', Daily Standard (Brisbane, Qld. : 1912 - 1936), 28 September, p. 16., http://nla.gov.au/nla.news-article178958356

lv 1941 'Late Mr. J. H. Stopford.', The Telegraph (Brisbane, Qld. : 1872 - 1947), 7 February, p. 11. (CITY FINAL LAST MINUTE NEWS), http://nla.gov.au/nla.news-article172720081

lvi DO THE AUTHORITIES WANT TO PROBE THE CUMMING MURDER? (1927, May 15). Truth (Brisbane, Qld. : 1900 - 1954), p. 13., http://nla.gov.au/nla.news-article203934759

lvii 1927 'MURDER ECHO.', The Brisbane Courier (Qld. : 1864 - 1933), 22 February, p. 12., http://nla.gov.au/nla.news-article21101950

lviii 1927 'DO THE AUTHORITIES WANT TO PROBE THE GUMMING MURDER?', Truth (Brisbane, Qld. : 1900 - 1954), 15 May, p. 13., http://nla.gov.au/nla.news-article203934759

lix 1927 'DO THE AUTHORITIES WANT TO PROBE THE GUMMING MURDER?', Truth (Brisbane, Qld. : 1900 - 1954), 15 May, p. 13., http://nla.gov.au/nla.news-article203934759

lx 1929 'THE TROCADERO', The Brisbane Courier (Qld. : 1864 - 1933), 2 February, p.15., http://nla.gov.au/nla.news-article21372371

lxi 1928 'RECKLESS MR. STOPFORD', The Telegraph (Brisbane, Qld. : 1872 - 1947), 6 February, p. 8. (CITY EDITION), http://nla.gov.au/nla.news-article179756526

lxii 1928. The True facts of Australia's greatest double murder mystery : who murdered Act. Sgt. Cumming and Mrs Eileen Walsh at Brisbane, 23rd December, 1926?, Commonwealth (ill.) 2nd ed, Nielsen & Simmons, Brisbane, Page 10

lxiii 1928. The True facts of Australia's greatest double murder mystery : who murdered Act. Sgt. Cumming and Mrs Eileen Walsh at Brisbane, 23rd December, 1926?, Commonwealth (ill.) 2nd ed, Nielsen & Simmons, Brisbane, Page 15

412

lxiv 1927 'The Bulletin SATURDAY, JUNE 4, 1927.', Townsville Daily Bulletin (Qld. : 1907 - 1954), 4 June, p. 4., http://nla.gov.au/nla.news-article60798326

lxv Queensland State Archives Item ID349443, Inquest file, Page a

lxvi 1927 'Southside Murders', The Week (Brisbane, Qld. : 1876 - 1934), 10 June, p. 7., http://nla.gov.au/nla.news-article187592722

lxvii Queensland State Archives Item ID349443, Inquest file, Page c

lxviii Queensland State Archives Item ID349443, Inquest file, Page g

lxix Queensland State Archives Item ID349443, Inquest file, Page e

lxx Queensland State Archives Item ID349443, Inquest file, Page f

lxxi Queensland State Archives Item ID349443, Inquest file, Page h

lxxii Queensland State Archives Item ID349443, Inquest file, Page j

lxxiii Queensland State Archives Item ID349443, Inquest file, Page k

lxxiv Queensland State Archives Item ID349443, Inquest file, Page m

lxxv Queensland State Archives Item ID349443, Inquest file, Page n

lxxvi Queensland State Archives Item ID349443, Inquest file, Page o

lxxvii Queensland State Archives Item ID349443, Inquest file, Page q

lxxviii Queensland State Archives Item ID349443, Inquest file, Page t

lxxix Queensland State Archives Item ID349443, Inquest file, Page u

lxxx Queensland State Archives Item ID349443, Inquest file, Page A

lxxxi Queensland State Archives Item ID349443, Inquest file, Page B-C

lxxxii Queensland State Archives Item ID349443, Inquest file, Page E-H

lxxxiii Queensland State Archives Item ID349443, Inquest file, Page I

lxxxiv Queensland State Archives Item ID349443, Inquest file, Page K

lxxxv 1928. The True facts of Australia's greatest double murder mystery : who murdered

Act. Sgt. Cumming and Mrs Eileen Walsh at Brisbane, 23rd December, 1926?, Commonwealth (ill.) 2nd ed, Nielsen & Simmons, Brisbane, Page 33

lxxxvi Queensland State Archives Item ID349443, Inquest file, Page L-Q

lxxxvii Queensland State Archives Item ID349443, Inquest file, Page S

lxxxviii 1928. The True facts of Australia's greatest double murder mystery : who murdered Act. Sgt. Cumming and Mrs Eileen Walsh at Brisbane, 23rd December, 1926?, Commonwealth (ill.) 2nd ed, Nielsen & Simmons, Brisbane, Page 35

lxxxix 1927 'UNCOMPLIMENTARY WITNESS', Truth (Brisbane, Qld. : 1900 - 1954), 12 June, p. 13., http://nla.gov.au/nla.news-article203941578

xc Queensland State Archives Item ID349443, Inquest file, Page -b-

xci Queensland State Archives Item ID349443, Inquest file, Page -f

xcii 1928. The True facts of Australia's greatest double murder mystery : who murdered Act. Sgt. Cumming and Mrs Eileen Walsh at Brisbane, 23rd December, 1926?, Commonwealth (ill.) 2nd ed, Nielsen & Simmons, Brisbane, Page 38

xciii Queensland State Archives Item ID349443, Inquest file, Page -k-

xciv Queensland State Archives Item ID349443, Inquest file, Page -n-

xcv Queensland State Archives Item ID349443, Inquest file, Page -o-

xcvi Queensland State Archives Item ID349443, Inquest file, Page -o-

xcvii Queensland State Archives Item ID349443, Inquest file, Page -p-

xcviii Queensland State Archives Item ID349443, Inquest file, Page -v-

xcix Queensland State Archives Item ID349443, Inquest file, Page -w-

c Queensland State Archives Item ID349443, Inquest file, Page -y-

ci Queensland State Archives Item ID349443, Inquest file, Page -z-

cii Queensland State Archives Item ID349443, Inquest file, Page -B-

ciii Queensland State Archives Item ID349443, Inquest file, Page -F-

civ Queensland State Archives Item ID349443, Inquest file, Page -Jcv Queensland State Archives Item ID349443, Inquest file, Page -P-

cvi 1928. The True facts of Australia's greatest double murder mystery : who murdered Act. Sgt. Cumming and Mrs Eileen Walsh at Brisbane, 23rd December, 1926?, Commonwealth (ill.) 2nd ed, Nielsen & Simmons, Brisbane, Page 55

cvii Queensland State Archives Item ID349443, Inquest file, Page -U-

cviii Queensland State Archives Item ID349443, Inquest file, Page -a-

cix Queensland State Archives Item ID349443, Inquest file, Page -b-

cx 1928. The True facts of Australia's greatest double murder mystery : who murdered Act. Sgt. Cumming and Mrs Eileen Walsh at Brisbane, 23rd December, 1926?, Commonwealth (ill.) 2nd ed, Nielsen & Simmons, Brisbane, Page 57

cxi Queensland State Archives Item ID349443, Inquest file, Page -e-

cxii 1928. The True facts of Australia's greatest double murder mystery : who murdered Act. Sgt. Cumming and Mrs Eileen Walsh at Brisbane, 23rd December, 1926?, Commonwealth (ill.) 2nd ed, Nielsen & Simmons, Brisbane, Page 58

cxiii Queensland State Archives Item ID349443, Inquest file

cxiv 1927 'BOMB OUTRAGE.', Morning Bulletin (Rockhampton, Qld. : 1878 - 1954), 15 August, p. 8., http://nla.gov.au/nla.news-article54609480

cxv 1927 'THE C.I.D. BOMB.', Cairns Post (Qld. : 1909 - 1954), 1 September, p. 4., http://nla.gov.au/nla.news-article40594685

cxvi 1927 'THE BOMB OUTRAGE.', Cairns Post (Qld. : 1909 - 1954), 16 August, p. 5., http://nla.gov.au/nla.news-article40587575

cxvii 1927 'THE C.I.D. BOMB.', Cairns Post (Qld. : 1909 - 1954), 1 September, p. 4., http://nla.gov.au/nla.news-article40594685

cxviii 1927 'FLEW FOR HIS GUN', Truth (Brisbane, Qld. : 1900 - 1954), 23 October, p. 21., http://nla.gov.au/nla.news-article203936309

cxix 1927 'FLEW FOR HIS GUN', Truth (Brisbane, Qld. : 1900 - 1954), 23 October, p. 21., http://nla.gov.au/nla.news-article203936309

cxx 1927 'C.I.B. EXPLOSION.', The Brisbane Courier (Qld. : 1864 - 1933), 3 November, p.14., http://nla.gov.au/nla.news-article21190458

cxxi 1927 'C.I.B. EXPLOSION.', Nambour Chronicle and North Coast Advertiser (Qld. : 1922 - 1954), 7 October, p. 9. http://nla.gov.au/nla.news-article76862220

cxxii 1927 'BETRAYED WOMAN SPEAKS FROM SCAFFOLD of SHAME', Truth (Brisbane, Qld. : 1900 - 1954), 6 November, p. 1., http://nla.gov.au/nla.news-article203941649

cxxiii 1927 'NEW CLUE IN CUMMING-WALSH MURDER', Truth (Brisbane, Qld. : 1900 - 1954), 30 October, p. 13., http://nla.gov.au/nla.news-article203934030

cxxiv 1927 'BETRAYED WOMAN SPEAKS FROM SCAFFOLD of SHAME', Truth (Brisbane, Qld. : 1900 - 1954), 6 November, p. 1. http://nla.gov.au/nla.news-article203941649

cxxv 1927 'BETRAYED WOMAN SPEAKS FROM SCAFFOLD of SHAME', Truth (Brisbane, Qld. : 1900 - 1954), 6 November, p. 1., http://nla.gov.au/nla.news-article203941649

cxxvi 1927 'Golden Casket', The Telegraph (Brisbane, Qld. : 1872 - 1947), 1 December, p.11. (5 O'CLOCK CITY EDITION), http://nla.gov.au/nla.news-article180789149

cxxvii 1927 'SEVERE SENTENCES.', Morning Bulletin (Rockhampton, Qld. : 1878 - 1954), 17 December, p. 9., http://nla.gov.au/nla.news-article55283337

cxxviii 1927 'NOLLE PROSEQUI.', Morning Bulletin (Rockhampton, Qld. : 1878 - 1954), 23 December, p. 8., http://nla.gov.au/nla.news-article55284132

cxxix 1928 'POLICE RE-SHUFFLE.', Maryborough Chronicle, Wide Bay and Burnett Advertiser (Qld. : 1860 - 1947), 12 April, p. 5., http://nla.gov.au/nla.newsarticle150992309

cxxx 1941 'POLICE INSPECTOR M. J. MELDON Notable Career in Police Force', Morning Bulletin (Rockhampton, Qld. : 1878 - 1954), 11 January, p. 3., http://nla.gov.au/nla.news-article56191138

cxxxi 1929 'Finance', The Telegraph (Brisbane, Qld. : 1872 - 1947), 11 February, p. 5. (5 O'CLOCK CITY EDITION), http://nla.gov.au/nla.news-article182371687

cxxxii 1930 '"SYSTEM PERFECT," SAYS MINISTER.', Daily Standard (Brisbane, Qld. : 1912 - 1936), 16 January, p. 7., http://nla.gov.au/nla.news-article186351793

cxxxiii 1930 'GOLDEN CASKET CASE', The Telegraph (Brisbane, Qld. : 1872 - 1947), 7 February, p. 5. (5 O'CLOCK CITY EDITION), http://nla.gov.au/nla.news-article182759763

cxxxiv 1930 'REFUSED TO ANSWER', Truth (Perth, WA : 1903 - 1931), 23 March, p. 3., http://nla.gov.au/nla.news-article210495273

cxxxv 1930 'GOLDEN CASKET.', The Central Queensland Herald (Rockhampton, Qld. : 1930 - 1956), 6 March, p. 50., http://nla.gov.au/nla.news-article70265677

cxxxvi 1930 'GOLDEN CASKET CASE.', Morning Bulletin (Rockhampton, Qld. : 1878 - 1954), 20 March, p. 6., http://nla.gov.au/nla.news-article55357687

cxxxvii 1930 'DEATH OF MRS. JAMES STOPFORD.', The Western Champion (Barcaldine, Qld. : 1922 - 1937), 14 June, p. 3., http://nla.gov.au/nla.news-article79650722

cxxxviii 1930 'Dr. J. Espie Dods', The Telegraph (Brisbane, Qld. : 1872 - 1947), 8 December, p. 16. (LATE CITY), http://nla.gov.au/nla.news-article188460377

cxxxix 1931 'AFTER SHORT ILLNESS.', Daily Standard (Brisbane, Qld. : 1912 - 1936), 28 September, p. 16., http://nla.gov.au/nla.news-article178958356

cxl Queensland State Archives Item ID565597, Police Service File

cxli 1932 'FORMER DETECTIVE.', The Brisbane Courier (Qld. : 1864 - 1933), 30 September, p. 14., http://nla.gov.au/nla.news-article22019868

cxlii 1932 'CROWN CASE ENDS', The Telegraph (Brisbane, Qld. : 1872 - 1947), 7 October, p. 8. (FINAL), http://nla.gov.au/nla.news-article180568242

cxliii 1932 'EIGHTEEN MONTHS', The Telegraph (Brisbane, Qld. : 1872 - 1947), 28 November, p. 1. (CLOSE OF PLAY), http://nla.gov.au/nla.news-article179529238

cxliv 1934 'EX-SERGEANT SEXTON'S APPEAL', The Telegraph (Brisbane, Qld. : 1872 - 1947), 31 May, p. 2. (LATE CITY), http://nla.gov.au/nla.news-article184727911

cxlv 1934 'SEXTON APPEAL.', Townsville Daily Bulletin (Qld. : 1907 - 1954), 1 June, p. 6., http://nla.gov.au/nla.news-article61790137

cxlvi 1936 'THE REAPER', Queensland Country Life (Qld. : 1900 - 1954), 3 December, p. 2., http://nla.gov.au/nla.news-article97162190

cxlvii 1941 'POLICE INSPECTOR M. J. MELDON Notable Career in Police Force', Morning Bulletin (Rockhampton, Qld. : 1878 - 1954), 11 January, p. 3., http://nla.gov.au/nla.news-article56191138

cxlviii 1939 'Obituary.', Daily Mercury (Mackay, Qld. : 1906 - 1954), 2 November, p. 8., http://nla.gov.au/nla.news-article170007300

cxlix 1941 'Late Mr. J. H. Stopford.', The Telegraph (Brisbane, Qld. : 1872 - 1947), 7 February, p. 11. (CITY FINAL LAST MINUTE NEWS), http://nla.gov.au/nla.news-article172720081

cl 1942 'EX-'TROC.' MAN TO PAY UP', Truth (Brisbane, Qld. : 1900 - 1954), 15 November, p. 23., http://nla.gov.au/nla.news-article202379538

cli 1943 'OBITUARY', Western Star and Roma Advertiser (Toowoomba, Qld. : 1875 - 1948), 31 December, p. 1. http://nla.gov.au/nla.news-article98107403

clii 1943 'Family Notices', The Courier-Mail (Brisbane, Qld. : 1933 - 1954), 29 June, p. 4. , http://nla.gov.au/nla.news-article42018761

cliii 1944 'DIGGER'S CASKET LUCK IS RECORD', Sunday Mail (Brisbane, Qld. : 1926 - 1954), 5 November, p. 4. , http://nla.gov.au/nla.news-article97945229

cliv 1945 'Family Notices', The Courier-Mail (Brisbane, Qld. : 1933 - 1954), 16 July, p. 6., http://nla.gov.au/nla.news-article50258356

clv 1946 '"Hit on Head With Piece of Piping"', The Telegraph (Brisbane, Qld. : 1872 - 1947), 8 May, p. 3. (CITY FINAL LAST MINUTE NEWS), http://nla.gov.au/nla.news-article201325020

clvi 1947 'Denial Of Gun Charge', The Telegraph (Brisbane, Qld. : 1872 - 1947), 18 November, p. 3. (CITY FINAL LAST MINUTE NEWS), http://nla.gov.au/nla.news-article187051420

clvii 1947 'Sent To Gaol For Wounding', The Telegraph (Brisbane, Qld. : 1872 - 1947), 28 November, p. 3. (CITY FINAL LAST MINUTE NEWS), http://nla.gov.au/nla.news-article187055128

clviii NAA: A9301, 6582, Item Barcode 4555212

clix NAA:B2455, HERBERT J.L. 1413

clx NAA:B884, HERBERT J. N279361

clxi 1928 'ITEMS OF INTEREST', Riverine Herald (Echuca, Vic. : Moama, NSW : 1869 - 1954), 27 November, p. 3., http://nla.gov.au/nla.news-article115116915

clxii 1932 '"INCENSED AT LIES AND PERJURY"', Truth (Brisbane, Qld. : 1900 - 1954), 21 August, p. 16., http://nla.gov.au/nla.news-article206124374

clxiii 1932 'BEFORE THE MAGISTRATES', The Brisbane Courier (Qld. : 1864 - 1933), 11 October, p. 15., http://nla.gov.au/nla.news-article22026932

clxiv 1936 'NOUMEA AS GAMBLING RESORT', Barrier Miner (Broken Hill, NSW : 1888 - 1954), 4 April, p. 3. (SPORTS EDITION), http://nla.gov.au/nla.news-article47927225

clxv 1940 'LAW REPORT.', The Sydney Morning Herald (NSW : 1842 - 1954), 23 October, p.6., http://nla.gov.au/nla.news-article17698246

clxvi 1942 '£90,000 GONE, SAYS EX-MANAGER OF BRISBANE TROCADERO', Truth (Brisbane, Qld. : 1900 - 1954), 8 November, p. 23., http://nla.gov.au/nla.news-article202379695

clxvii Queensland State Archives Item ID349443, Inquest file, Exhibit 1

clxviii John Oxley Library, State Library of Queensland Neg: 8028

clxix Queensland State Archives Item ID349443, Inquest file, Exhibit 19

clxx Queensland State Archives Item ID349443, Inquest file, Exhibit 16

clxxi Queensland State Archives Item ID349443, Inquest file, Exhibit 9

clxxii Queensland State Archives Item ID566416, Police service file

clxxiii 1927 'MIDNIGHT EXPLOSION', The Telegraph (Brisbane, Qld. : 1872 - 1947), 15 August, p. 9. (5 O'CLOCK CITY EDITION), http://nla.gov.au/nla.news-article181394963

www.ingramcontent.com/pod-product-compliance
Lightning Source LLC
Chambersburg PA
CBHW050449270326
41927CB00009B/1661

9 780992 563783